THE EARLY FACTORY MASTERS

THE EARLY FACTORY MASTERS

The Transition to the Factory System in the Midlands Textile Industry

STANLEY D. CHAPMAN

REPRINTS OF ECONOMIC CLASSICS

AUGUSTUS M. KELLEY • PUBLISHERS
NEW YORK • 1967

Printed in Great Britain by
Latimer Trend & Company Limited Plymouth
for David & Charles (Publishers) Ltd
South Devon House, Railway Station,
Newton Abbot, Devon

Contents

5

List of Illustrations

PLATES

7

IN TEXT

Acknowledgements

THIS book contains the substance of a thesis entitled 'The Midlands Cotton- and Worsted-Spinning Industry, 1769–1800', which was accepted for the Ph.D. degree of the University of London in January 1966.

In the course of my research, I have sifted through the resources of borough, county, ecclesiastical and private record depositories in the Midlands and the Public Record Office and Guildhall Library in London. I should like to record my debt to librarians and archivists, whose kindness has frequently extended beyond the bounds of duty.

I must also record my thanks to the people who have allowed me to study documents and business archives in their private possession. A full list of manuscript sources and their location will be found at the end of the book.

My research has also benefited from the friendly suggestions of a number of local historians, among whom I would particuarly like to mention Miss M. H. Mackenzie (North Derbyshire), Mr M. W. Spick (Arnold) and Mr W. Clay Dove (Sutton-in-Ashfield). Professor J. D. Chambers and Professor A. H. John have made valuable suggestions which improved earlier versions of the text. Finally, my thanks are due to Mr R. E. Forder and my brother, Mr F. R. Chapman who took the photographs, except for Plate 1 which is the crown copyright of the Science Museum, South Kensington; Plate 6, a painting reproduced by permission of the owner, Mr. G. Gopsill, of Burton-on-Trent; Plate 8 which is reproduced from the Boulton & Watt collection at Birmingham Reference Library; and Plate 14 which is from a painting by a French prisoner-of-war named Lequesne, by kind permission of the owner, Mr F. H. M. Fitzroy Newdegate, of Arbury Hall, near Nuneaton, Warwickshire.

S.D.C.

9

Sources

ONLY a few business records have survived from the second half of the eighteenth century, the period covered by this book, and these are invariably only fragments. Consequently, most of the evidence has been drawn from scattered sources such as local topographical works, government reports, local newspapers, directories, wills, and insurance records. The use of footnotes would have resulted in more notes than text in some places, particularly where there are references to a large number of mill-owners in connection with some particular development. A full list of firms is given at the back of the book (Appendix A), together with the sources of evidence on each. The sources of other evidence are grouped in the notes at the end of the text.

Introduction

THE main centres of the English cotton industry in the eighteenth century were in the north-west of England, centred on Manchester, and in the east Midlands, centred on Nottingham. Until the last two decades of the century, the Manchester trade was principally in fustians, or woven-cotton fabrics, while the Nottingham speciality was cotton hosiery. In both regions the last thirty years of the century witnessed a fairly rapid transition of the cotton-spinning industry from a domestic environment to newly-built, power-driven factories. In view of the importance that historians and economists have long attached to the subsequent changes in organization of industry, it is surprising that the Midlands industry —which, in Lombe and Arkwright, can claim a priority in the chronology of factory production—has received little more than passing consideration. This work is an attempt to remedy that deficiency by offering a detailed study of the transition to the factory system in the Midlands cotton- and worsted-spinning industry, and seeking to analyse the reasons for the early decline of the Midlands industry in face of the competition of Lancashire and the West Riding.

The early development of the Midlands industry is very poorly-documented, largely because it had contracted to small proportions before the age of Victorian chroniclers and commentators, and only a handful of firms survived into the twentieth century. However, sufficient evidence remains to trace the concentration of production and capital up to the time of Hargreaves and Arkwright, and to examine the impact of these two innovators on the Midland region. It has also proved possible to discern the main lines of development from a study of the career-patterns and enterprises of the entrepreneurs known to have been spinning cotton by power in the region before the close of the eighteenth century. No complete list of firms has survived for the Region, but it has proved possible to compile a list from a variety of sources.

For the purpose of this study, the Midlands Region is taken to include Nottinghamshire, Derbyshire (except the large parish of Glossop, which falls within the orbit of Manchester), Staffordshire, Leicestershire, Northamptonshire, Warwickshire, Worcestershire, Lincolnshire and Shropshire. This definition of the Region is not without precedent. It has proved necessary to make the geographical area as wide as this to comprehend all the scattered outposts of the industry as they developed in the latter part of the eighteenth century. In spite of the scattered nature of the industry on the margins of the Region, the Midlands cotton- and worsted-spinning

TABLE I

Firms and Mills Established to Spin Cotton and Worsted by Power in the Midlands,
1769–1800

	Cotton		Worsted	
	No. of Firms	*No. of Mills*	*No. of Firms*	*No. of Mills*
Nottinghamshire	28	42	3	5
Derbyshire	24	39	1	1
Staffordshire	10	15	1	1
Leicestershire	4	5	1	1
Northamptonshire	3	3	—	—
Warwickshire	3	3	2	2
Worcestershire	—	—	1	1
Lincolnshire	2	2	2	2
Shropshire	1	1	—	—
	75	110	11	13

Source: see Appendix A.

Notes: (*a*) Four worsted-spinners were first cotton-spinners. They have been included in both categories, i.e., counted twice, so that the total number of firms is 82.

(*b*) Firms have only been counted once if they operated in more than one county. All firms are listed under county of origin. The details are set out in Appendix A.

(*c*) The list includes all water-powered and steam-powered mills known to have existed in the Region during the period. Workshops housing hand-operated jennies are not included.

industry has been found to be an integrated manufacture, isolated mills having close links with the centres of the industry. The relative importance in cotton- and worsted-spinning in the counties comprising the Region is suggested in Table 1.

To avoid any possible confusion, the Midlands, as defined for this study, are indicated by spelling the word 'Midlands' with a capital 'M'. Similarly, the word 'Region' is spelt with a capital 'R' when it is intended to indicate the specific part of the country under review. The common use of the phrases 'east midlands' and 'west midlands' has no special validity in the context of this study. Hence, if the eastern side of the Region is mentioned, the phrase 'east Midlands' is used; similarly, there are references to the 'west Midlands' in some parts of the study.

CHAPTER ONE

The Domestic Textile Industry

1. Handloom-Weaving

HANDLOOM-weaving was a common occupation throughout the Midlands until the beginning of the seventeenth century, after which it was gradually superseded by other branches of the textile industry, as well as by regional specialities such as pot-making, leather goods, and the metallurgical industries. The earliest major innovation in the textile industries of the Region was the introduction of the stocking-frame. The hosiery industry established itself in Nottingham before the Civil Wars, and in Leicester and Derby after the Restoration.[1] Coventry became one of the early centres of the English silk industry, gradually displacing the old woollen industry of the town. At Newcastle-under-Lyne, the celebrated hat-making industry of that town was well-established by the period at which this study commences. However, in parts of the Midlands remote from the centres of industry and commerce, the original clothing industry survived into the nineteenth century, in some places on the basis of a local speciality, such as the carpet-weaving industry of Kidderminster, Worcester, and (of less importance) Chesterfield.[2] It is useful to notice some of the locations of these survivals of the earlier textile industry as, in a few cases, they formed the basis for the establishment of a worsted-spinning factory, while in others the handloom weavers were induced to transfer their interest to cotton, and so encourage the growth of mechanized spinning.

The limited evidence suggests that there were handloom weavers thinly scattered over the whole region up to at least the end of the eighteenth century, with concentrations in certain districts. A few old market-towns retained a colony of weavers. Derby and Leicester had small numbers of tammy weavers but they were rapidly giving way to the framework knitters.[3] Within the hosiery districts, the only concentration of weavers appears to have been at Southwell, twelve miles north-east of Nottingham. In 1792, the Southwell weavers were strong enough to organize their own association and to advise the public of 'the necessity of raising their wages' by increasing the price of their products. Among these they mentioned 'plain linens', 'woolseys', 'woollens', and 'figured work'.[4]

The weaving of 'tammy', a worsted cloth commonly worn by working-class women in the eighteenth century, is supposed to have originated at Tamworth in South Staffordshire, and the district retained a residual interest up to the end of the eighteenth century.[5] The parish registers of nearby Burton-on-Trent record the marriages of weavers, feltmakers, woolcombers, clothiers, cordwainers and flax-dressers, but between 1780 and 1800 these entries are less numerous than those for shoemakers and screwmakers. There was also a family of tammy weavers at Tutbury, important because they transferred their interests to cotton-spinning in 1781. Elsewhere in Staffordshire, Wolverhampton was a flourishing centre of the wool trade in the Middle Ages. Although the local textile industry was superseded by the iron manufacture before the end of the seventeenth century, the woollen and worsted industry was still represented in a list of occupations given in the town's rate-book in 1792, and this continuing interest was no doubt important for the establishment of a worsted mill in the town the previous year.

In Warwickshire, the Coventry silk industry did not entirely supersede the old clothing industry. At Bedworth, just to the north, a strong cloth called 'duffle' supplied the special needs of the local mining community, and encouraged the establishment of mechanized worsted-spinning in the district. The woollen industry also survived at Birmingham and Warwick, but a far more important survival was that of the carpet weavers at Kidderminster and Worcester. The weavers' demand for yarn gave employment throughout the district of north Worcestershire, particularly in

Bromsgrove, Pershore and Shipston-on-Stour.[6] The carpet-weaving industry exercised an important influence on the location of worsted-spinning factories during the period covered by this study.

In Northamptonshire, the weaving of woollen goods was still the leading industry in Kettering, Rothwell, Desborough and district at the end of the eighteenth century. The *Universal British Directory*, III (1794) records that 'The manufacture of the town (of Kettering) is sorting, combing, spinning and weaving of tammies and lastings; . . . About 500 weavers are employed'. Whether the Northampton-shire cotton mills owed anything to this traditional industry is not clear.

Another rural district in which handloom weavers survived into our period in significant numbers was the north-west of Derbyshire. Very few of the parish-registers in this district give occupations, but those that do confirm the impression of a diminutive industry. The Tideswell marriage-registers, for instance, list ninety-five occupations from 1759 to 1780, among which there are only ten weavers. Nevertheless, this declining industry was an asset to the Derbyshire cotton industry between 1788 and 1803 when, in a general shortage of labour and loomshops, the resources of the old textile industry were transferred to the new. Though the fabrics made from wool or linen vanished by 1800, the old skills played an important part in the transition to the new, many of the manufac-turers and workers having learned their craft with the traditional yarns.[7]

2. The Hosiery Industry

The merchant hosiers, and the country mercers and drapers who dealt in hosiery, played a leading role in the transition to the factory system in cotton- and worsted-spinning. It is therefore important to trace the origins and development of this class of wholesalers in the provinces, and to chart the accumulation of capital in their hands. This need not involve recounting the history of the machine-wrought hosiery industry so much as recalling those features which are relevant to an understanding of the transition to factory production.

The hosiery industry owes its original location in the east Midlands to an accident of birth. The Reverend William Lee, the Renaissance genius who invented the stocking-frame, was born and spent most of his life in Calverton, a village four miles to the north of Nottingham. In the seventeenth century, however, the industry was concentrated in London, then as now the centre of fashion, and it was not until after the Restoration that the industry's centre of gravity shifted to the provinces, as stockings became cheaper and more standardized. From the Restoration until the Napoleonic blockade, a period of 150 years, the hosiery industry enjoyed almost continuous expansion in the provinces, first in Nottingham and its environs, then in Leicester and Derby and the surrounding market towns and rural areas.[8]

As evidence of the industry's growth, the number of stocking-frames employed in the provinces is said to have increased from about 150 in 1664 to 25,000 in 1812. After a famous test-case in 1728, in which Nottingham magistrates refused to recognize the validity of the restricting ordinances of the London Company of Framework Knitters, the migration of the hosiery trade from London accelerated, and a new class of provincial merchant hosiers began to emerge. In Nottingham the number of hosiers rose from just over fifty at the middle of the eighteenth century to seventy in 1771, and then leaped to 199 at the end of the century. In Leicester there were eighty-five firms of merchant hosiers in 1794. About the same period Hinckley had twenty-three hosiers and Derby thirteen.[9]

The increase in the number of frames and wholesalers was paralleled by the geographical dispersal of the industry over an increasing number of towns and villages within the counties of Leicestershire, Nottinghamshire and Derbyshire. Though the trade remained centred on the three county towns, small groups appeared at Alfreton, Chesterfield, Bakewell, Litton and Youlgreave (in the Peak district of Derbyshire), and Hinckley, Ashby-de-la-Zouch and Loughborough (Leicestershire) during the course of the eighteenth century. Sutton-in-Ashfield, with the adjacent town of Mansfield (Nottinghamshire), was also an early centre. (These country locations are important for this study as the country hosiers played a prominent role in the development of factory spinning, having the initial advantage of good sites for the development of water-mills.) Net made on the stocking-frames was finished, and much of it hand-embroidered, by large numbers of women and children working in their own homes, scattered through the villages of Nottinghamshire, Derbyshire, Leicestershire, Yorkshire, Staffordshire and even beyond.[10]

Further evidence of the hosiery industry's growth from 1660 to 1810 lies in the adaptation of the versatile stocking-frame, first to new fibres 'notably cotton and silk, both in the early part of the eighteenth century' and then, in the second half of the eighteenth century, to the production of new meshes and new garments. The initial stimulus was provided by the success of Jedediah Strutt's 'Derby rib' hose (1758). The continuous experiments of framework knitters during the next generation extended the use of the frame from stockings to underwear, breeches, gloves, handkerchiefs, waistcoats and elasticated knitwear, and various imitations of cushion-lace. In 1812, some forty distinct fabrics were being knitted on the frame, despite some contraction due to the war. In the second half of the eighteenth century, hosiery was a dynamic industry in which the ingenuity of the workmen was constantly producing new modifications to the frame, which the hosiers were eager to patronize where they saw a market for the new product.[11]

In the early decades of the eighteenth century, many hosiers climbed from the ranks of frame operatives to the position of merchants. In the seventeenth century, frames were expensive to build or buy (£80 is mentioned in 1658) and the knitters appear to have been men of some substance. Before the outbreak of the Civil Wars, master framework-knitters sold their own hose direct from stalls or shops in Nottingham, and the practice continued, though on a diminishing scale, until the end of the eighteenth century.[12] Two men who rose from the ranks of the knitters, Samuel Need (Arkwright's future partner) and Samuel Unwin of Sutton-in-Ashfield, were also among the pioneers of mechanized spinning in factories. It is clear from Unwin's case that, rising from the status of a 'stockiner' (as he described himself in 1735) to that of a merchant hosier, was not the same as rising from rags to riches. Unwin became a wholesaler about 1740, according to one tradition as a result of inheriting money from his uncle, a wealthy Sutton farmer and hosier, and according to another by borrowing £200 from two Duffield (Derby) farmers. Whichever story is true—and perhaps they both are—the would-be hosier clearly needed capital.[13]

So it was that a number of other early merchant hosiers began their careers as mercers and drapers. From the time of the Restoration, Nottingham mercers, drapers, and grocers began to travel to London to purchase their supplies, and this extension of wholesaling activities coincided with the rise of the provincial hosiery industry, and was almost certainly stimulated by it. Very likely the mercers and drapers learned to fill their pack-horse bags with hose on the outward journey. Nicholas Allsop, who is generally supposed to have introduced the stocking-frame into Leicester, was apprenticed to and first in business as a mercer, and some of the most prosperous Leicester hosiers at mid-century also began their careers as mercers. A substantial number of early factory masters followed this route into the hosiery industry.[14]

In the second half of the eighteenth century the area of recruitment extended considerably as many of the established hosiers became wealthy. During the first thirty years or so, apprenticeship premiums were fairly low; the records of Leicester Corporation show that £3 to £10 was paid according to the status of the hosier, and most of the apprentices were the sons of artisans and tradesmen. However, in 1732, Joseph Craddock (of E. & J. Craddock, 'mercers and hosiers') charged a hundred guineas, and thereafter premiums began to rise rapidly. In the second half of the century, premiums of a hundred to three hundred guineas became common, so that hosiers were necessarily recruited from wealthy homes. An analysis of the occupations of the fathers of 146 apprentices bound to Leicester merchant hosiers between 1750 and 1800 shows that more than one-third (thirty-four per cent) of the apprentices were sons of landed proprietors of one kind or another. Another third of the apprentices (thirty per cent to be precise) were sons of leaders of the textile industry.

Mercers were drawn from similar backgrounds, and although there was a continuous flow of recruits from more lowly homes, it was the gentry who paid the highest premiums and so secured places in the leading firms for their sons.[15] Though no comparable figures are available for Nottingham, one gains the impression from a number of instances that recruitment there was from similar social strata. The significance of this for future economic development was that a high proportion of the hosiers had family resources which might be mortgaged for major industrial expansion. Indeed, in one or two cases, the country estates of hosiers and mercers or their families provided sites for the building of mills.[16]

Apart from family connections and previous occupations of hosiers, two other sources of capital are important. One was provided by the London agents of the provincial hosiers, the other by the country banks. Although the hosiery manufacture had all but deserted London by the middle of the eighteenth century, the hosiery market remained centred on the City of London until after the Napoleonic wars.[17] The bulk of the hosiery manufactured in the east Midlands was sold through commission agents in the City who specialized in this commodity, one of whom inserted the following advertisement in a provincial newspaper:

Commission in the Hosiery
Wanted, by a person who has a warehouse in the most eligible part of the City of London; who having been brought up in the trade in London, and lately come from a very capital manufacturing house, has a thorough knowledge of, and an extensive connection with the first wholesale and retail houses in the line.

The importance of the connection between the provincial hosier and the City commission agent was that it sometimes constituted a channel for the flow of capital from London to the provinces. As early as 1753, five London hosiers, all 'considerable dealers' in their speciality, declared before a House of Commons committee that they employed 'great numbers of manufacturers in different parts of England', no doubt some of them in the east Midlands, the main location of the hosiery industry in the provinces. The practice was not extinct by the end of the century for, in 1794, Timothy Harris, a City hosier, owned '70 or 80' silk-stocking-frames in Nottingham.[18]

A number of east Midland hosiers are also known to have entered into partnership with their City agents, the most interesting example from the perspective of this study being Samuel Unwin of Sutton-in-Ashfield, who was in partnership with James Heygate, an Aldermanbury (City) warehouseman by 1781. Heygate was subsequently in partnership with John Pares, a leading Leicester hosier and cotton-spinner at Calver, in the Peak district of Derbyshire. Heygate's partnerships were formed specifically to finance development of the large cotton mills in the Midlands, and his interest was by no means unique among City warehousemen. Thus the flow of capital from London to the Midlands textile industry, which probably began with Samuel Fellows and Sir Thomas Lombe, found fresh channels when the Midlands cotton-spinning industry got under way, and continued to be a feature of the development of the hosiery districts of the east Midlands throughout the eighteenth century.

The country banks also played a remarkably active role in the development of the hosiery industry in the provinces, particularly through the enterprise of Smith's bank at Nottingham, said to have been established as early as 1658. A general ledger of Smith's bank relating to the period 1748–52 has survived and shows that more than forty of the bank's customers were hosiers and 'framework knitters', i.e., hosiery manufacturers on a considerable scale, and as Smith's were the only bankers in Nottingham and district until

1760, this figure probably reflects the total number of hosiery merchants and manufacturers in the town who were availing themselves of banking facilities. At the middle of the eighteenth century there were few more than fifty 'putters-out' (or larger hosiery manufacturers trading with London) in Nottingham, so that a high proportion, perhaps eighty per cent, were bank customers. Moreover, the records of Smith's bank show that a number of hosiers and mercers were availing themselves of borrowing facilities even at this early period, some for quite substantial sums. Thus Samuel Need had an overdraft of £910 in January 1748, when the ledger opens, and Burden and Wright, Mansfield hosiers and bleachers, had an overdraft of £668 at about the same time. Another hosier who was subsequently connected with the development of cotton-spinning, and had an active account at this period, was John Killingley (later of Killingley, Green & Co.). He had an overdraft of £80 in June 1752 when the surviving ledger closes. At this period Smith's customers were scattered over a wide area, extending far beyond the hosiery-manufacturing districts of the east Midlands. Among the country customers revealed in later accounts were Samuel Unwin of Sutton-in-Ashfield and John Gardom of Bakewell. At Derby, three of four hosiers had accounts with Crompton, Evans & Co. (founded about 1771) and a surviving day-book relating to the late 1770s shows that overdrafts were sometimes allowed. The bank's most important customers were Jedediah Strutt and his partners.[19]

The scale on which merchant hosiers operated varied considerably. At the top, the trading wealth of the most prosperous could bear comparison with that of the 'merchant princes' of the West of England clothing industry, while at the bottom end the hosiers merged into the ranks of independent framework knitters. In examining the scale, it is useful to distinguish between three categories of hosiers in the industry. The merchant princes consisted of a handful of hosiers who were leaders of the industry and controlled a large part of the trade in their respective centres. The majority of them were patrons, or purchasers, of some innovation in the trade, the most successful firm being that of the Hayne brothers, who held the patent for point-net lace for eleven years, until it was nullified at law in 1789.

William Hayne came of a family of gentry at Ashbourne and is said to have started in the hosiery trade in Nottingham in 1773 with an estate worth £7,000. In 1782, Hayne & Co.'s warehouse and offices were insured for £500, and their stock and machinery at the warehouse for £4,000. By 1812, the firm owned nearly a thousand net-frames, worth £24,000, and located as far out of town as Mansfield (14 miles) and Melbourne, Leicestershire (16 miles). In addition to knitters, the firm employed an army of women and girls to embroider the net by hand, and its pattern-book is said to have contained 11,930 varieties. The value of the firm's work in progress and credit is beyond guessing, though it is some indication of magnitude that it had £25,000 worth of net confiscated in Paris in 1809, and this was only one export market.[20]

Another merchant prince was Robert Wright, a Hull linen-draper who came to Nottingham about 1748 and 'acquired a handsome fortune' as the Nottingham proprietor of the patent for 'knotted and double loop work' for ribbed silk-stockings, breeches and waistcoat pieces. A local historian recorded that 'So great was the demand for these beautiful and durable goods that, in 1797, a thousand silk-knotted-frames could furnish but a scanty supply'. Wright's account with Smith's bank stood at £8,000 plus for most of the 1790s.[21]

Though the Hayne brothers and Robert Wright had no connection with factory spinning so far as is known, other leaders of the hosiery industry recognized it as a suitable channel for their capital. The best-known example is that of Samuel Need and Jedediah Strutt, owners of the 'Derby rib' patent of 1758, whose experience with this early patent in the hosiery trade encouraged them to form a partnership with Arkwright. Samuel Unwin, whose early career has already been mentioned, won a Royal Society of Arts prize for the best improvement to the stocking-frame in 1758, and held a patent for fancy knitted-waistcoats. Though the scale of Strutt's and

Unwin's businesses is not known, analogy with other leaders of the industry suggests that it was considerable, and that ownership of new techniques could generate considerable capital.

The second group of hosiers comprises the substantial number of wholesalers whose trade and assets placed them below the leaders of the industry but above the petty or 'bag' hosiers of the manufacturing villages. They constituted the great majority of merchant hosiers in the main centres of the industry at Nottingham, Leicester and Derby, and in the various subsidiary centres like Hinckley, Mansfield, Chesterfield and Bakewell. Only a rough estimate can be made of the scale of a typical hosier's business, but contemporary accounts suggest that Nottingham hosiers regularly paid out £200 a week in wages before the French wars. They might employ 200 frames, each of which gave employment to a knitter and three more hands. Altogether, such a hosier would employ 800 domestic workers, men, women and children.[22] To judge from occasional advertisements in the local newspapers for the sale of frames, the hosier often owned 50 to 100 of the frames he employed. The books of Coltman & Gardiner, a Leicester firm of hosiers whose history will be discussed in Chapter Six in connection with the origins of mechanized worsted-spinning, reflect a financial structure which was probably typical of dozens of firms in the east Midlands. This structure can be illustrated by financial data from three years:

	1783		*1792*		*1800*	
	£	%	£	%	£	%
FIXED CAPITAL						
Warehouse (at cost, 1760)	580		580		580	
Frames and utensils	186		896		823	
	766	15	1,476	19	1,403	14
CIRCULATING CAPITAL						
Raw materials, work in progress, and stock	1,319		2,305		2,967	
Customers' debts	3,125	85	3,844	81	5,874	86
TOTAL CAPITAL	5,210	100	7,625	100	10,244	100

The partnership of Coltman & Gardiner began about 1766 and ended with John Coltman's death in 1808. In 1783, the partners probably owned only ten or a dozen stocking-frames but, by 1792, when the first detailed record occurs, they had forty-three frames and, in 1800, forty-five stocking- and two lace-frames. Though the firm's sales seem to have been considerable—rising steadily from £6,679 in 1791–92 to £13,818 in 1801–02—the partners found it prudent to withdraw only £200 to £250 a year each from the business. This may appear a modest income for a merchant but most hosiers who became factory owners were drawn from the middle range of enterprise, and it is likely that many would have been operating on a similar annual income.

The third group of hosiers, known as 'bag' hosiers, were really middlemen who organized the local hosiery industry in villages where there was a large population of framework knitters. They acted as agents to the merchant hosiers, distributing yarn and forwarding the finished goods to the warehouses, deducting a commission which, in 1783, was alleged to be as much as twenty per cent of the price paid by hosiers. In time, they began to acquire frames and sell directly to local shopkeepers and the travelling agents of London hosiers, thus competing with the 'gentlemen hosiers' of the towns. There is no record of any bag hosier investing money in the cotton- or worsted-spinning industry; their interest lies in a rather different direction. As early as 1790, the framework knitters at Sutton-in-Ashfield and Ilkeston were complaining that it was impossible for a man to maintain himself and his family 'with honesty and decency' because the bag hosiers, 'beginning the business with a small capital . . . make use of every oppressive stratagem to lower the workmen's price, and advance the quality of the hose, in order that they may undersell the old-established hosiers. . . .'[23] Relations between knitters and their employers became particularly embittered in the bagmen's villages where, twenty years later, in the period of slack trade which followed the Napoleonic blockade of the Continent, the Luddite gangs began their nocturnal attacks. In the intervening two decades, deteriorating relations were a potent factor in the labour problems with which the early factory masters had to contend, a subject considered in greater depth in Chapter Ten.

3. The Lace Industry

The lace industry had a history of its own quite distinct from that of cotton- and worsted-spinning until 1804, when machine-spun cotton finally achieved sufficient fineness to be used in the manufacture of Nottingham lace.[24] The relevance of the lace industry's machinery to this study turns on the employment of scarce resources. The excitement aroused by the first production of lace on a machine diverted interest and resources from cotton-spinning to lace, and the artisans on whom the merchant hosiers relied to keep abreast of technical progress turned their attention to the more dazzling rewards offered by the fashion market. The period of expansion in the lace industry began in 1784 and continued its erratic course until the late 1830s. In the first phase, between 1784 and 1802, the demand for lace machines crowded out the sporadic orders for spinning plant and encouraged local spinners to buy their machinery in Lancashire. Thus the early technical leadership of Nottingham in cotton-spinning rapidly gave way to that of Manchester. To develop this point further it is necessary to survey the origins and growth of the lace industry to about 1815.

The social origins and capital outlay of Hayne & Co., the innovating entrepreneurs in the point-net (lace) manufacture have already been mentioned. The accomplishment of the Hayne partnership was to manufacture and develop a market for an hexagonal silk-mesh which was perfectly fast, i.e., would bear cutting in any form without the web being deranged by the loops being set free. Although the first patent for point-net was taken out in 1773, the technique was not really perfected until 1786. A court case (Hayne v. Maltby) led to the patent being nullified three years later, and triggered off a long period of rapid (though erratic) expansion in the industry. According to Henson, point-net was in such demand that its sale doubled yearly for a decade after 1786. It entered upon a new phase of development in 1804, prior to which the extra fineness of the frame on which the net was made had confined it to the use of silk. By 1804, however, the cotton-spinners had succeeded in spinning yarn of such fineness that the lace manufacturers were able to produce a much cheaper net, and one which preserved a more 'perfect whiteness' than silk-net. The subsequent growth of the point-net trade was so rapid that the industry developed from hardly more than twenty frames in 1786 to nearly 1,200 frames in 1802–03, and then to 1,500 frames in 1810. The machines themselves developed over this period from 18–20 inches width to 30 inches wide and above. In 1810, the Nottingham lace manufacture, 'taking the business in all its branches, gave employment to from 10,000 to 15,000 persons, including women and children', who were employed to embroider patterns on the net.

Other branches of the hosiery trade which came into existence in the last quarter of the eighteenth century had a more ephemeral existence, but were also responsible for a considerable diversion of capital and labour within the period covered by this study. There was no attempt to make a complete census of the hosiery trade until 1812, by which time 'the French war, the Spanish war, and a change of fashion attendant upon a war system had nearly destroyed every branch of the fancy trade in stockings'. Even so, the census revealed that there were still forty-one different branches of the hosiery manufacture in existence. Though the trade historians are silent on the size of almost all of them, even the 1812 figures show that most gave employment to hundreds of frames.[25] Moreover, these lucrative fashion branches of hosiery competed strongly with cotton- and worsted-spinning for capital provided by the merchant hosiers, for skilled artisans and, probably most significant of all, for orders with the framesmiths.

The constant introduction of new branches and new machinery stimulated a machine-building industry which grew rapidly during the second half of the eighteenth century; in 1807 there were forty-seven master framesmiths in Nottingham, 'many of whom had large establishments of journeymen and apprentices'. The vanguard of the technical development consisted of a relatively small number of the most able framesmiths and knitters who lived close to each other in Nottingham, feeding on each other's ideas and stimulated by the patronage the merchant hosiers offered to the most successful. Technical progress was extraordinarily rapid from the middle of the eighteenth century, and inventors and manufacturers who broke out of the circle soon ceased to contribute to the flow of ideas.[26] The trade historians insist that the mechanical problems involved in producing lace-net on a machine called for continuous and intense mental exertion, so it is not surprising that few of the Nottingham machine-builders had time to notice the progress that was being made in developing spinning machinery in Lancashire and the West Riding, let alone try to keep up with it.

The rewards offered by the new lace industry after 1786 were sufficiently high to attract several hosiers who had embarked on cotton-spinning. Four Nottingham hosier-spinners are known to have become lace manufacturers, and there may well have been others. At least one firm attempted to make cotton-spinning and lace-manufacturing complementary by training some of their girl apprentices who had completed their time as net embroiderers.[27] But the two activities can hardly be regarded as complementary before 1804, and it is probably true to say that lace-manufacturing diverted the attention and capital of entrepreneurs from cotton-spinning.

Information on the relative level of earnings in the hosiery and spinning industries is fragmentary, but it is possible to discern a pattern. The position in the hosiery trade was summarized by Sir F. M. Eden in 1797: 'The price of labour is very variable in this town (Nottingham) particularly in the stocking line: some weavers [i.e., framework knitters] earn 40s a week and others only 8s: this disparity is occasioned in some through want of industry; but chiefly arises from the nature of the different branches of the manufacture. It is thought two-thirds of the weavers do not, upon an average, earn more than 10s weekly. Lace workers earn from 20s to 40s.' This differential between the more- and less-skilled did not, however, originate with the point-net branch of the hosiery trade, but dated back to the earliest varieties produced on the stocking-frame in the middle of the eighteenth century. Thus workmen employed in knitting Spanish eyelet-hole silk mitts earned as much as 50s weekly for a decade after 1772. The best-paid workers of all would be the highly-skilled framesmiths who made the new machines, and at about the turn of the century their wages ranged from 25s to three guineas, according to the skill of the worker.[28]

By comparison with these earnings of skilled operatives and craftsmen in Nottingham, the wages of the best-paid mill workers were paltry indeed. The wage-books of Arkwright's Bakewell mill for periods from 1786 to 1811 show that mechanics at the top of the wage-scale earned only 10s to 15s weekly. At Arkwright's Cressbrook mill, William Newton, who took control of machine building, earned 20s a week. It seems unlikely that other cotton-spinning firms would pay more than the innovating entrepreneur, and a few remarks in Eden seem to confirm this. At Derby, those who worked in mills and cotton mills earned about 16s a week, and at Wirksworth overseers in cotton works were paid only 12s a week. The workers most at a premium in the early mills were the combers demanded by the worsted manufacturers, but even the skilled comber could earn no more than a guinea a week, and that at a mill located within four miles of Nottingham. It is, of course, true that men employed at cotton and worsted mills could readily find emment for a wife and children, so that family earnings could be much larger than those of the artisan alone, but this does not alter the substance of the argument because there was no shortage of work for women and children in the hosiery industry.[29] (Indeed, the rates of pay for female and juvenile labour were generally higher in the hosiery industry than in the mills.)

A train of fires, bankruptcies, and closures of mills for other reasons, and reports of laying-off of hands and apprentices reveal that, whatever the intentions of the entrepreneurs, employment in cotton- and worsted-spinning was no more permanent than in the hosiery industry. Linked with the well-known antipathy of the workers to the factories, all the evidence points to the lace trade drawing the best workers from the hosiery trade, and the cotton- and worsted-spinning industry being able to offer little competition to them.

Later in this book it will be seen how, in the hosiery districts of the east Midlands, it was all but impossible for the framework knitter or framesmith to become an entrepreneur in the warp-spinning industry. Nevertheless, the aspiration remained for a journeyman to become a master and in the lace and fancy hosiery trade, where earnings were frequently three to five times as high as the traditional wage in the common branches of the hosiery industry, numbers of skilled and enterprising workmen did succeed in establishing themselves as independent masters. It is difficult to obtain precise details for the period before 1810, but, as an example in one trade, an advertisement in the *Nottingham Journal* in 1796 gave the names of sixty-nine master-manufacturers of twilled work,[30] a substantial number of whom the burgess records show to have been originally framework knitters. The merchant hosiers were personally responsible for few technical discoveries and most of the continual experimentation to produce new meshes and garments on the stocking-frame was undertaken by the knitters and smiths. The fact that there was so much less opportunity to become an independent master in the spinning industry than in the hosiery industry served to direct nearly all the mechanical ingenuity of Nottingham and the hosiery districts into the established industry.

The chronology of technical innovation and development of the new branches of the hosiery industry, and their subsequent decline, is worth tracing. The trade's historians suggest that, Strutt apart, most of the important new techniques in hosiery were introduced in the 1770s and 1780s. Lists of patents registered show two phases of innovation, the first from 1777–84, the second (and rather less-important period) from 1788–92, and these are precisely the periods of maximum growth in the Midlands cotton- and worsted-spinning industry.[31] Basic wage rates were maintained from 1787 until 1809, though the onset of the French wars in 1792 caused a contraction in the market for fancy hosiery.[32] Point-net manufacture, however, maintained its momentum for a period, while mechanical ingenuity was concentrated on an intense effort to imitate the motions of the cushion-lace maker on a machine. And in 1809, Heathcoat, the pioneer of the modern lace industry, finally succeeded in making a commercial proposition of what became known as 'twist net'. Thus, during the two phases in which the warp-spinning industry was establishing itself, it had to compete with hosiery and lace for scarce resources of mechanical ability and suffered for twenty years subsequently from the contraction of its main market. The introduction of cotton to the point-net frame offered only temporary relief. No more than 600 frames were in production in 1815, the best year for this speciality, and the trade in point-net collapsed when it came into competition with the superior French product.[33]

Turning, finally, to the Nottingham industry's recruitment of its highly-paid innovators and mechanics, although the new branches of the hosiery industry were highly concentrated in Nottingham, the town attracted mechanical talent from a much wider area. The pages of the trade historians are filled with the stories of artisans who took the golden road to Nottingham. They came not only from the framework-knitting districts, but also, in a few cases, from regions beyond; indeed, by the early 1820s Nottingham was even attracting German clockmakers.[34] In the west Midlands, Birmingham also acted as a magnet for mechanical ability over a wide area, and Sheffield and Manchester wage-rates were probably a source of attraction to able mechanics born on the northern margins of the

Region covered by this study. There may have been some remote parts of the Region where artisans of ability did not know of the opportunities offered by the large towns—the industry around Tideswell and Hartington may fall into this category—but, in general, it seems that the cotton- and worsted-spinning industry had to compete with other industries, especially the Nottingham lace industry, for resources, particularly mechanical ability, which were in short supply. And the fact that rewards in the lace industry were much higher than those in spinning goes a long way towards explaining the collapse of cotton-spinning in the Region at the beginning of the nineteenth century.

CHAPTER TWO

The Concentration of Production up to 1769

ALTHOUGH the domestic hosiery and clothing industries were predominantly cottage industries, there was already a marked degree of concentration in workshops and factories by the time Arkwright and Hargreaves came to Nottingham. Hosiery frames were already being concentrated in workshops, some of them employing juvenile and female labour. In Nottingham, a number of manufactories were opened, primarily to maintain innovations in secrecy, while in Derby, and elsewhere in the hosiery districts, Lombe's silk mill found numbers of imitators, though on a more modest scale than the prototype. All these provided important precedents for the development of the cotton- and worsted-spinning industries and are considered in this chapter, together with a reassessment of the significance of the Paul-Wyatt mills.

1. Framework-Knitters' Worshops

The framework-knitters' workshops of the hosiery districts were by far the most common form of industrial concentration in the Midlands during this period and were to be found in three distinct locations. Most merchant hosiers seem to have maintained their own home department, a workshop where they kept a dozen or so frames to execute special orders. The warehouse of Alderman William Wilson of Nottingham was probably fairly typical in this respect and consisted of 'a long narrow room up a yard, with a length of counter and a few racks at one end and a counting-house at the other; an attic overhead with a dozen or so of hand-frames would represent the home department of machinery'.[1] Many of the hosiers kept premises which, like Wilson's, were nothing more than converted tenements. But, as their prosperity increased, some began to occupy more substantial dwelling-houses, and a few purchased mansions built by the gentry as town-houses and converted them for their own use.[2] A fairly early example of a converted property was advertised for sale in the *Nottingham Journal*, 11 March 1769. It was described as:

> A new re-built house, well situated on the Back-Side, consisting of a cellar, pantry, kitchen and large house [-space]; first floor three entire chambers, on the second floor one large work room (perhaps the best in town) which will hold 13 frames completed; the tiled floor and two large garrats over it will hold four or five beds.

However, only a small proportion of the total number of frames in the industry were located in the hosiers' workshops, most of them being in the homes of the knitters. In the manufacturing villages, four-roomed cottages, consisting of a house place, weaving-shop, scullery and the bedrooms, were still being built by the knitters up to the last decade of the eighteenth century. The weaving-shop was intended to accommodate one or two, sometimes three frames. In Nottingham, where the failure to enclose the common fields was driving up the price of land, cottages of this kind were less common than in the country districts, certainly by the second half of the eighteenth century. About 1784, terraced houses of three storeys, built back-to-back in courts, began to appear as the characteristic form of working-class dwelling, and this kind of house is illustrated in Figure 1. The small size of the second-floor rooms limited them to two or three frames. A few more substantial (five-roomed) houses were built with larger workshop accommodation. Thus, in general, the rapid growth of Nottingham during the last quarter of the eighteenth century did not lead to any considerable concentration of hosiery frames.[3]

In Leicester, and most of the manufacturing villages, land was less scarce than in Nottingham, and workshops were much less commonly built above dwelling-houses. In Leicester, larger work-

FIGURE 1

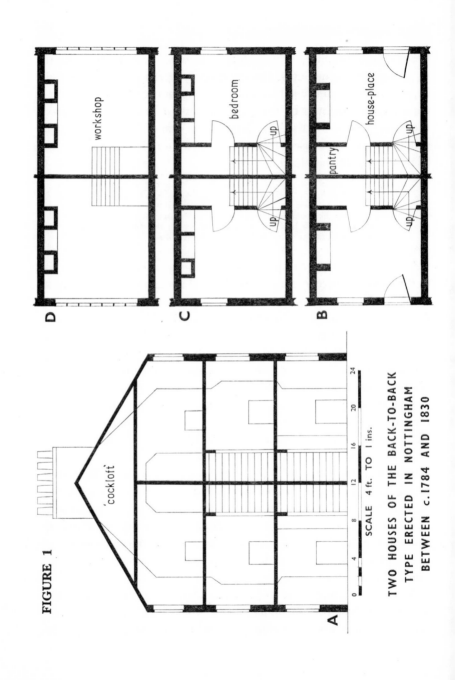

workshop

bedroom

pantry   house-place

D

C

B

'cockloft'

A

SCALE 4 ft. TO 1 ins.

0   4   8   12   16   20   24

TWO HOUSES OF THE BACK-TO-BACK
TYPE ERECTED IN NOTTINGHAM
BETWEEN c.1784 AND 1830

shops containing a dozen or more frames, were built as an annexe to workers' houses and cottages, though this development was only just beginning at the end of the eighteenth century.[4]

Advertisements for the sale of hosiery- and lace-frames appear frequently in the local newspapers after the middle of the eighteenth century. They usually indicate where the frames were located, and it is possible to gain a fairly accurate impression of the overall concentration of frames in workshops. The great majority of workshops held from one to four frames, and there appears to have been no very striking change over the thirty years covered by this study. Any workshop with more than six frames was unusual, and likely to be owned by a framesmith or bag hosier. The domestic organization of industry, as such, offered little by way of precedent for the development of factory industry.

2. Factories and the Employment of Parish Apprentices

The concentration of machinery in factories, usually associated with the name of Arkwright, was anticipated by earlier developments in Nottingham. The hosier who pioneered the concentration of production in the textile trades in the town was Samuel Fellows (1687–1765). Fellows was born in London and, after serving his time there as a framework knitter, migrated to Nottingham in about 1705 or 1706. Two separate, but not necessarily conflicting accounts are given of his removal. Henson related that Fellows was threatened in the riots that took place in the London parishes of St Luke, Cripplegate and Shoreditch at the beginning of the eighteenth century. The journeymen framework knitters were demonstrating against the employment of an excessive number of apprentices by certain masters, and Fellows is said to have been one of those who agreed in future to observe the regulations of the London Company of Framework Knitters. A second account says that he moved to Nottingham when his father died, to claim some property left to him near Selston, in the county. Quite possibly he sold the land to

establish himself as a master in Nottingham, where he thought he
would be free from the Company's regulations.

In Nottingham, Fellows resolutely defied the Company by establishing a workshop where he boarded numbers of apprentices on his
frames. The stocking-frame, though a complicated mechanism, was
not difficult to operate, its basic motions being simple and rhythmic,
and a strong boy, aged ten to twelve, could become proficient in six
or nine months. The parishes paid masters £5 for each apprentice
taken off their hands, and clothed them during their period of
apprenticeship. Fellows' apprentices, of whom he was employing
more than forty by the early twenties, generally earned 8s a week
for their task work and, when employed on better work, 9s or 10s a
week. From this sum, 3s or 4s was deducted for their board and
lodging. As journeymen at this time earned 10 to 12s a week
Fellows and those who followed his lead must have found their
apprentice workshops very profitable. The London Chartered
Company brought a test-case in 1728 against one such employer,
Cartwright, but the Nottingham justices, pleased with this creation
of new employment, refused to recognize the legal validity of the
Company's ordinances.[5]

This decision prompted Fellows to expand his business still further, and it was probably at this time that he began to specialize in
silk hosiery, a lucrative branch of the trade in which his knowledge
of the fashion-conscious metropolitan market would be of special
value. His daughter, Hannah, who appears to have supervised her
father's silk spinsters, was said to have had the greatest skill of any
woman in the town connected with the silk trade.[6] It is likely that he
developed a second workshop for his silk spinsters.

When the success of Strutt's 'Derby rib' precipitated an era of
experimenting in the production of new meshes on the frame,
Fellows was ready to purchase artisan ingenuity. The first major
innovation after Strutt's was a device attached to the frame by
which it was possible to imitate 'Spanish' eyelet-hole mitts. Different ways of making these fashion goods are said to have been con-

trived by Samuel Betts, a Nottingham framesmith, and Ferdinando Shaw, a Mansfield artisan. Shaw sold his method to Fellows who built 'a large factory' near Weekday Cross, Nottingham, for their reception. This is the first recorded occasion on which a large work-shop was built as a 'safe-box' for an innovation in Nottingham. The idea was taken up by successive hosiers who sponsored innovation so that, by the time Arkwright came to Nottingham, the factory could be recognized as a location of production commonly used by innovators. The Strutt's 'Derby rib' machines were first put in a room lit only by skylights, but this attempt to ensure secrecy failed when some of the local population climbed on to the roof to look down at the frames. This failure may well have inspired Arkwright's attempt to achieve greater security for his innovation. A Chester-field hosier, John White, also learned the technique of making eyelet-hole work about the same time as Fellows and he, too, built a factory in his own locality to keep the process secret. The hosiery factory was not unknown to the country hosiers, as well as to those in Nottingham.[7]

Before long—certainly by 1778—girls as well as boys from the parishes were being apprenticed in the frames. According to a Nottingham framework knitter who appeared before the House of Commons committee on the knitters' petition of 1778, boys of ten or eleven years of age, recruited from the parish workhouses, were made to work until eleven or twelve o'clock at night to complete their tasks. Girls and women worked in separate workshops, en-gaged on the easiest work, that of making small worsted stockings. However, 'Amicus', a correspondent of the *Nottingham Journal*, maintained in the same year that, 'It is well-known that this work —which an apprentice has generally performed for his task—was [worth] no more than 6s per week, out of which 2s or near it must be deducted for frame rent etc. Then the master has only 4s for the maintenance of his apprentice—so that unless he has a number of them and all prove diligent and faithful, the profits are not worth the trouble and expense'.

This conflict of views is largely reconciled by evidence of the general practice of parish apprenticeship in Nottingham. In January 1775, the three parishes of the town advertised that they had 'Several healthy boys of eleven and twelve years of age to be apprenticed—N.B. Money will be given with each boy'. The appearance of the advertisement suggests that demand for juvenile labour was limited and a month later the parish officers complained to the Corporation that 'Several of the poor manufacturers are daily taking parish apprentices from country parishes, merely for the sake of a little money, and then turning them loose, so that they become a burden on the Nottingham parishes.'[8]

No doubt the country apprentices were preferred because they were removed from the immediate supervision of their parish overseers. This evidence, and the lack of considerable concentration of frames, suggests that apprenticeship of paupers did not exist on a large scale, and that the exploitation of juvenile labour was largely confined to a number of small masters, among them several unscrupulous framework knitters. Very likely, Fellows and Cartwright had few imitators because the hosiers found that there was little profit and a great deal of trouble attached to keeping numbers of parish apprentices. In later years, towards the end of the eighteenth century, it was the practice of 'colting' (or training and employing youths as knitters without formal apprenticeship) which attracted the wrath of the framework-knitters' unions. For the hosiers, this was a lot cheaper way of meeting the shortage of labour than by boarding numbers of apprentices.

3. Silk Mills

The first silk-reeling mill in the country, which was built at Derby between 1718 and 1721, has deservedly attracted a great deal of academic attention. It was the first successful power factory in England and the model for industrial units set up in the last three decades of the century. It is said to have employed about 300 people, the same number as Arkwright's first mill at Nottingham, which was, in turn, the prototype for numerous cotton mills in town and country.[9]

Silk remained the staple industry of Derby throughout the eighteenth century. The Spitafields silk industry, and the growing hosiery industry of the east Midlands, provided an expanding market for the reeled silk. During the second half of the eighteenth century, a number of mills were opened but, as Hutton recorded in 1791, 'they are all on a diminutive scale compared with the original Derby mill'. Pilkington, writing in 1789, makes a similar comment on the Derby silk industry, and implied that eleven mills employed some 900 workers between them. Nevertheless, even these small mills provided some precedent for factory industry. Strutt and Woollatt had a silk mill in Derby by 1771, before Strutt had embarked on his programme of factory-building at Belper, and possibly prior to his experience at Nottingham and Cromford in partnership with Arkwright.

The influence which the Derby silk mill exercised on the Strutts is suggested by some remarks which the firm made on working conditions at Belper and Milford in 1816. 'The working hours (at the Strutt mills) are twelve', W. G. and J. Strutt declared, 'six before dinner (which is from twelve to one), and six after, each of which six includes time for breakfast and tea. This has been the invariable practice at the original silk mill in Derby (and) in this neighbourhood for more than a hundred years'. The details of working hours are not our concern here; what is significant is that the second generation at Belper should attempt to justify their practice by allusion to the Derby silk mill. The impression given from the Strutts' remarks is that not only the design of the buildings, but also the details of administration and organization at the Derby mill had been absorbed by the local business community and accepted as precedents.[10]

Only a few silk mills were built outside Derby (but within the Midlands) before the end of the century. The earliest may have been that of Samuel Unwin of Sutton-in-Ashfield. Local tradition maintains that his first mill was opened in 1740, but the records of Unwin's joiners first mention the setting up of a 'silk engine' in 1753. Little is known of the scale of this enterprise, though it is clear that the bucket water-wheel was also used to give power to fulling stocks and to what were known as 'twist mills' a simple apparatus used by knitters to twist thread. Another early silk mill was built at Chesterfield about 1757. This four-storey factory stood athwart the River Hipper and was owned by the Tucker family for several generations. There is also believed to have been a silk mill at Tutbury, Staffordshire, built before 1781 on the River Dove, and this enterprise may have been conducted by John Bott & Co., though the facts are not clear.[11]

The other silk mills outside Derby were all built in and about Nottingham, where the silk branch of the hosiery industry gave extensive employment. The introduction of silk point-net lace in 1784 considerably increased the demand for reeled silk and one of the first mills was built in Sheep Lane, Nottingham, sometime before 1792. It may have been opened by Joseph Hopkinson, who was later forced to sell it on becoming bankrupt. It was then purchased by William Stanford, a Nottingham silk merchant, and William Elliott, who had retired from the hosiery trade after making a fortune as a dyer, and had previously (1782) owned a cotton mill in the town. Another Nottingham silk mill opened by John Fellows, a silk hosier and son of Samuel Fellows, was converted from a lace factory about 1800. Blackner, writing about 1812, mentions two other small mills, and one at least was in existence in 1799, owned by a hosier called Bolton.[12]

Three of the owners of the silk mills identified had connections with the cotton-spinning industry. Bott & Co. opened a large mill at Tutbury, and William Stanford, in partnership with a Mansfield hosier called Burnside, opened a cotton mill adjoining his silk mill and another at Mansfield. John Fellows' brother, Elihu Samuel Fellows, was partner in an early cotton mill at Wirksworth.

Nevertheless, there is no evidence of experience in silk-reeling leading to interest in cotton-spinning, except in the case of Unwin of Sutton-in-Ashfield. Unwin was an unusual entrepreneur in several respects (as will be seen in Chapter Five, where his career is examined at length), but his opportunities as a country hosier were paralleled in many other parts of the hosiery districts. In the absence of more definite evidence, it is only possible to make a tentative conclusion. In Derby, the silk-reeling industry was prosperous for most of the eighteenth century, and there was little incentive for the mill-owners to divert their capital into cotton-spinning. Derby provided few recruits to the cotton industry. Silk-reeling did not arrive in Nottingham until towards the end of the eighteenth century, and there is no evidence of any transfer of experience from the organization of a silk mill to that of a cotton mill. However, the case of Unwin suggests the possibility of a number of other merchant hosiers having installed reeling-machines on the Lombe principle. The use of power (horse capstans or water-wheels) to motivate these machines might form a precedent for cotton-spinning by power, following the success of Arkwright's roller-spinning factories.

4. Early Factories in Birmingham

It has not always been appreciated that cloth-making was still an important industry in Birmingham and the vicinity at the middle of the eighteenth century. Most of the products were traditional ones for the local market, heavy fabrics in linen, wool and hemp, but they gave rise to an early concentration of capital. The linen yarns had to be twisted to make warp threads and from 1730 we hear of machines being invented to twist a number of threads simultaneously. These machines were known as twist mills (or twisting mills); in Lancashire they were used for twisting warp threads for cotton looms. Before Arkwright began his career in cotton, twist mills with forty or fifty spindles were common and 200 spindles were not unheard of.

These large machines had to be motivated by horse capstans or water-wheels. There were more than a dozen threadmakers at work when Birmingham's first directory (Sketchley's) appeared in 1767. The local linen-thread industry declined after about 1782 (as cotton became progressively cheaper) but it was not until 1809 that the last thread mill was sold up.[13]

The contribution of John Wyatt, the Birmingham inventor, and his partner, Lewis Paul, to the textile industry is best understood in the context of this local industry. In the first half of the eighteenth century cotton was being mixed with linen to produce lighter cloths, and there was clearly a good market in Birmingham for anyone who could spin cotton cheaply. The idea of spinning cotton by rollers was first conceived by Paul, who came to Birmingham from London to secure mechanical assistance and formed his partnership with Wyatt in 1731. However, it was not until the end of the decade that their first small factory was opened in Birmingham.

During this long interval Paul is heard of in London and Nottingham experimenting to improve the technique and also, subsequent events seem to suggest, trying to recruit capital. The early failure of the Birmingham factory was partly due to lack of capital, but more particularly to the failure of either Paul or Wyatt to bring the machine to a point at which it was workable without great expense and frequent mishaps. When the partners became bankrupt in 1742, Edward Cave, better known as the editor of the *Gentlemen's Magazine*, opened a mill at Northampton with a water-wheel giving motivation to 250 spindles. The mill was badly managed and did not prove a commercial success.

Before the Birmingham and Northampton factories were projected, Paul spent some time in Nottingham trying to establish mechanized spinning there. Henson relates that, for a while, Paul directed his experiments to spinning cotton for use on the stocking-frame. Though Paul's first experiments were conducted in London (presumably with the London hosiery industry in mind), he moved to Nottingham about 1739, no doubt because the hosiery manufacture was then in process of migration to the Midlands, and Nottingham had begun to specialize in cotton industry. In Nottingham (again according to Henson), 'he attempted to spin four threads at once; but the defect of his method of cleaning and carding the wool (i.e., raw cotton), and his imperfect machinery made his productions higher in price than yarn spun by hand'. This record is supported by Charles Wyatt's account of his father's invention of a carding and roving 'box' later in his career. Though Paul returned to Birmingham, his invention is said to have been responsible for initiating an era of experiments in mechanized spinning in Nottingham. The failure of these experiments served to create a climate of of expectancy, in which Arkwright and Hargreaves found little difficulty in securing patrons in the town.[14]

CHAPTER THREE

The Spinning-Jenny and the Evolution of the Factory System

IT is a striking fact that most of the key figures in the development of the Midlands spinning industry were not natives of the Region. Samuel Fellows, Sir Thomas Lombe and his half-brother John, and Lewis Paul, all came from London, though the Lombes originated in Norwich and Paul is supposed to have come of a Huguenot refugee family. In the next stage of development three of the major innovators, Hargreaves, Arkwright and Peel migrated into the Region from Lancashire where the development of the cotton industry had anticipated that in the Midlands. James Hargreaves was born in the semi-moorland district of Oswaldtwistle, near Blackburn, Lancashire, and became a handloom weaver. He acquired a reputation for mechanical ingenuity by introducing one, and possibly two, improved methods of carding cotton by hand.

After the middle of the eighteenth century the demand for spun-cotton yarn began to outstrip the supply in Lancashire, partly because of the expansion of the domestic and overseas markets, and more particularly because of the widespread adoption of Kay's flying shuttle in the 1750s, which doubled the capacity of the weavers. This expansion created a bottleneck at the previous stage of production, that of spinning and, in about 1764, Hargreaves contrived a hand-machine to duplicate the work of the old spinning-wheel (Plate 2). The invention was disclosed to Robert ('Parsley') Peel (grandfather of the future Prime Minister, Sir Robert Peel), who helped Hargreaves while he was perfecting his invention and protected him from the fury of the mob during the jenny riots in Blackburn in 1778. Shortly after the riots, Hargreaves left secretly for Nottingham, where a crisis in the supply of yarn had also developed, though for rather different reasons. It is not clear whether he was invited to Nottingham, or merely followed in the footsteps of Arkwright, who was already familiar with the hosiery districts. At any rate, neither Hargreaves nor Arkwright had difficulty in securing patrons once the value of their techniques had been demonstrated.

During the early 1760s a crisis had broken in the Nottingham hosiery trade. The Tewkesbury hosiers began to undersell their Nottingham rivals when it was discovered that their country spinsters could readily accommodate themselves to spinning cotton because they were used to handling short-staple Spanish wool. The women in the Midland counties were only familiar with long-staple wool, and 'could not be brought to spin a thread that would bear the least resemblance to India's cotton', which the Nottingham hosiers were thus compelled to import. The Indian cotton was of much superior quality, but it was difficult for the customer to detect the difference in the knitted garment. The Nottingham hosiers succeeded in securing an Act of Parliament (known as the Tewkesbury Act, 1766) by which all hose had to be marked, but as Wadsworth and Mann remark, the Act 'can have done little to help them, since, as in the case of most legislation of the time, there was no machinery for putting it into force'.

As a result of Mr Aspin's reconstruction of the machine using the patent specification of 1770, we now know exactly what the original jenny looked like and how it worked. 'The world's first successful spinning-machine', Mr Aspin points out, 'can hardly be said to have been the work of a mechanical genius.' It was a hand-operated machine, smaller than the stocking-frame and weaving-loom in use throughout the Region, clumsy to operate but requiring no special skill. Its use was not restricted by the patent of 1770, and it could, therefore, be used freely in hosiers' warehouses or framework-knitters' shops. Thus the jenny itself could not have been immediately responsible for transforming the spinning industry from a domestic to a factory situation. The enlarged and improved (vertical wheel) jenny demanded more space than most cottage workshops could have provided, but these machines were slow to be introduced into the Midlands and, by then, the Hargreaves jenny was already becoming redundant in the hosiery districts of the east Midlands. It is true that Hargreaves and James put up a building, known as Hockley Mill, to house the first jennies they built, though it could more accurately be described as a workshop since it only became a mill in 1777, when it was converted to warp-spinning. At the time it was built, it was merely an attempt to keep the invention secret, a 'safe-box' to which only trusted workmen would be admitted, at least until a patent could be established. When Hargreaves declined to defend his patent against the 'coalition' of Nottingham hosiers that rose against him, there was no longer any need to guard against industrial spies or machine-breaking mobs and other jennies could be more conveniently worked in existing industrial premises.

Finally, it is necessary to reconsider the reasons for the early decline of Hargreaves' and James' Nottingham enterprise. The fact is that within eight years of Hargreaves's migration to Nottingham, his partner, Thomas James, was compelled to abandon jenny-spinning to become one of Arkwright's earliest licencees. As a result of Mr Aspin's researches, it seems indisputable that roller-spinning was a superior technique to jenny-spinning. With both the early and the improved jenny, the range of yarns that could be produced varied from No. 7 to No. 20; while Arkwright's machines could produce as fine a thread as No. 60. Moreover, experiments with the reconstructed jenny confirm Henson's allegation that the machine produced uneven and lumpy yarns. Henson, whose history of the hosiery trade was drawn from the oral testimony of Nottingham framework knitters, noted that the 'cotton yarn spun by Hargreaves, though much superior to the Nottingham spinning (of the local spinsters) was still a poor article, being full of tender, thin places, bumps and burs, and was with difficulty wrought into

Plate 1. Stocking frame, c. 1770. A hand-operated machine similar to the original stocking frame invented by William Lee in 1589.

Plate 2. Hargreaves' Jenny, reconstructed by Messrs Textile Machine Makers from the Patent Specification of 1770

stockings'. These two sources, corroborating each other, seem more reliable than other evidence.[1]

On Hargreaves' death, the *Nottingham Journal* said that stockings made of jenny yarn 'are esteemed over all Europe to be far superior in neatness and more durable than any cotton-hose manufactured in any part of Great Britain'. A year earlier, when the jennies were offered for sale, Hargreaves and James had claimed that their machinery for making and 'finishing cotton-yarn for hosiery' was 'fully employed by a set of the very best workpeople, and the yarn then produced, finds a ready sale, being of the first quality'.[2] Clearly it is not possible to reconcile these two statements with the other sources, other than to suggest that the jenny patentee may well have over-rated the value of his plant.

For technical reasons, the jenny proved less valuable in the Midlands than in the cotton industry of Lancashire and the north-west. In Lancashire, the jenny was used for more than a generation after its invention to supply weft to the weavers, and proved complementary to the activities of the warp-spinning mills until after the introduction of the mule. (Crompton's mule was slow to supersede the jenny because of its much higher building cost.) In the east Midlands, cotton-yarn was knitted, not woven, and only one thread was used in the process. Yarn spun on the water-frame was quite suitable for the stocking-frame, and because roller-spinning was a continuous, power-driven process it soon proved cheaper to produce yarn by this method than by the intermittent motions of the hand-operated jenny. However, the hosiers and lace manufacturers of Nottingham, whose main interest lay in producing fine goods for the fashion market, would not have been very interested in the coarse thread produced by the jenny. Quality hose and lace-net demanded a fine cotton-thread which the jenny was incapable of producing. It was not until the mule was perfected that a thread fine enough for the fashion specialities could be produced, and by this time the east Midlands had already lost its early lead in the spinning industry.

D

The initial superiority of Arkwright's technique, reinforced, no doubt, by his business acumen, rapidly brought him other advantages. In Samuel Need, he secured the patronage of the leading hosier in Nottingham, whereas Thomas James, Hargreaves' partner, was a relatively insignificant framesmith. In 1772, Arkwright already employed three times the labour force of James and Hargreaves in Nottingham alone, and that on machines needing less attention than the jenny required. The registration of Arkwright's carding patent (1775) dealt Hargreaves and James the final blow. This patent, a legal manœuvre by which Arkwright sought to monopolise the whole spinning process, including older inventions than his own, finally forced the reluctant partners to become licencees of the leviathan patentee.[4]

In the second part of this chapter it will be seen that the spinning-jenny was widely distributed in the north and west of Derbyshire and in the adjacent parts of Staffordshire in the last two decades of the eighteenth century, and indeed appears to have survived in the Region until the close of the Napoleonic wars. It may seem anomalous that these machines should have continued in production for more than a generation after the collapse of Hargreaves' and James' enterprise, and the explanation is to be found in the geographical specialization within the Region. In Nottingham, the centre of the cotton-hosiery manufacture, only the finest and best-paid work was undertaken. The town was a magnet for mechanical ingenuity in the trade, and new branches of the fashion industry were constantly being born under the patronage and immediate supervision of the merchant hosiers and lace merchants. In the surrounding rural areas, only the coarser and less well-paid work was undertaken. Consequently, the Nottingham trade demanded the finest spun-yarn for its specialities, while the remote Derbyshire spinners satisfied demand for the coarser yarns.

The Peak district was also peripheral to the Lancashire cotton-manufacturing region, and here, as in the Midlands, the coarser spinning was left to the geographical margins of the region. (Samuel

Crompton's census of the cotton industry in 1811 shows that most of the surviving jennies were located in Stockport and Wigan.) Hargreaves' and James' jennies ceased production just about the time the machine was becoming popular in Derbyshire as the demand for the coarser yarns migrated to the margins of the Region. The jenny survived in the hands of these marginal producers—the phrase is used in both the geographic and economic sense—while it was gradually overtaken by the more efficient techniques developed by Arkwright and Crompton and their successors.

The Hockley Mill represented a transitional stage between the domestic industry and the factory system in two important respects. In the first place, it contained fifty spinning machines and 100 workers, a concentration probably without parallel in the Regional textile industry up to that time, apart from the Derby silk mill and Arkwright's Nottingham mill. The concentration of machinery did not create a precedent in the district for reasons that have already been explained, but the size of the building doubtless helped to familiarize the Nottingham manufacture with the idea of factory production. Secondly, the partners used a horse capstan for driving the carding engines which Hargreaves had developed.[5] When the jennies became obsolete, the premises and the source of power were available and readily adaptable for warp-spinning. It was in this process of transition that the Hockley Mill provided a pattern which, if not emulated, was certainly repeated in many locations of the jenny-spinning industry.

Wadsworth and Mann, in their *Cotton Trade and Industrial Lancashire, 1600–1780*, observe that Nottingham, like Lancashire, 'also had its jenny mills', but this statement is supported by only one advertisement, in the *Manchester Mercury*, referring, in fact, to the Hockley Mill machinery, which was offered for sale when James and Hargreaves turned to roller-spinning.[6] The paucity of advertisements in the *Nottingham Journal* and *Derby Mercury* suggests that jenny mills were practically unknown in and about Nottingham. The only advertisement for a jenny-workshop in the

Nottingham Journal refers to one owned by Samuel Walsh, a Bulwell calico printer. Walsh worked eight jennies and a number of calico looms in a 'large-sashed dwelling-house'. His manufacturing interests and his connections were not typical of the Region, for his partner was a London merchant and one of his family had a calico warehouse in Manchester. His jennies were built by a Stockport machine-builder and the business had such a short life that one might justifiably imagine that it was a Lancashire import which did not prosper in the Midlands environment.[7]

The *Derby Mercury* contains only two advertisements for the sale of jennies in workshops. In 1782, an advertisement appeared for the sale of three jennies and 'implements for the cotton business' at Coal Bridge, near Derby, and in 1787 John Ward, a Derby joiner, offered for sale a 'Cotton Works' containing four spinning-frames.[8] The available evidence suggests that Walsh was planning to open a warp-spinning mill when he sold his jennies, and that Ward's workshop was converted to a roller-spinning plant by the purchasers. It is significant that none of these jenny-workshop owners was a merchant hosier, most of whom were readily able to absorb such jennies as they needed into the existing fabric of their businesses without erecting new buildings. As they were the sole purchasers of spun-cotton in the east Midlands, they were largely able to determine the source of their supplies and hence the location of the new techniques.

The coalition of Nottingham hosiers that prevented Hargreaves from exploiting his patent cannot be identified with certainty, but were probably the same militant association which was in conflict with the framework knitters at this time. The association would no doubt have been sufficiently powerful to intimidate all but the most resolute patentee with extensive financial backing, and it is not surprising that Hargreaves shrank from the prospect of an expensive contest. In 1772, this association of hosiers was confident enough to publish a list of its members which contained seventy names and included most of the leading merchant houses in the town.[10] At least ten of those listed, excluding Samuel Need, subsequently became partners in cotton-spinning mills on Arkwright's principle. Probably the jenny was the link between the merchanting activities of the hosiers and the factory enterprises in which a significant number invested their capital.

The merchant hosiers at Nottingham, Derby and Leicester exercised some control over the domestic industry throughout the three counties, but their interest in the more distant parts of Derbyshire, particularly the High Peak Hundred, was weak. Nottingham hosiers employed women in Derbyshire, Leicestershire, Staffordshire and Yorkshire for embroidering lace-net at the end of the century, but few knitters lived more than a dozen miles from the centres of the hosiery industry at Nottingham, Derby, Leicester, Mansfield, Bakewell and Hinckley. Handloom-weaving was the more usual form of domestic industry in those remote parts of the Region up to the second decade of the nineteenth century, and here, beyond the orbit of hosier control, the jenny was widely used and independently owned, playing an important role in the evolution of factory industry.

Evidence of the existence of the jenny in Derbyshire is contained in several topographical works of the period, though the record is confused by the vocabulary used. James Pilkington, Derbyshire's first historian, recorded in 1789 that 'a considerable quantity of cotton is . . . spun upon hand-machines or wheels in the north-west part of the county', and makes it clear that he is not referring to the old spinning-wheels in his comments on Tideswell, where he says there are 'a few hand-machines or jennies for spinning cotton'. He mentions a large number of villages and hamlets in the Peak district where cotton-spinning, evidently by jennies, was being carried on. The cotton mills are given distinct mention, so that he is obviously not confusing warp-spinning (in mills) and jenny-spinning (in cottages or workshops).

Pilkington's commentary is supported by some interesting autobiographical details in William Radcliffe's polemical *Origin of*

Power-Loom Weaving. Radcliffe came of a farming family at Mellor (Derbyshire) which, like so many of their neighbours, supplemented their agricultural income by their earnings as spinners and weavers. In the family workshop, Radcliffe acquired 'a practical knowledge of every process from the cotton bag to the piece of cloth, such as carding by hand or by the engine, spinning by the hand-wheel or jenny, winding, warping, sizing, looming the web, and weaving either by hand or fly-shuttle'. In 1785, at the age of twenty-four, he became an independent manufacturer, putting out work in the surrounding district and 'in all parts of the hill country of Derbyshire within the distance of a day's journey from Mellor'. Radcliffe claims that his career, at any rate in its early stages, was fairly typical of that of a great many other small manufacturers in northwest Derbyshire. In 1800, there was not a village within thirty miles of Manchester on the Derbyshire and Cheshire side', Radcliffe asserted 'in which some of us were not putting out cotton warps and taking in goods, employing all the weavers of woollen and linen goods who were declining those fabrics as the cotton trade increased . . .'. Though Mellor itself is not within the Midland Region as defined here, a thirty-mile radius takes in something like a third of the whole of Derbyshire, and includes such places as Bakewell, Hartington, Tideswell, Bamford and Chapel-en-le-Frith, all of which are considered in this and some subsequent chapters.

Recalling local tradition about the history of the district in the later eighteenth century, Redferd mentions in his *History of Uttoxeter* that there were several jenny-shops in the town, and that these later gave way to the cotton mills on a stream just outside the town. In the course of compiling his *Agriculture of Derbyshire*, John Farey made a tour of the county in 1807–09 and listed the locations of 107 cotton mills. Forty-nine of these were in the parish of Glossop, beyond the purview of this study, and most of the remaining fifty-eight can be identified with known enterprises or with surviving mill buildings. There is, however, a residue of eleven locations, all in the High Peak area, which cannot be identified with either the names of firms or any physical remains, except a collection of farm buildings.[11] The word 'mill', as used in the textile industry at this period, sometimes meant no more than 'a machine which performs its work by rotary motion'. The assumption must be that Farey listed a number of surviving jenny-shops, and this is supported by other evidence.

The manuscript sources and local newspapers convey some further information. A letter in the Barker manuscripts records that spinning-jennies had been introduced at Bakewell—the centre of the small hosiery industry of the Peak district—and at Youlgreave sometime before 1776. The Land Tax returns for the occasional parish give details of industrial buildings, and from this source it appears that, at Tideswell, six small land-owners operated 'cotton mills' at the end of the eighteenth century. Only one mill building survives in the village, and it seems reasonable (in view of Pilkington's remarks) to suppose that the tax returns are referring to jenny- and weaving-shops. In the nearby parish of Beard (Glossop) there were eleven such 'mills' mentioned in the Land-Tax returns in 1799, and it may well be that some of this enterprise spilled over from Glossop into the adjacent parishes.

The Derbyshire jenny-spinners, however, were by no means confined to the north-western periphery or to the parish of Glossop. In 1788, the firm of Dakeyne & Sons of Darley Dale, three miles north of Matlock, inserted a long notice in the *Derby Mercury*, calling on 'the Cotton-Jenny Spinners of the County of Derby . . . to assemble in your several districts' to prepare petitions to submit to Parliament against the import of calicoes. The political intentions of Dakeynes are not important for the moment; the point being that the firm clearly knew of the existence of a substantial number of jenny-spinners in that area, sufficient at least to be politically significant. In other parts of Derbyshire, Pilkington refers to a cotton industry at Wirksworth, Matlock, Hartington and Ashford, and an advertisement in the *Derby Mercury* in 1796 reveals a factory employing jennies and looms at Winster.[12] Samuel Crompton's census of the cotton industry in 1811 revealed a jenny-shop of a thousand spindles at Chapel-en-le-Frith.

According to William Radcliffe, the years between 1788 and 1803 were the 'golden age' of the small rural manufacturer who employed domestic spinners and weavers. The age was created by Crompton's mule, a machine which was employed in domestic workshops but was sufficiently versatile to produce yarns for every description of clothing 'from the finest book muslin, lace, stocking, etc., to the heaviest fustian'. However, Radcliffe was writing primarily of Mellor, a village only fourteen miles from Manchester, and it is not clear how far this prosperity was shared by remoter Derbyshire villages, even though the mule was just as valuable to the hosiery industry as to the Manchester trade. The only lead on this point is the apparent connection between Radcliffe's remarks on the rapid fabrication of workshops during this period and the conversion of premises in other parts of Derbyshire. Radcliffe recalled that in the years after 1788 'the old looms being insufficient, every lumber-room, even old barns, outhouses and outbuildings of any description were repaired, windows broke through the old black walls, and all fitted up for loom-shops. This source of making room being at length exhausted, new weavers' cottages with loom-shops rose up in every direction . . .'. In the parts of Derbyshire that fall within the Midland Region, workshops were also being converted from cottages or farm outbuildings. Thus a small farm advertised for sale at Wirksworth in 1794 was described as a 'small house and large barn, lately converted into a cotton factory'. Characteristically, this 'factory' was offered for sale with 'five closes of rich land'. A house offered for sale near Winster in 1797 was described as 'suitable for some branches of the cotton manufacture'. Another house at Ashover, which was 'used to spin hurds', was advertised for sale with the facility of water-power from the adjacent River Amber, an advantage which points to the line of development of many of these rural workshops.[13]

There were, in fact, several methods by which such workshops were adapted to the growing scale of the cotton industry. The adoption of steam-power is illustrated by the development of a workshop at Winster. In 1795, the local press announced the sale of all the machines and implements used in the workshop, 'consisting of carding engines, billys, jennies, looms, reeds and gears, warping-mills, bobbins, etc., etc., . . . Also a . . . steam-engine complete, fixed at the end of the said mill, of sufficient force to work the machines'. Evidently the partners in the enterprise had introduced a Newcomen engine to drive their carding engines, but were over-sanguine of its value for driving the other machines. The pur-chasers of this factory (one of whom was a Winster grocer of some fortune) subsequently opened a water-powered mill at Matlock, which suggests that this was the more profitable line of develop-ment in a county where good water-mill sites were so abun-dant.[14]

The usual pattern of development was for the owners of country workshops in the Peak district to turn over to mules or, even more frequently, to harness an adjacent stream to a water-wheel for warp-spinning. Lancashire-built mules could be purchased in the Mid-lands, and indeed were advertised in the *Nottingham Journal* as early as 1793. Mules are heard of as far afield as Chesterfield where, in 1797, Mary Haslam advertised for sale two mules built by Shel-don & Co. of Manchester.[15] Another instance of the transition from jenny- to mule-spinning is provided by Thomas Taylor of Warslow, near Hartington. He probably came to the cotton industry from malting, for he advertised for a partner or purchaser for 'a brew-house and cotton business for mules and jennies', offering the facilities of a five-storey building.[16]

It was, however, more common to utilize the power of a stream to convert buildings for warp-spinning, and the best-documented ex-ample of this pattern of development occurs at Hartington. Thomas Cantrell appears to have come of a family of yeoman farmers at Kniveton, a village just to the north of Ashbourne. In 1776, he moved to Hartington to purchase a farmhouse, barn stables and outbuildings. There was only half an acre of land with the property; so obviously Cantrell's main interests were outside farming. Pilkington, visiting Hartington about 1783, recorded that in the village and its neighbourhood 'about sixty hands are employed in the manufacture of cotton, thread, linen and check'. This writer was quite explicit when recording the existence of cotton mills, so clearly he saw only jennies and looms at Hartington. When the 'check manufactory' was burned down in 1786 it was said to be worth £2,000. Four years later, Cantrell and his three sons leased a corn mill on the River Manifold, a mile and a half away from their home, and built a 'large and extensive' cotton mill, with warehouses and workshops, to spin cotton and make calicoes. The partners borrowed £500 from a neighbouring clergyman in 1792, but were forced to sell out in 1794 and Cantrell ended his days as a farmer at Bakewell.[17]

Most of the manufacturers who employed jennies and looms or stocking-frames were probably too small to employ their own agents to secure supplies of cotton and to market their product. Instead, they were linked with the centres of the cotton industry by a number of middlemen. The earliest trade directory to cover the region lists cotton factors at Wirksworth, Chapel-en-le-Frith and Uttoxeter, and there was at least one family of cotton merchants in existence in Bakewell by 1781. The factors had merchant contacts with Nottingham, Leicester, and no doubt Manchester.[18] Some sold direct to large firms of merchant-manufacturers, like McConnel & Kennedy of Manchester.

The limited evidence thus shows a jenny-spinning industry scattered over many villages and hamlets in the northern and western parts of Derbyshire and the Staffordshire borders, originating perhaps in Ashbourne and Bakewell in the middle seventies but spreading also from Manchester via Glossop. Almost from the first, it faced competition with mills on the Arkwright pattern, and was already in decline by the time Pilkington made his itinerances in the middle 1780s. It was probably extinct by the conclusion of the Napoleonic wars. However, the jenny industry is of more than ephemeral interest, and is of permanent importance in that a handful of these cotton-shops were able to keep pace with the rapid technical progress of the cotton industry, utilizing the many fast-flowing streams to provide power for warp-spinning until they later turned to mules and steam-power. The documentary sources are supported by the evidence of field work in the Peak District, which seems to confirm that a few factories evolved from the nucleus of an isolated farmstead or village workshop.

Probably the best surviving example occurs at Bamford, in the Peak, where from about 1782 a local miller and farmer, Christopher Kirk, operated a cotton mill whose construction, Pilkington noted, was 'very different from that at Cromford'. When it was burned down in 1791, the workshop and machinery were insured for only £500. The enterprise was rebuilt and enlarged and probably at this period turned over to power-spinning. Cotton is still being spun in a mill on the site.

The fully-evolved mill can also be studied on the ground at Edale. The enterprise probably originated with Nicholas Cresswell, a substantial freeholder on these high moorland pastures. The Land Tax records show a 'miln' among his freehold property for the first time in 1790. In 1795, the valuation of this property increased suddenly; it was no doubt at this period that Cresswell took three partners and substantially enlarged the plant, perhaps on the model of Arkwright's Cressbrook Mill, to which it bears a striking resemblance. His partners were James Harrison, Robert Blackwell and Joseph Fletcher who were already in business as cotton carders and spinners in Manchester, where they had workshops insured for £2,000. In 1795 Edale Mill, machinery and stock were valued at only £1,000. The mill was spinning until 1933. Another example occurs at Tideswell, where there is a spinning-mill still in production, standing astride a tiny stream just to the north of the town. The mill probably belonged to Thomas Frith, a Tideswell farmer who

was in partnership with the notorious Ellis Needham of Litton
Mills from 1782 to 1799. At his death in 1820, Frith, describing
himself as a cotton manufacturer, left not only extensive farming
stock but also his 'dwelling-house . . . with the outbuildings,
factory, garden, lands and appurtenances . . .'. The factory, with its
'stock in trade, machinery, looms, materials and other effects belonging to my trade' figures here, as in other legal documents of the
period, as an integral part of the farming unit.[19]

These three instances of mills that survived in production until
recently, and the other examples from Tideswell and Hartington,
suggest that in these parts of Derbyshire men of small capital were
able to become entrepreneurs in the cotton-spinning industry. The
jenny could be built locally and cheaply, and it enabled farmers,
local tradesmen and artisans to enter or retain their interest in the
textile industry and, given skill and economy, to graduate to more
capital-intensive forms of spinning.

Information on the distribution of the jenny and its ownership in
the Midlands is scarce, so that it is useful to draw additional details
from the adjacent Lancashire textile region. Stockport and Mellor
were peripheral to the Lancashire region, as Tideswell and Hartington were to the Midlands. The large concentration of jennies in
Stockport and its 'circuit' (fifty-five workshops in 1811) was owned
and operated by men who were originally local artisans, tradesmen
and small farmers. Clockmakers, joiners, weavers, hatmakers and
shoemakers all appear to have provided recruits to this new group
of entrepreneurs. The insurance records give substance to these
local traditions, showing that in Stockport in 1795 a well-established
jenny-spinner might have as little fixed capital as £115.[20] Stockport
is only fourteen miles from Chapel-en-le-Frith, where the Midland
Region may be said to end and the Lancashire region to begin.
This distance is small enough for news of the opportunities opened
up by the invention of the jenny to have been well-known. There
can be little doubt that, in Derbyshire, local and petty capital, as
well as capital generated in the centres of the Midlands' textile in-

dustry, was recruited to establish and develop a new workshop- and factory-spinning industry. The generation of capital in the major centres of the Midland industry is more fully analysed in Chapter Five.

CHAPTER FOUR

The Impact of Arkwright

RICHARD Arkwright, as his most recent biographers have pointed
out, remains one of the enigmas of the eighteenth century. A semi-
literate tradesman, he left few personal papers and almost all his
business records have perished. Among the numerous accounts of
him there is considerable conflict and it is difficult to distinguish
fact from legend. Almost all that can be drawn from the various
accounts of his early life was that he was born in Preston in 1732 and
served an apprenticeship as a barber before opening his own shop
in Bolton. Marrying for a second time, he acquired sufficient capital
to become an itinerant dealer in hair for wigs. His first connection
with the spinning industry is a matter for speculation, and there has
long been a debate about his contribution to the development of
roller-spinning, originating with the legal disputes over his patents
between 1781 and 1785 and maintained by journalists and historians in every generation since.[1] The evidence presented in this
study gives weight to the view that Arkwright's genius lay in his
capacity for recognizing the value of other men's technical and
managerial ideas, and in exploiting them on a greater scale.

From the perspective of the Midlands, the initial problem in
plotting Arkwright's career is to decide why he should have wanted
to leave Lancashire for Nottingham, and then shortly move again to
remote Cromford, in the Derbyshire dales. In those days, an un-
educated Lancastrian would have had difficulty in making himself
understood in the Midlands, and Arkwright's technique (like Hargreaves') was far from being perfected by the time he arrived in
Nottingham.

The clue to Arkwright's contact with the Midlands is given in
Stephen Glover's first *Derbyshire Directory*[2]. A native of Wirks-

worth, Glover records that Arkwright carried on his early trade as an itinerant hair-dealer at Wirksworth for some time before 1768, no doubt travelling the principal markets of the area, and very likely reaching as far as Nottingham bargaining for unwanted feminine locks. Here, he would no doubt have heard of the crisis in the Midlands hosiery industry, which followed the success of Tewkesbury hosiers in spinning their cotton-yarn locally. The hosiers were desperate for a solution to the impasse, and Arkwright recognized that, once he could demonstrate the value of a spinning-machine, he would have little difficulty in finding a hosier patron. In Samuel Need he secured the support of the wealthiest hosier in Nottingham, and in Jedediah Strutt the leader of the Derby trade.

The one characteristic of Arkwright which, above all others, emerges from the various accounts of him is his social vanity. Henson, drawing on the legend of Arkwright current among his fellow-workmen in Nottingham, tells how he craved to be a member of the gentry and to enjoy the luxury of living in a mansion and riding in a carriage. In Nottingham, it was a long and expensive process to buy one's way to the pinnacle of the local establishment, for the Corporation was a self-perpetuating oligarchy, its members being elected for life. Samuel Need and Ichabod Wright, the banker who was Arkwright's earlier contact in the town, were members of Castle Gate Congregational Chapel, and excluded by resolution of their own Society from membership of the Corporation. Arkwright's residence in Wirksworth would have lead him to appreciate the possibilities of the district to a manufacturer needing water-power, but more especially to a social-climber. Cromford, two miles north of Wirksworth, was also the next village to Matlock Bath, which was already popular as a spa town and near the centre of an area where many of the gentry owed their positions to their interest in the lead- and calamine-mining industries.[3]

Established in Cromford, Arkwright wrote to Strutt, 'I can't think of stopping this concern here as that at Nottingham is not nor

ever will be anything in comparison to this . . .'.[4] Clearly, Need was
sceptical of the value of the distant and isolated Derbyshire factory
and Arkwright was trying to defend his insistence on the location.
In fact, the Nottingham mill was quite a substantial four-storey
building, employing 300 people by 1772.[5] The surviving buildings
at Cromford suggest that the first mill built there was not much
larger than the Nottingham mill, and Bray records that, as late as
1777, it employed only 'about 200 persons, chiefly children'. The
second Cromford mill was larger than the first, but the buildings
were not completed until the end of 1777, and it probably took until
the end of the decade to build up the total labour force of 800
which Pilkington noticed in 1783. The cost of community-building
at Cromford probably made the investment less profitable than that
at Nottingham, at least until the second mill was in full production.

The legend that Arkwright chose the Cromford site because of its
unique source of power—a warm-water sough from the Cromford
lead-mines—still persists, but the record is clear that the first of
Arkwright's mills at Cromford was powered by a small stream, the
Bonsall brook, a tributary of the nearby River Derwent. This
brook, to judge by its present appearance, was similar to dozens of
others much nearer to Manchester and Nottingham. Two early
maps of Cromford show that the second, or Lower Mill (which was
not built until 1777) used water from the Cromford Moor Long
Sough, but that the first mill relied on the Bonsall brook alone.[6]
Part of the stone channel and the iron aqueduct which carried water
from the Sough can still be seen to enter the site of the Cromford
mills at a point below where the remains of the Upper Mill stand
but above the Lower Mill, thus confirming the evidence of the maps.

In fact, Cromford proved a poor site for water power and Arkwright would have foreseen this if he had had any real understanding of water mills. The water supply of the Bonsall brook was so
small that, when additional factory accommodation was projected
in 1776, all kinds of technical and legal problems arose. The brook
did not provide sufficient power to drive a second wheel, and even

Plate 3. The earliest surviving illustration of Arkwright's first mill at Cromford (1771) reproduced from The Mirror, *22 October 1836. The present building has evidently had the top two storeys removed at some time*

Plate 4. Stramshill corn mill, Uttoxeter, Staffordshire, which was converted for use as a cotton mill in 1783. The wheel-house is on the left of the buildings. The earliest spinner on this site was Thomas Parkes, a local plumber and glazier. The mill and house contained 600 spindles and 20 calico looms in 1798

Plate 5. *Robert Peel's cotton mill as it is today. The lintel on the ground floor marks the site of the first water-wheel. A second wheel stood on the side of the mill. Its position can be seen from the abrasions left on the wall*

Plate 6. *Robert Peel's third cotton mill (1791) at Burton-on-Trent, from a mid-nineteenth century painting by an unknown local artist. The cottage at the centre of the picture was the original corn mill on the site.*

when Arkwright demolished one of the old corn mills to release more water, the augmented flow was still inadequate. He enquired into the cost of steam-engines for pumping back water into the old mill-race, but for the time being the cost deterred him. Ignorant or impatient of legal negotiation, he seized the water supply from the Cromford Moor Sough, the mouth of which was very close to the village millpond. He diverted the flow of water from the 'tail' of the Sough into the old millpond and regulated the flow by means of floodgates. As the result of this was to raise the water level in the lead-mines after rain, the miners soon retaliated by sabotaging Arkwright's floodgates, and his new mill-wheel ground to a halt. When the Sough owners took up the miners' case, he replied by installing an 8 hp Boulton & Watt engine to return water to his reservoir, and by enclosing and roofing his channel from the Sough. The dispute dragged on for five years, and then went to arbitration when it was decided in favour of the Sough proprietors, since Arkwright would give no 'proofs or evidence' of his claims.[7]

A common method of providing a regulated flow of water to turn a mill-wheel was to cut a leat (or channel) just above a steep section of a river, and lead the diverted flow over the wheel and back into the natural water-course. As early as 1780, part of the course of the Trent was diverted for this purpose by Peel at Burton, but at Cromford, though the waters of the Derwent were available, the river flows through a narrow gorge and a diversion was clearly impossible. Moreover, the swiftness of the river was a very real threat to all buildings erected near it; Arkwright's nearest neighbour, Peter Nightingale, lost his cotton mill in a flood in 1785.

Having lost his dispute with the Sough owners, Arkwright began to look for sites in other parts of Derbyshire, and in 1777 he was negotiating for land adjoining a more promising stretch of river at Bakewell, a market-town at the centre of communications in the Peak District, where a labour force might more easily be recruited. But here again he ran head-on into legal opposition to his appropriation of water supplies, this time with a hostile Duke of Rutland,

E

one of the major landowners, who 'was well persuaded that it was not for the interest of his estates to encourage manufacturers upon them'. He did not return to Cromford to build until 1783, and then only to erect a paper mill, not a cotton-spinning plant.[8] For this project, he chose the only possible site in Cromford, alongside the Derwent itself. The site was a very difficult one, and the cost of damming the river and making the building secure must have been considerable.

It is possible to argue that Cromford had other economic assets which attracted Arkwright. Wirksworth was one of the principal centres of the lead-mining industry; between Cromford, Wirksworth and Stoney Middleton there were over a hundred shafts and more than a score of veins being exploited at about the time Arkwright moved to Cromford. This small area employed six pumping-engines and a smithy, evidence of engineering skill in the locality.[9] Even so, the skills and labour force of one smithy must have been paltry indeed compared with the resources of the textile-machine makers of Nottingham, Derby or Leicester, not to mention other centres of the industry. The lead-mining industry was contracting towards the end of the eighteenth century, and it has been pointed out that this situation may have seemed to offer a pool of unskilled female and juvenile labour. In point of fact, however, Arkwright had to draw a large part of his unskilled as well as skilled labour force from the main centres of the textile industry at Manchester and Nottingham, and at least one first-class mechanic refused to accompany him from Nottingham to Cromford.

In the event, the most useful asset probably proved to be one of Cromford's older industries. That part of the parish of Cromford between the village and the River Derwent, the site of the two earlier Arkwright mills, is known locally as Smelting Mill Green. There is no evidence of a smelting mill being on this site during or since Arkwright's time at Cromford, but in the later part of the sixteenth century the heavily-wooded Derwent valley did become the site of a number of lead-smelting mills. It seems likely that Arkwright, in fact, took over a declining works and employed its power for his own purpose, as Strutt was to do at Milford, Robinson at Bulwell and Toplis at Cuckney.

The only other possible attraction of Cromford was its isolation, which could have made it a good location for developing new techniques in secret, and relatively safe from rioting spinners and knitters.[10] However, this advantage seems small indeed compared with the very real handicaps which transport costs and isolation from the centre of the cotton textile industry imposed on the Cromford enterprise.

Thus, although the cotton-spinning industry was established at Cromford, and still remains there, the conclusion that it was taken there for non-economic reasons, or under a misapprehension of the economic advantages of the site, seem inescapable. Arkwright moved to Cromford because he was familiar with that part of the country, and recognized it as an appropriate district for the gratification of his social ambition. In this, at least, his expectations were amply fulfilled and he was duly knighted during his term of office as High Sheriff of Derbyshire. The second Richard later used his immense inherited wealth to complete the building of Willersley Castle—suitably out of sight of Cromford village and works—and to promote the interests of his large family by buying more land and acquiring positions for them in local government, in Parliament, in the Established Church, and in the legal profession.[11] In a word, he proved himself the true heir to his father's ambitions.

1. Influence on the Location of the Midlands Industry

In view of the interest attaching to Arkwright as the 'father of the English factory system', it is strange that no one has attempted a complete catalogue of his enterprises. In the Midlands, he seems to have been responsible for building ten cotton mills. Fitton and Wadsworth list some of these: Nottingham (1769), Cromford Upper Mill (1771), Cromford Lower Mill (1777), Cressbrook, near

Tideswell (1779), Bakewell (1782), Wirksworth (about 1783) and Masson, Matlock in 1784. In addition, there was a mill on the Dove at Rocester, Staffordshire (1782), and possibly also at Ashbourne (about 1781). There was also a small mill at Bromsgrove, Worcestershire, opened about 1783. Only the first three or four were built in partnership with Arkwright's Midland partners, Need and Strutt. Strutt and his son built five mills before the end of the century—at Belper (1778, 1786 and 1793), Milford (*c.* 1779) and Derby (1793)—and the evidence of the insurance records suggests that he did so independently of his partnership with Arkwright.[12]

Arkwright travelled all over Derbyshire, Yorkshire and Lancashire to find streams to turn his mills and by 1780[13] was diverting his attention to other counties; the Keighley (West Riding) mill is said to have begun work in 1780 and the Arkwright mill at Manchester was opened, after some delays, in 1783. After 1784, he may have decided that he had exhausted the possibilities offered by the Midlands, for in that year his last mill in the Region was completed and his interest switched to his Scottish projects.[14]

The geographical distribution of Arkwright's mills largely determined the location pattern of the Midlands cotton-spinning industry. Table 2 shows that, with one exception, the main centres of the Midlands industry remained where he and his partners and connections established them: in Nottingham and its district; along the Derwent valley from Derby up to Edale, but with a strong concentration around Matlock; and in the Dove valley, particularly between Ashbourne and Uttoxeter. The considerable development in and around Mansfield originated with Samuel Unwin, who may have been a Matlock connection of Arkwright's, and with William Toplis, a Mansfield mercer who was uncle to John Toplis, the Wirksworth banker, and a social connection of Arkwright's. The last two categories in the table serve to lump together a number of scattered locations.

TABLE 2

Location of Cotton Mills in the Midlands, *1769–1800*

Nottingham and South Nottinghamshire	25
Mansfield and North Nottinghamshire	14
Derwent Valley	31
Dove Valley	9
Remainder of Trent Valley	16
Outlying locations	15
Total number of mills	110

If, as the evidence suggests, it is true that the centre of Arkwright's empire at Cromford was selected from motives that were not primarily economic, it must follow that the firms which sprung up around the Arkwright mills in the Derwent and Dove valleys also occupied sites that would ultimately prove uneconomic, unless the industry in these areas could establish some internal economies before the competition of the Manchester and Nottingham mills overtook them. An exception must be made in the case of Evans' and Strutts' mills which, though situated on the Derwent, were fairly near to Derby, and were linked with the county town by valley roads. But for other mills in the Peak District, the generalization can be made that their uneconomic locations were a factor in the early decline of the Midlands cotton-spinning industry. This point will be taken up in the last chapter of this book, when the reasons for the early decline of the Midlands' cotton industry are considered.

2. Influence on the Future Development of the Midlands Industry

The significance of Arkwright in the development of modern industry is that he demonstrated the profitability of warp-spinning by power and thus induced others to attempt to follow his path to fortune. His genius, that is to say, was that of the successful innovating entrepreneur; for while there are several witnesses to his mechanical ability, he could lay small claim to the title of inventor and, indeed, showed little originality as a mechanic. Certainly, he did not originate or develop the idea of roller-spinning; the testimony of Matthew Boulton leaves no doubt that this was accomplished by Louis Paul. Arkwright's achievement was to translate Paul's mechanical success into the factory system of organization, and into commercial success.

This is now generally accepted by economic historians, but is repeated here to help explain why Arkwright did not for long maintain his technical leadership. There are clear signs of decline in his position from 1784; in particular, he failed to modify his warp-frame to spin worsted, he failed in his first attempt to apply rotary steam-power to his frames, and he failed to adopt the mule. It is important to examine some of the details and assess their impact on the Regional industry.

According to one authority, the modification of Arkwright's warp-spinning machinery for worsted 'involved no more than making the front rollers of greater diameter and adjusting the distance between the back and front rollers'.[15] Arkwright did not lack inducement to apply his frame to worsted-spinning, for at one period (1784–85) he was partner (with Josiah Wedgwood and Sir Joseph Banks) in a scheme to establish a statutory monopoly of worsted-spinning. Banks offered to use his influence to introduce a Bill into Parliament and, with his friends among the Lincolnshire gentry, to put up £10,000 for the establishment of the industry in that county. The terms could hardly have been more favourable; Arkwright's only obligation was to produce a machine that was mechanically sound.[16] The offer was attractive even without Parliamentary protection, and it is difficult to resist the conclusion that Arkwright lost the opportunity through his failure to perfect the process of worsted-spinning on his machine.

His failure to apply steam-power to the plant at his Manchester mill is equally striking. The enterprise was begun in 1780 and not completed until 1783, sufficient evidence of delay. According to Joseph Wilkes, writing to Boulton & Watt in 1783, Arkwright was obliged to alter the rotary steam-engine to a water-wheel, and it was probably for this reason that, until 1790, Arkwright 'could not be brought into a belief that a good thread could be spun by that means' (i.e., rotary steam-power).[17] The failure was a set-back to the Manchester as well as the Midlands industry.

Arkwright's failure to use the mule was admitted after his death by his son, who found himself excluded from the market for the finer counts of yarn, and quickly contracted the spinning business. By 1803, it was reduced to three mills, two at Cromford and one at Bakewell, the latter in partnership with Samuel Simpson. At Cromford mills, the number of people employed fell from 1,150 to 725 in 1816, by which time Arkwright & Co. were reduced to the status of producers of cheap, coarse yarns. The son wisely diverted his capital to finance, as is seen from his loans to Samuel Oldknow and his partnership (1802) in Toplis's bank at Wirksworth. Towards the end of his long life, he became a regular money-lender of substantial amounts to the aristocracy.[18]

The failure of Arkwright and his son to keep abreast of technical developments and to maintain their position in the industry seems all the more remarkable when their careers are compared with those of Jedediah Strutt and his three sons. While the Arkwright empire reached its meridian in 1784, Strutt's business continued to develop through the 1790s and in the early years of the nineteenth century; and when many firms in the Region were closing down William Strutt became the outstanding figure of the Midlands industry. Before 1790, he was experimenting with the mule and produced a self-acting model, though (according to his son) the inferior workmanship of the day prevented the invention from being a success. However, his design of iron-framed fireproof factories with heating systems was successful and was immediately copied. He embarked on mule-spinning at Derby in 1795 and built the Calico Mill, later referred to as the Derby Mill.[19]

This contrast between the careers of the Arkwrights and Strutts is no doubt partly a reflection of differing abilities, but must also be connected with Arkwright's migration from the industry's centres of progress. Most important inventions are the product, not of one mind, but of a number of inventors working together in close proximity, feeding on each others ideas and often stimulating one another by their rivalry. Cotton-spinning was no exception and, by moving to Cromford, Arkwright cut himself off from the centres of invention at Nottingham and Manchester. By exchanging the company of mechanics for that of the Derbyshire gentry, he forfeited his place as a leader of the industry. William Strutt on the other hand, living in Derby and attending meetings of the Derby Philosophical Society, was able to maintain his family's interest in the technical progress of the cotton industry.

Summarily, then, the influence of Arkwright on the development of the Midlands' industry was confined to the initial stimulus his early success gave to others in the Region. Had he remained in Nottingham, the history of the Midlands spinning-industry might well have been different. However, it must not be assumed that his early departure for Derbyshire was entirely responsible for the decline of the Midlands industry in the early years of the nineteenth century. The analogy of John Heathcoat, the Nottingham frame-smith who perfected and patented the bobbin-net lace-machine and then took his firm to Tiverton, suggests that the community of inventive minds in Nottingham was perfectly able to survive the loss of one of their number, however outstanding.[20] The lace industry survived and flourished in Nottingham, in spite of Heathcoat, and although Arkwright's migration to the remote Derbyshire dales must be counted a cause of the early decline of the Midlands cotton industry, it was not the only, nor indeed the decisive factor.

2. Licencees and Infringers of Arkwright's Patents

A number of entrepreneurs began spinning on the model of Arkwright's successful mills before the first court decision against his patents in 1781. The existence of both pirates and licencee cotton-spinners has been recognized by several historians; the difficulty is to identify the firms with any degree of certainty and to chart their influence on the early development of the industry in the Region. In addition to pirates and licencees, three Midlands spinners succeeded in by-passing the Arkwright patent of 1769 by obtaining patents of their own for some minor variation of the specification.

The pirates necessarily kept their activities secret and their identity can only be guessed at. Peter Nightingale of Lea, the defendant in the Arkwright test-case of 1785, may be thought to have been one, but the fact is that Lea mills were not opened until 1784, and Nightingale was probably chosen as an opponent because he was one of the ten proprietors of the Cromford Sough. The agreements between Arkwright and his licencees were confidential, and the patentee's only recorded statement on the subject was that he had sold licences to 'numbers of adventurers' in Nottinghamshire, Derbyshire, Leicestershire, Staffordshire, Worcestershire, and several other counties outside the Midlands.[21]

So few firms were established in the last three counties that it is possible to infer the names of the licencees in the light of other evidence. The only firm in Leicestershire that could have opened before 1781 was that of Smith Churchill, a Nottingham hosier who moved his business to his native village of Shepshed (near Loughborough) after a mob had demolished his house during the frameworkknitters' riots in Nottingham in 1779. In Staffordshire, Robert Peel's first mill at Burton-on-Trent opened in 1780, after an earlier attempt at roller-spinning at Altham (Lancashire). The only spinning-mill opened in Worcestershire was the one already noticed at Bromsgrove, built by Arkwright but later operated by John Adams.

The Pares manuscripts contain tantalizing allusions to licensed mills in Nottinghamshire and Derbyshire, among which the names of three early firms can be recognized: Robinsons at Papplewick (Nottinghamshire), James at Nottingham and Gardom, Pares & Co. at Calver, near Bakewell (Derbyshire). The Pares correspondence also confirms that Arkwright's premiums were very costly. Gardom, Pares & Co. paid £2,000 premium for the use of Arkwright's first patent (1769) and £5,000 for the use of his second (1775), plus an annual royalty of £1,000. Such expensive royalties seemed unreasonable to the licencees and made legal resistance worth while. They began to act together to resist the leviathan patentee in 1782, and their attitude no doubt encouraged the trade's growing opposition to Arkwright.[22]

Three patents were taken out by spinners in an attempt to avoid royalties, the earliest of which was registered by Samuel Unwin at Sutton-in-Ashfield, near Mansfield (Nottinghamshire). Unwin's first mill was built about 1770 and, like Arkwright's first mill at Nottingham, was powered by a horse capstan. The connection between Unwin and Arkwright is a matter for speculation. The two may have been friends and Unwin may have been Arkwright's first licencee, for Unwin had a country house at Tansley, a village just two miles to the north of Arkwright's cotton-spinning community at Cromford, and Arkwright enjoyed fraternizing with the local gentry and people of substance. It seems more likely, however, that they were rivals for the blue riband of cotton-spinning, which Arkwright won by a short lead. Unwin already had a reputation as an inventor and, as a hosier, he could hardly have ignored the competition of Tewkesbury in the middle 1770s. Unwin experimented to improve the early roller-spinning machinery and, early in 1772, his own patent (No. 1,009) was registered. The idea was to minimize breakages in the yarn by eliminating the use of cogwheels in winding and doubling; instead, the bobbins were turned by the friction of a drum's rotation. The improvement, though useful, seems fairly obvious to the layman, and one is tempted to imagine that Unwin had secured the patent in order to avoid expensive royalty payments to Arkwright. Certainly, a few years later, he refused to pay more modest sums to the steam-engine patentees, Boulton & Watt.

Another patent was taken out in 1772 by Coniah Wood, a turner who at one time worked for Arkwright at Nottingham. Wood's patent suggests an attempt to combine the principles of the jenny and roller-spinning, and he may have been supported by one or more of the Nottingham manufacturers.[23]

Another manufacturer who almost certainly infringed the Arkwright patents with one of their own was Robert and Thomas Barber, worsted-spinners of Derby. The partners were probably the sons of John Barber, a 'gentleman' of Bilborough (Nottingham) who 'spent a fortune of £50,000 in mechanism, and in permitting knaves to impose on his credulity'. Patents were taken out in the name of each son in turn (1777 and 1783), but the contemporary reader is likely to be sceptical about a machine said to 'spin and embroider threads of silk, worsted, hemp, flax, gold or silver wire'. In January 1779, 'Messrs Barbers of Derby, Proprietors of the Manufacturing Mills near the said town' announced in the *Derby Mercury* that, 'having been informed by their friends, that they would certainly be prosecuted by the Cromford Company for infringing upon their patent', they would assure the public that they had not 'in the least encroached on the said patent'. This is difficult to believe, since the jenny was unsuitable for worsted-spinning and, in any case, the partners were spinning by power. The jenny and Arkwright's patent were the only successful techniques of mechanized spinning that emerged before the mule. In 1784, one of the Barbers tried to adapt his machinery to Sir Joseph Banks' project for introducing worsted-spinning by power into Lincolnshire. The owner of a rival machine wrote to Banks that 'the original principle both of Mr Barber's and mine is Arkwright's'.

Thus nine firms working on the Arkwright model before 1781 have been identified, and there may well have been others. For instance, a local tradition at Church Wilne insists that Wilne Mill (near Draycott, Derbyshire) was the first country mill to be built after Cromford. This is quite feasible, since one of the original partners at Wilne built Arkwright's first mill at Nottingham. What is certain is that from the publication of his first patent (1769), Arkwright was plagued by infringers. It is not too fanciful to suppose that his second patent (1775) was less a reflection of his 'monopolizing tendencies' than an attempt to anticipate further encroachments on the rights conferred by his existing patent. The three firms mentioned in Pares' letter as Arkwright licencees all began production within a year or two of the publication of the carding patent (April 1776), and there is no evidence of the existence of licencees before then. This suggests that Arkwright finally gave way to pressure and began to confer licences after he had taken the precaution of a further patent. However, his foolish insistence on prohibitive premiums, and his claims to inventions that were not his own, brought the wrath of the whole trade upon him, and led to the early invalidation of his patents at law.

CHAPTER FIVE

The Early Factory Masters
(1) in Cotton-Spinning

ARKWRIGHT'S first defeat at law in 1781 precipitated a rush to make fortunes in warp-spinning, and the origins of the entrepreneurs who entered the industry in the Midlands between 1769 and the close of the century are summarized in Table 3. This chapter is devoted to discussion and interpretation of the various trades and occupations that provided recruits for the new industry of spinning cotton by power, and some of their possible motives for entering the industry.

In interpreting Table 3, two qualifications must be born in mind. The occupations listed are those of the principal partner, or group of partners. Where there were other partners with different occupations, this is mentioned in the text or footnotes to this chapter. The second qualification is that the analysis includes only those firms who originated a cotton-spinning concern, and not those who acquired an established mill. However, where the second or subsequent owner is of some particular interest, attention has been drawn to this in the text. Only a handful of firms were established in the years after 1800, most of which were small and short-lived, and had no significant effect on trends already apparent in the Midlands industry. In the circumstances, the year 1800 seemed to set an appropriate chronological limit for the analysis.

(A) Bleachers and Country Hosiers

Country hosiers are distinguished from hosiers operating in the towns because, in the early phase of development of cotton-spinning, the country hosiers were favoured by operating water (fulling) mills, or by occupying sites suitable for development. The rapid expansion of the hosiery industry in the second half of the eighteenth century, and the failure to enclose the common fields of Nottingham, compelled the subsidiary processes of bleaching and fulling to move into the country parishes outside the town. Bleachers and country hosiers found sites along the River Leen (a stream which originally skirted Nottingham Castle) in Basford, Bulwell and Linby, and a number collected in and around Mansfield, a local centre of the hosiery industry. Smith Churchill's migration from Nottingham to Loughborough in 1779 may have been inspired by the need for space for expansion, as well as affording a political escape route.[1]

TABLE 3

Occupations of the Principals of Cotton-Spinning Firms Established in the Midlands, 1769–1800

		Number of Firms	Number of Mills
(A)	Bleachers and Country Hosiers	5	13
(B)	Merchant Hosiers	15	17
(C)	Mercers, Drapers	7	10
(D)	General Merchants	2	3
(E)	Lancashire Cotton Manufacturers	3	7
(F)	Silk Trade and Manufacture	3	6
(G)	Other Textile Manufactures	4	4
(H)	Former Managers of Cotton Mills	2	2
(I)	Framesmith	1	1
	All textile occupations	42	63
(J)	Retail Trade (other than mercers and drapers)	4	5
(K)	Potters	3	3
(L)	Lead and Iron Industry	2	2
(M)	Gentry, Farmers, Miller	8	8
(N)	Building Trades	2	2
(O)	Brewers	1	1
(P)	Birmingham Trades	1	1
(Q)	Miscellaneous	1	1
	All non-textile occupations	22	23
	All categories	64	86
	Not classified (Arkwright, Strutt and partners)	2	15
	Occupation unknown	9	9
		75	110

The most successful country hosier was Samuel Unwin, whose early rivalry with Arkwright has already been referred to. The leading role which Unwin played in the history of the Midlands cotton and worsted industry makes it necessary to examine his career in rather more detail. He came of a family that had been in the hosiery manufacture at Sutton-in-Ashfield since at least the Restoration, and his great-grandmother is said to have introduced the stocking-frame into the village. At the beginning of the eighteenth century, his father built up the business and evidently became a 'putter-out' or agent to a Nottingham or Leicester factor, for he is said to have opened a warehouse in the village. The ancestral farmlands were increasingly used as tenter-fields and, about the middle of the eighteenth century, when Unwin took over the business, he built his first water-powered mill. The water-power was employed to drive silk-reeling machines, fulling stocks and twisting mills. About the same period, Unwin built Sutton Old Hall, an imposing mansion largely used as a warehouse and office. The extension of Unwin's interests to cotton-spinning was thus a natural development of his earlier interest in power-operated machinery. In partnership with his son-in-law James Heygate, a London hosier and banker, Unwin opened a second mill at Mansfield (1782). Before the close of the century he had built two other mills near his country residence at Tansley and, at Sutton, had turned to the manufacture of nankeens and ginghams.

The Leen valley produced two firms who extended their activities as bleachers and country hosiers into factory spinning. Robert Hall was a Nottingham mercer and hosier who, sometime before 1761, had opened a 'thread mill' at Basford, two miles up the River Leen from Nottingham. The water-wheel of this mill appears to have been used to prepare thread for the hosiery trade, but the precise nature of the machinery is not known. In 1766, Hall appears as a bleacher at Basford and, by 1783, he and his sons were describing themselves as 'bleachers, thread manufacturers and yarn merchants'. The Basford site was used to build a cotton mill about this period. A memoir of Robert Hall junior says that the mill was built in 1787, but a letter dated 1781 from Robert Hall & Co. in the Boulton & Watt manuscripts suggests that a cotton mill may possibly have been opened at this time. The third partner in the cotton mill was John White, a son-in-law of Samuel Unwin. White was a Chesterfield hosier who, in 1766, had built a 'safe box' workshop in the town to keep secret the technique of knitting Spanish lace gloves. It is interesting to note that Robert Hall junior was one of the first to apply chlorine to bleaching on a commercial scale, but the profits he earned as an innovating entrepreneur probably came after the cotton mill was erected.

Two miles farther up the Leen, George Robinson (1712–98) of Bulwell developed a business along parallel lines. He is said to have been a Scots migrant who settled at Bulwell in 1737, but there is no record of his occupation until 1771, when he was noticed as a bleacher. By 1783, Robinson and his son were describing themselves as 'merchants and thread manufacturers', as well as bleachers, so that, like Halls', they may have had a thread mill. Between 1776 and 1791 Robinson and his two sons, John and James, built six mills strung along three miles of the River Leen between Bulwell and Lord Byron's Newstead Park. As in the case of Hall's mill, the enterprise appears to have come from the second generation of a well-established business.

The firm of Charles & George Stanton, Mansfield cotton manufacturers, appears to have developed along similar lines to those of Hall and Robinson. In 1774, Wright, Stanton & Co. of Mansfield had a bleach-yard in the town, and in 1790 Charles Stanton appears as a thread merchant. Four years later, the brothers appear in the directory as cotton manufacturers.

The only other country hosier who became a cotton-spinner was Smith Churchill. The migration of this firm to Shepshed has already been noticed, suggesting that the framework-knitters' riots of 1779 may have been the occasion rather than the reason for moving. It is relevant to notice that John Churchill, who may have been a relative, was a Nottingham thread merchant. Without doubt, the firm prospered in Shepshed, and by 1812 the village possessed 900 stocking-frames, the largest number in any place apart from Nottingham, Leicester and Hinckley.

(B) Town Hosiers

Fifteen of the cotton-spinners who established themselves in the Midlands were also merchant hosiers operating in the main centres of the industry. Of the fifteen, eleven were based on Nottingham, one on Mansfield, one in the City of London, one in Leicester and one was a partnership linking a Leicester hosier with a Bakewell family of country hosiers. The concentration on Nottingham is a striking comment on the specialization within the east Midlands hosiery manufacturing area. Apart from the Strutt family, the interest of Derby's hosiers remained with silk.

The fifteen hosiers differed considerably in their financial re-sources and business experience, and the size of the factories they built reflected this variation. Four of the group built small mills in Nottingham and Leicester on the model of Arkwright's first mill. Pearson and Grimshaw's mill at Nottingham was powered by a horse capstan, and Timothy Harris was about to install a capstan when (in 1785) he heard of the success of the Boulton & Watt engine. Cox and Halls of Nottingham opened their factory in a small tenement building measuring fifty by twenty-four feet. Miller, Howe & Co. occupied a slightly larger factory in Northgate Street, Leicester, containing 684 spindles. All these firms in turn installed Boulton & Watt engines, beginning with Harris.

The owners of these small enterprises give the impression of fairly humble origins. George Lisant Cox was apprenticed to a frame-work knitter before becoming a hosier. He evidently drew capital from Edward Hall, a City warehouseman who was probably his London agent. Samuel Howe was the son of a framework knitter and it is quite likely that he was apprenticed to his father before he

F

became a Leicester hosier. His partner, Thomas Miller, was a Leicester brewer turned banker. Pearson and Grimshaw are more difficult to trace. Henry Pearson was the son of a prosperous Nottingham brass-founder and ironmonger. The son was a City merchant before returning to Nottingham as a hosier. His Nottingham partner was probably the John Grimshaw who built machinery for James and Hargreaves in 1773. Timothy and William Harris were Nottingham hosiers who became wholesale hosiers in London, but apparently continued to employ numbers of stocking-frames in the Midlands. They had no local partner, but no doubt employed a local manager.

The evidence of these four firms shows the City of London contributing capital to factory developments in Nottingham, notably for men who could not raise enough from their own businesses. The contribution of London may well have been even more extensive, as the following advertisement which appeared in the *Nottingham Journal* in 1794 suggests:

> To Hosiers. Any gentlemen in the hosiery business residing in the metropolis or elsewhere who would chose to employ a person to superintend a manufactory at Nottingham . . . will find their proposals duly attended to by directing to M.M. . . .[2]

However, most of the hosiers who entered cotton-spinning acquired local partners and opened mills on streams in the country districts of Nottinghamshire or Derbyshire, their prototype being Arkwright's Cromford mills, rather than his first factory at Nottingham. Nine firms, out of the fifteen in this group, established mills on this pattern, six in Nottinghamshire and three in Derbyshire. These firms are listed in Appendix A and the histories of most of them were very similar to that of Almond & Lambert, whose origins are fairly well documented, particularly in the first chapters of the *Memoir of Robert Blincoe*. Richard Lambert senior built up a hosiery warehouse in St Mary's Churchyard, Nottingham, and in due course the prospering business was taken over by his three sons, who branched out into the fancy hosiery and lace trade. Drawing capital from Robert Almond, a Nottingham linen draper and hosier, they opened a small mill and bleach-ground at Gonalston, a hamlet on the Dover Beck, eight miles east of Nottingham, in 1784. Before long, it proved necessary to augment the water-wheel by a Newcomen engine. The five other firms who established mills in Nottinghamshire followed a similar pattern, except that Davison and Hawksley began with a small mill at Nottingham (1788) but moved to Arnold when they found the power of the River Leen inadequate.

The three hosiery firms who opened mills in Derbyshire had a different partnership pattern, no doubt because of the remoteness of their mills. John Pares, a Leicester hosier, went into partnership with the Gardoms of Bakewell, a family of country hosiers and bleachers, and with James Heygate, the London hosier and banker who has already been noticed as a partner of Samuel Unwin. The firm built Calver mill. Elihu Samuel Fellows, hosier and grandson of the Samuel Fellows whose career is discussed in Chapter Two, went into partnership with another Nottingham hosier and a Nottingham dyer, and with John Dalley, a cotton factor of Wirksworth, to build a mill at Wirksworth. The Gardoms and Dalley were probably local agents of the hosiers whom they later joined in partnership. The competition which Arkwright's mills at Bakewell and Wirksworth presented to the local jenny-spinning industry galvanized these Derbyshire employers into action. John Cooper, the other hosier who invested in cotton-spinning in Derbyshire, opened mills at Woodeaves (1784) and Mayfield (1793), both near Ashbourne. Cooper had married into the Strutt family, and one of his partners (Dale) was probably a member of a landowning family at Ashbourne. Such families possessed sites for mills, and the location of an Arkwright mill at Ashbourne is not without significance.

In the final decade of the eighteenth century the country mills were already giving way to new multi-storey factory blocks, generally built in or close to the towns of the Region. The new factories were sited along the banks of projected or recently-

opened canals. In Nottingham the development of this new scale
of enterprise began in anticipation of the cutting of the Nottingham
Canal, and two Nottingham hosiers built factory blocks with easy
access to the wharves that were under construction. The larger
factory, built by Denison & Oates (a partnership between a second-
generation Nottingham merchant, related to the Denison family of
Leeds, and a Leeds merchant), was a seven-storey block containing
3,024 spindles powered by a 30 hp Boulton & Watt engine and gave
employment to about 300 people. The smaller mill was built by
Alderman Henry Green and John Killingley, the former a first-
generation hosier whose political career suggests an ambitious and
forceful personality. It is interesting to note that these two enterprises ante-dated William Strutt's multi-storey factory at Derby—
the celebrated fireproof factory—by a year.

(C) Mercers and Drapers

The emergence of the merchant hosiers as a distinct class has
been discussed in Chapter One. The hosiers did not begin to appear
as a distinct and specialized trading group in the Midlands until the
second quarter of the eighteenth century, when the manufacture
was migrating from London to the provinces. Numbers of hosiers
were originally mercers and drapers who took to specialization in
hosiery as the provincial manufacture developed. It seems that
mercers were still active in the hosiery trade in the later decades of
the eighteenth century, especially in the smaller towns, where the
division of labour in merchanting was more limited.

The significance of these local variations in the organization of
the hosiery industry becomes clear when it is stated that six out of
the seven mercers who became cotton-spinners had their original
businesses in the smaller towns of the Region. The Nottingham
mercer, Thomas Oldknow (uncle of the better-known Samuel
Oldknow of Stockport and Mellor), was the only partner from one
of the large towns, and he took two Mansfield drapers (as well as a

Nottingham ironmonger) for his partners at Pleasley Mill. The other mercers who became cotton-spinners were William Toplis of Mansfield, who built cotton- and worsted-spinning mills at Cuckney and Worksop (Nottinghamshire); Hewitt & Bunting and Radley & Chapman of Chesterfield, who opened mills near the town, Anthony Bradley & Co. of New Mills, Mayfield, near Ashbourne, Green & Brockshaw of Alfreton, and Parkes, Brookhouse & Crompton of Warwick, cotton- and worsted-spinners. These mercers may have recruited additional capital from local gentry. Oldknow, Cowpe & Co. drew their capital from trade in Nottingham and Toplis had family banking connections at Wirksworth. The five other firms had second partners (third in the case of Parkes, Brookhouse & Crompton) who have not been identified in local industry or trade.

(D) General Merchants

Several of the hosiers noticed and all the mercers dealt in other goods besides hosiery. The two firms classified as general merchants differed in that their connection with the textile industry prior to entering manufacturing was only marginal, and because they entered industry as an investment for their capital. They are included in the textile group in Table 5 because they may have traded in wool and raw cotton. Both the general merchants were River Trent traders who were responsible for taking the cotton-spinning industry into hitherto rural parts of the Midlands, so that their careers merit some attention.

Joseph Wilkes came of a family of farmers at Overseal (near Measham, Leicestershire), and climbed to fortune through his enterprise in extending the canal and turnpike network of the Midlands. In 1763, he went into partnership with Sampson Lloyd of Birmingham, 'the true founder of Lloyd's Bank', and four Burton-on-Trent tradesmen to buy a twenty-one years' lease of the nineteen miles Trent Navigation (Wilden Ferry to Burton) from the

Earl of Uxbridge for £2,500. It was the profit and confidence which this venture brought to Wilkes that made him a principal promoter of canals, turnpikes and railroads in the Midlands, and provided the capital or connections for his purchase of the parish of Measham for £50,000 in 1783.

Wilkes set out to exploit the resources of the parish with characteristic energy and intelligence. A friend of Robert Bakewell of Dishley Grange, he enjoyed some celebrity as an improving farmer and landlord, having reclaimed part of the Ashby Wolds and other heath and waste for agricultural use. He worked the coal-seams of the parish, opened a successful brickworks, established a barge-building industry (for the canals) and built a corn mill. It may have been this mill which prompted his entry into cotton-spinning, for he economized in the use of a Boulton & Watt engine by harnessing its power to the cotton mill by day and corn mill by night. Women and children provided labour for the cotton mill, men for the corn mill. His first mill was built in (or before) 1783, and a second and larger mill in 1802. Wilkes' early partners in the cotton mill were his brothers, John and Thomas, but sometime after their death Wilkes' factory manager (and former colliery manager), Thomas Jewsbury, became a partner. Joseph Wilkes also operated a number of banks in the Burton area; these will be considered in Chapter Seven.

The careers of the principal partners in Handley, Sketchley & Co. of Newark show business interests almost as diverse as those of Wilkes. William Handley was a Newark mason who somehow became a successful merchant, trading up and down the Trent, perhaps mostly in grain as his partner (Samuel Sketchley) and his sons were brewers. Sketchley was the son of a Nottingham man who was in turn painter, signwriter, engraver, auctioneer and general dealer, and proprietor of the first public brewhouse in the town. The auctioneer's business was modelled on that of his brother at Birmingham, the author of the first Birmingham directory of 1767. It is interesting to notice that John Sketchley advanced money on security, performing a function somewhere between that of a pawnbroker and a banker. Samuel Sketchley was a brewer and iron merchant at Burton before joining the Newark cotton mill enterprise. The mill was a large one, and was employing some 300 people by 1797.

(E) Lancashire Cotton Manufacturers

Although a number of Lancashire cotton manufacturers built mills in the Glossop district of Derbyshire, only three (excluding Hargreaves and Arkwright) penetrated the Midlands region. These three were Robert ('Parsley') Peel, who migrated to Burton-on-Trent about 1780, his son (Sir) Robert Peel, who bought the manor of Tamworth in 1790, and William Buszard, a Manchester dimity and fustian manufacturer who opened a mill at Lutterworth (Leicestershire) with the aid of his brother Marston Buszard, 'surgeon and banker' of the town.

The link between the two Peels and the Midlands was provided by Wilkes of Measham. All three of 'Parsley' Peel's mills at Burton were built on sites provided by the Trent Navigation Co., and water-power was provided in each case by cuts from the River Trent arranged with the company. Peel left Blackburn because of his losses in the jenny riots of September and October 1779, and later recorded his obligation to the rioters for having destroyed his machines and so turned him to Arkwright's invention. However, it is unlikely that this semi-literate, mechanical genius would have been so successful in the Midlands had it not been for Burton's perfect situation abreast of the canal routes between Nottingham and Lancashire. The opening of the Trent and Mersey Canal (1765) and its link with Burton made the town an ideal intermediate location between the two English centres of the cotton industry.

Sir Robert Peel's motives for establishing himself in the Midlands were quite different from those of his father. By 1790, he had 'capital overflowing in his hands', and coveted Tamworth as the basis for a political, rather than a new industrial career. The cotton mills and calico works built in and about the town gave him a further hold over the Parliamentary borough. In 1790 he spent £15,500 on property in the borough (including 120 houses) and then, jointly with Joseph Wilkes, bought the Thynne estates (belonging to the first Marquis of Bath) in the area for £123,000. The canal linking Birmingham with the Trent and Mersey Navigation passed through Tamworth and gave it a good commercial link. During the last decade of the century, Peel and Wilkes opened calico works in Tamworth Castle and Castle Mill, and spinning-mills in the town and at nearby Fazeley and Bonehill. Bleaching and calico-printing were also carried on at Fazeley.

(F) Silk Trade and Manufacture

The Midlands silk industry at Derby and Nottingham probably suffered a slight decline after about 1780 as cotton stockings became cheaper and more fashionable.[3] Moreover, the power-driven silk-reeling frames may have provided the individual manufacturer with a precedent for warp-spinning, as we have noticed with Unwin and Strutt. Three silk merchants attempted to diversify their interests by extending their activity into cotton, and the firm of Stanford & Burnside present the most illuminating example of this.

William and Thomas Stanford and John Taylor began their careers as apprentices to their uncle, William Elliott, a Nottingham silk-throwster who discovered a superior technique of dyeing and finishing black silk stockings. The discovery was made towards the middle of the eighteenth century and for the next twenty years Elliott undertook the major part of the work of finishing silk hose for Leicester as well as Nottingham. In 1768, the Stanford brothers and Taylor established their own business as dyers and silk merchants and, judging by the wills of the partners, the firm was at least moderately successful. However, in or before 1782, Taylor had built a cotton mill in Nottingham, apparently with the support of Elliott, who had by now retired to a country seat at Radford. It was probably at this period that William Stanford built his silk mill in Sheep Lane, Nottingham, with a smaller building for spinning cotton (500 spindles) adjoining. Stanford's interest in cotton was considerably extended in or about 1788 when he entered into partnership with his son-in-law, John Burnside, a Nottingham hosier who was establishing a foundry and cotton mill on the River Maun at Mansfield. In 1800, Stanford's two sons, who had inherited Elliott's fortune, opened a third cotton mill at Leenside, Nottingham. Thus were the profits of an innovating entrepreneur in the silk industry channelled into the cotton industry.

The firm of Daintry & Ryle of Macclesfield was well-known at the end of the eighteenth century as the largest merchants and manufacturers in the silk industry of that town. Their 'handsome' silk mill on Park Green, Macclesfield, began its work in 1775, and although their main interests were in the silk industry, and (after 1800) in banking, they built (or acquired) two cotton mills within the Region. One of these was a very small mill at Endon, near Leek (Staffordshire), which they may have bought to develop. The other was a larger mill at Eyam, in the Peak District of Derbyshire, which in 1808 employed a hundred people. In 1805, Daintry and his son went into partnership with Charles and Richard Wood, who owned the Old Mill Lane cotton-spinning mills in Macclesfield. Like Stanford, Daintry did not lack capital, and it is not difficult to recognize his ventures into cotton-spinning as an insurance against the decline of the silk industry.

Much less is known about the third entrepreneur included in this category than about the other two, but the limited information hints at a parallel career pattern. Charles Callow was a Derby silk-, cotton- and worsted-dyer of some substance. In 1792, he had built a cotton mill alongside his house and warehouse in the town.

(G) Other Textile Manufacturers

Four entrepreneurs moved into cotton-spinning from other

branches of the Midlands textile industry. According to the historian of Tutbury (Staffordshire), John Bott & Co. operated silk mills in the town before diverting their interest in 1781 to the more prosperous cotton industry. However, Bailey's *Midland Directory* and the partnership agreement of the firm (1783) refer to John and Charles Bott as tammy weavers, and this occupation seems more consistent with Tutbury's long-established woolcombing industry. In 1780, a petition from the principal inhabitants of Tutbury was sent to the King, praying him to grant a lease of land on the Duchy of Lancaster estate to build a mill for the spinning of cotton and worsted. There is no evidence to show that Botts ever spun worsted, but the reference is interesting because it points again to the firm's earlier interest in the wool rather than the silk industry. When the petition was granted, a five-storey, water-powered mill was built on the Dove in 1781.

A small mule-mill at Newark also began with an attempt to divert capital from the declining woollen and worsted industry. John Hardcastle, a wool-stapler of Newark, made a partnership with William Walker of Woolsthorpe, near Grantham (Lincolnshire), who was probably a landed proprietor. The partnership went bankrupt shortly after its foundation in 1793.

The other two textile manufacturers included in this group entered cotton-spinning by extending their existing interest in the previous stage of production. Samuel Walsh, a Bulwell (near Nottingham) calico-printer, purchased spinning machinery to open a small mill on the River Leen. John and Thomas Turton of Crich (Derbyshire), owners of 'the hat factory' there, opened a water-powered mill near their factory about 1799. Both enterprises were small and had very short lives.

(H) Former Managers of Cotton Mills

The early Lancashire cotton industry is supposed to have recruited a number of entrepreneurs from a new class of cotton-mill managers, some of whom came of wealthy families and chose this way of entering the industry, while others were artisans whose mechanical skills were necessary to keep the mills going. The Midland Region can furnish two examples in the period covered by this study of mill managers who became successful owners.

By the end of the eighteenth century, the younger Robert Peel and his partners owned no less than twenty mills in Lancashire and the Midlands, and in 1803 employed some 15,000 people. Several managers were recruited from among the relatives of Sir Robert Peel and his partner, William Yates, but others were recruited from among talented employees. In Lancashire, Haliwell, who became a partner 'was originally a menial in the warehouse at Manchester; from this he rose to packer, then traveller, then partner'. Yates, who became a partner with £200 capital, was once a cotton-mill apprentice. Greaves, of Peel, Greaves & Co., Manchester bankers, began his career as a bank-clerk. In due course, the firm adopted a policy of giving shares to its managers, who thus became junior partners. In the Midlands, the conspicuous product of this policy of internal promotion was Richard Thompson, who first appears as 'Superintendent at Peel, Yates & Co's cotton manufactory' at Burton. He subsequently became a partner in Sir Robert Peel's business, and in 1795 opened his own multi-storey cotton mill in the hat-making town of Newcastle-under-Lyme.

Sir Richard Arkwright had only one son, and from the outset had to employ managers with a high degree of autonomy in the scattered units of his industrial empire. John Adams of Arkwright's Bromsgrove mill, John Simpson and Robert Heptinstall all acquired ownership or part-ownership in Arkwright's mills. The surviving evidence provides only one instance of an Arkwright employee establishing his own cotton mill, but there may have been others. George Trueman features in three letters to Boulton & Watt in 1790 as Arkwright's manager at the Nottingham mill. Little more than a year later, Trueman was establishing his own mill in Coalpit Lane, Nottingham, a few dozen yards from his former master's mill.

(I) Framesmiths

The only framesmith to establish his own cotton-spinning business was Thomas James, the Nottingham partner of James Hargreaves, inventor of the spinning-jenny. James and Hargreaves abandoned jenny-spinning for warp-spinning in 1777, as a result of the developments described in the previous chapter.

Framesmith is the only one of the fifteen occupations summarized in Table 3 which could be described as working-class; all other occupations required capital to enter them. James was quite untypical of his occupation in so far as he was able to utilize the family's holding of land to raise capital to build his mill. The difficulties of a framesmith who attempted to establish himself as a partner in a cotton mill without any such family heritage is illustrated by the career of William Newton (1750–1830) of Tideswell. Newton was apprenticed to his father, a country carpenter, but 'very early became so ingenious, skilful and industrious, as to be employed by some few genteel families of the neighbourhood', including the Duke of Devonshire, who was then building at Buxton. When Arkwright's Cressbrook mill was opened in 1779, he became 'machinery carpenter' at a salary of £50 p.a., but lost his position and everything he had in a fire which burned down the mill and cottages in 1785. When the site was bought by Barker Bossley (brother of Alexander Bossley of Bakewell, Arkwright's attorney), Newton was offered a 'third partnership' on the condition that he found £200—but mainly because the daughter of the Rector of Eyam had recognized his genius as a writer of sonnets! Subsequently, Newton became well-known as an enlightened mill manager, and his sons bought Litton Mills, but he undoubtedly owed his original preferment to a few lines of poetry published in the *Gentleman's Magazine* rather than to his ability as a mechanic.[4]

There was also a joiner among the five partners in the Chesterfield mill originally opened by Radley & Chapman. The partners valued this small country mill at £1,500 at the time and it employed about a hundred people. There may also have been one or two other joiners and framesmiths who secured partnerships in small Derbyshire mills.

(J) Retail Trade (other than Mercers and Drapers)

The excitement accompanying Arkwright's spectacular success attracted into cotton-spinning speculators without previous contact with the textile industry, but with money to invest. Three such speculators entered cotton-spinning after a career in retail trade.

The partners in Markland, Evison & Little, of the Maythorn Mill, near Southwell (Nottinghamshire), were Jonathan Markland, a Nottingham wine merchant, Thomas Evison, proprietor of the 'Spread Eagle Inn', Nottingham, and Robert Little, a retired surgeon who owned land at Southwell. The mill opened in 1786 and ran into financial difficulties within three years; in the following years it was advertised for sale several times. Another enterprise with a short life was begun by Thomas Burdett, a Nottingham ironmonger. In 1791 he opened a small mill at Burton Latimer near Kettering (Northamptonshire) which was up for sale in 1794 and later became a corn mill. Robert Lowe, a Lincoln ironmonger, also set up a small mill in his native town, but its fate is unknown. Probably the most successful of the retailers' ventures into cotton-spinning was that of Henry Wooley, a grocer at Winster, near Matlock. By 1803, he owned mills in Winster and Matlock. The occupation of his partner, James MacQueen, is not known, but it may be surmised that he was the managing partner who provided the technical knowledge that Woolley lacked.

(K) Potters

The contraction of the pot-making industry outside Stoke-on-Trent and its district caused capital to be diverted into the cotton industry, and the Morley family provide an interesting illustration of this transition from the one industry to the other. Successive generations of the family worked a pottery at the Beck Barns, just outside Nottingham, from at least the sixteenth century. During the first half of the eighteenth century, the family opened a glasshouse and 'Nottingham brownware'—especially beerhouse mugs—was in great demand throughout the Midland counties. The family's first links with the hosiery trade were made in this heyday of the local pottery industry, when Charles Morley I (1702-42) married the daughter of a hosier. One of Morley's sons became a hosier, the other (Charles Morley II) carrying on the family business except for the glasshouse. The pottery was built alongside a minor tributary of the Trent, and harnessed its power to grind down the materials used in making the pots. About 1780, Morley was clearly attempting to diversify his trading interests, for he described himself as 'merchant'. By 1783, one of the buildings was being used for cotton-spinning and Morley was describing himself as 'cotton manufacturer and potter', having joined in partnership with his hosier brother. In 1788, when a Boulton & Watt engine was installed, the power was harnessed for grinding as well as spinning cotton.

Another Nottingham potter, Thomas Wyer, was the leading partner of a quintet that opened a mill at Ilkeston, adjoining the Erewash Canal, in 1792. Like Morley, Wyer described himself as a merchant shortly before he became a spinner, which suggests that he may have gradually extended into textiles as the market for local earthenware fell away. Yet another potter, John Bacon of Alfreton (Derbyshire), built a small mule-factory at Sutton-in-Ashfield, near Unwin's factory. A manufacturer of Nottingham brownware, his career seems to have paralleled that of the Morleys.

(L) Lead and Iron Industry

The Derbyshire lead and iron industries were also contracting in the later decades of the eighteenth century, which helps to explain the establishment of two other mills in the county. Thomas

Evans (1723–1814), the owner of lead and calamine mines at Bonsall and slitting- and rolling-mills at Derby, is remembered because his Derby bank (Crompton, Evans & Co., 1771) provided capital for both Arkwright and Samuel Oldknow. Evans and his two sons built their own cotton-spinning community at Darley Abbey, a mile north of Derby, in 1783. The Evans inter-married with the Strutts, and William Strutt and his sister Elizabeth 'seem at one time to have been partners in the Evans bank and mills'.

The name of Peter Nightingale, lead merchant at Lea, near Cromford, is usually connected with another incident in Arkwright's career, for he was the defendant when Arkwright attempted to re-establish his patent in 1785. Lea Mills were only established the year before, and probably on a limited scale, as the weaving-shop contained only eleven calico looms. Like the Evanses, Nightingale maintained his interest in the traditional Derbyshire staple trade.

It is worth noticing here that John and Samuel Simpson, who had close business and social ties with the Arkwrights, came from a family with extensive mining interests. Their father, Adam Simpson of Bonsall, had shares in lead mines at Wirksworth, Matlock, Middleton, Elton and Brassington, and owned a cupola and slug mill at Matlock. On his death in 1782, neither son tried to maintain his business, for all his property was sold off. J. L. Thacker, of Stretton, Thacker & Co., a firm discussed below, also appears to have sold out a family interest in the iron industry in favour of cotton.

(M) Gentry, Farmers, etc.

The landed interest played a minor role in the textile enterprise of the Midlands in this period. Several members of the gentry became cotton-mill owners, but with one or two possible exceptions they were buyers of established concerns or sleeping-partners, rather than originators of new enterprises. The principal exception was Ellis Needham, the allegedly sadistic factory master of the infamous *Memoir of Robert Blincoe*. The history of his firm is considered in detail in Chapter Ten, and it is sufficient here to state that both Needham and his partner were substantial landowners, though they were seldom accorded the status of gentry in the surviving records. The only other possible recruits from the gentry were George and Charles Lowe, who opened the large Amber Mill at Shirland (near Alfreton) about 1794. It seems likely that they came of the Lowe family of Locko, but the name is a common one in the district, and it is not possible to make any positive connection between the family and this enterprise.

Chapter Three has already recorded the existence of four cotton-spinners in the Peak District who had farming backgrounds and probably graduated to warp-spinning through jenny-spinning. Two other Derbyshire farmers may have entered warp-spinning direct from handloom-weaving or some other traditional textile occupation. The general availability of water-power in the Peak District suggests that there may have been others like them. Abraham Flint, of Darley hillside (near Matlock), was a small grazier who happened to have a fast-flowing stream running through his upland pastures. He opened a small mill (400 spindles) in 1785, but two years later financial pressure compelled him to sell out to Daniel Dakeyne, the local squire. The Dakeynes added a flax mill and apparently experimented with worsted-spinning, but went bankrupt in 1801. A surviving legal document shows how the buildings of a seventy-two-acre farm at Hartington, near Chapel-en-le-Frith, had been added to establish a warp-spinning mill sometime before 1799, but nothing is known of its subsequent history. The mill, like that at Darley, owed its existence to a stream which flowed by the farm buildings, though the previous interest of the farmer in the textile industry can be guessed at.

(N) Building Trade

This category links two speculators without previous experience in the textile industry, but whose interest was probably aroused by their employment in mill-building. William Stretton was an architect and builder who, in partnership with his father, was responsible for some of the best architecture in and about Nottingham in the latter part of the eighteenth century, obtaining commissions from the aristocracy, Corporation and Church. His interest in cotton-spinning no doubt originated in 1767, when he was commissioned to build Arkwright's first cotton mill at Nottingham. In 1781, he became a partner in Wilne Mills on the Derwent, near Draycott (Derbyshire) and ten miles south-east of Nottingham. His partners were J. L. and Joseph Thacker, members of a local family who appear to have had an interest in a rolling- and slitting-mill at Wilne. Stretton dropped out of the partnership in 1787, but the mills continued for many years afterwards.

The other cotton spinner who originated from the building industry was Thomas Parkes, a plumber and grazier of Sudbury, near Uttoxeter (Staffordshire). A member of his family owned land through which the Tean brook meandered, and he opened a very small enterprise a mile north of Uttoxeter in 1783.

(O) Brewers

Mention has already been made of several cotton-spinning firms whose partners had connections with the brewing industry, as well as one which was founded on capital from the retail liquor trade. As a consequence of the enterprise of Joseph Wilkes and 'Parsley' Peel, Burton-on-Trent became a centre of the Midlands cotton industry. It is not therefore surprising to find two Burton brewers joining to establish a cotton mill. Thomas Dicken appears in Bailey's *Directory* (1783) as a 'brewer, mercer, draper and manufacturer', an interesting link between the old textile industry of the area and the rapidly-growing Burton brewing industry. Dicken and his brother made a partnership with Benjamin Wilson, one of the three leading Burton brewers in 1784. The Dicken brothers took

G

charge of the mill, which was on the Trent and Mersey Canal at Alrewas, seven miles south-west of Burton, while Wilson employed his extensive market connections to take charge of the raw cotton buying.

(P) Birmingham Trades

Despite the existence of several thread mills there is only one recorded attempt to spin cotton in Birmingham after the failure of Paul and Wyatt. Thomas Gill is first noted as a file-cutter and maker in Dale End, Birmingham, in 1767. Between 1780 and 1783, he discovered or perfected a method of making superior swords, and secured contracts first with the East India Company and then with the Board of Ordnance. By 1788, he was a 'manufacturer of swords, guns, pistols, saws, files, elastic spurs, pistols with bayonets and unparalleled snuffers', and a merchant supplying the Board with all their ironmongery stores. However, contraction in the sale of arms after the American War of Independence caused him to look elsewhere for new trade, and he turned to experiments with spinning cotton and wool. He rented room and steam-power in a £5,000 factory built in Fazeley Street and employed about two-dozen girls on various processes culminating in the spinning of cotton 'for fine muslins'. He soon gave up the enterprise himself, but the owners of the factory continued it for a few years afterwards.

(Q) Miscellaneous and No Information

A cotton-spinning firm whose previous activities can only be classified as 'miscellaneous' is that of William, John & Joseph Fowler of Tamworth. In 1794 they described themselves as 'cotton-spinners, mealmen, oil-pressers and paper-makers' at Alber Mills, near Tamworth.

No biographical details have come to light for ten firms in this sample, and in two of these cases not even the name of the entrepreneur is known. The firms are listed in Appendix A, so there is no need to recite them all here. The interesting enterprise of Benjamin Stone and Edward Harrison at Winster, whose entrepreneurs have not been identified, has already been mentioned in Chapter Three.

Surveying the details of all these firms, it seems possible to surmise that there were, basically, three motives for entering the cotton-spinning industry in the Midlands during the period under review. These may be summarized as follows:

(i) The largest group numerically, and responsible for the major initiatives in following Arkwright, were those who entered warpspinning as a means of maintaining or increasing their leadership of the hosiery industry. The wholesale merchants of the hosiery industry (country hosiers, merchant hosiers, and mercers) had been gradually extending their control over the framework knitters and processes of the hosiery industry through the eighteenth century. Most hosiers were familiar with the technique of workshop management and some with juvenile employment. It was easy to incorporate the jenny in the workshop and, where water-mill sites were available, it was not a difficult step from jenny to warp-spinning. As yet, the technical problems were simple, and a skilled and intelligent workman could be hired to supervise the plant.

The isolated Derbyshire handloom-weaving and hosiery industry provided the context for a parallel development beyond the control of the hosiers. Here the independent farmer-manufacturers were responsible for the main initiative. Many of them became jennyspinners, and a few succeeded as warp-spinners, in an attempt to maintain their position in rural industry. The farmer-manufacturers had the advantage of good sites, but suffered from poor communications, slender capital and isolation from the centres of technical progress. Four of them are shown as establishing themselves as warp-spinners in Table 3, under the heading 'Gentry, farmers, miller', but there may have been others, as most of the entrepreneurs whose earlier occupations have not been traced had mills in rural Derbyshire.

(ii) A second, and numerically small group of entrepreneurs diverted capital from declining industries in the Region into cotton. These industries were silk, Derbyshire lead-mining and iron-smelting and, very likely, the woollen and worsted industry which, like silk, was temporarily losing ground to cotton. Those who transferred their interest from some other branch of the textile industry no doubt utilized market connections as well as capital and mercantile experience derived from their earlier trading interest. The two entrepreneurs who recruited capital from the extractive and mineral industries had the benefit of an early contact with Arkwright.

(iii) The remainder of the entrepreneurs, with the exception of the Peels, can only be described as speculators. They varied considerably in their economic backgrounds and resources; all they had in common was that they possessed capital and recognized in cotton-spinning a good investment. 'Parsley' Peel's motives were similar to those of the merchant hosiers: he was attempting to maintain his existing interest in the textile industry. His son's motives were political rather than economic; he saw Tamworth primarily as a means of entering Parliament, and only secondly as a potential centre of the cotton industry.

CHAPTER SIX

The Early Factory Masters
(2) in Worsted-Spinning

DURING the second half of the eighteenth century the manufacture of worsted hosiery became increasingly concentrated in Leicester, though Nottingham was never completely devoted to cotton hosiery and the Derby specialization in silk stockings did not exclude other branches. The merchant hosiers who traded in worsted stockings connected combing and spinning jersey with their business, and though there was some tendency to specialization after mid-century, hosiers and woolcombers still worked in close liaison. The rapid growth and concentration of the worsted hosiery manufacture led to a bottleneck in the supply of worsted-yarn in the Midlands, and before the end of the century Leicester hosiers were said to be employing 'some 18,500 married and unmarried women, widows, aged and infirm persons and children' on the task. Even so, the supply of yarn proved insufficient and orders were sent as far as Bristol and Aberdeen. A similar scarcity apparently prevailed in Nottingham, for J. & H. Hadden moved there from Aberdeen in 1787 to channel supplies from Scotland to the Midlands.[1]

The spinning machines patented by Hargreaves, Arkwright and Crompton were designed for and achieved their first success in spinning cotton, but attempts were quickly made in each case to apply the machine to the spinning of woollen- and worsted-yarns. The jenny was easily applied to spinning wool and rapidly became as popular in the West Riding as it was in Lancashire. However, unsuccessful experiments in the Midlands and in Yorkshire soon showed that this machine was unsuitable for worsted-spinning. Arkwright's frame, on the other hand, was adaptable to the spinning of worsted, but not of woollen-yarn. The Midland counties specialized in worsted-yarns for hosiery (at Leicester and elsewhere in the east Midlands), and for carpets in the neighbourhood of Kidderminster and Worcester. After the invalidation of Arkwright's patent, a number of worsted-spinning plants were established, in several cases in association with cotton-spinning mills.

The worsted-spinning plants and mills opened before the end of the eighteenth century were not so geographically concentrated as were the cotton mills. Their dispersion is illustrated in the following table:

TABLE 4
*Location of Worsted Mills Established in the Midlands,
1769–1800*

	Number of Firms	Number of Mills
Leicester	1	1
Nottinghamshire (Arnold, Cuckney, Worksop, Retford)	3	5
Derbyshire (Derby)	1	1
Worcestershire (Bromsgrove)	1	1
Warwickshire (Warwick, Bedworth)	2	2
Staffordshire (Wolverhampton)	1	1
Lincolnshire (Raithby, Louth)	2	2
	11	13

Source: Appendix A.

There were several reasons for this dispersion of the industry. Arkwright tried to adapt his roller-spinning machine to the spinning of wool (and probably of worsted) but apparently without any commercial success. His failure, and the invalidation of his patent, opened up the field to other inventors and speculators. As it happened, no very outstanding figure emerged from among those who strove to become the Arkwright of worsted-spinning; certainly no single entrepreneur came to dominate this branch.[2]

The earliest attempt of which we have any record was that of Coniah Wood, a Nottingham turner who had assisted Arkwright with his experiments in roller-spinning at Nottingham. Wood, as we have seen, refused to move to Cromford with Arkwright, but continued to experiment after Arkwright had left and took out a patent in 1772 (No. 1,018) for a machine for spinning wool or jersey. The patent suggests an attempt to combine Arkwright's principles with those of the jenny but it does not appear to have had any success. In Derby, Robert and Thomas Barber, sons of a 'gentleman' of Bilborough (near Nottingham), established a small mill to spin worsted by 1779. Their machines were described as jennies, but as we have already noticed, the original principle, of their machine was Arkwright's. The yarn was very coarse and had to be sent to Yorkshire for carpet-weaving.

The first real success was achieved in Leicester, where John Coltman (1727–1808), a leading hosier with a scientific turn of mind, conducted a series of experiments first with the jenny and then with Arkwright's roller-spinning apparatus. His work was taken up by one of his woolcombers, Joseph Brookhouse, who perfected a machine in 1785. He entered into partnership with Coltman and Joseph Whetstone, a master-comber who is said to have employed between a thousand and fifteen hundred spinners at this time. The partners' plans were frustrated in December 1787 when, as a consequence of a fortnight of riots in Leicester, the Corporation forbade them to operate the machine within fifty miles of the town, despite Coltman's attempt to negotiate terms with the combers. The infant industry was thus dispersed from its natural centre at Leicester, and remained so for more than a quarter of a century.

The third cause of the dispersion of the Midlands worsted-spinning industry lies in the needs of other surviving branches of the Midlands textile industry. During the course of the eighteenth century, the hosiery industry was spreading into the surrounding county areas from the centres at Nottingham, Leicester, Derby and Hinckley, gradually displacing the older woollen industry. Hand-loom-weaving thus became peripheral to the growing hosiery industry. The mills opened at Bedworth, Louth and Wolverhampton appear to have originated with the idea of supplying a local industry, or reviving its importance. Each of these mills not only spun but also manufactured some kind of fabric: worsted-cloth at Bedworth, 'common narrow stuff' at Louth, and carpets at Wolverhampton. Raithby was (as we shall see) an off-shoot of Louth. The Midlands carpet industry at Kidderminster and Worcester, with its growing demand for coarse worsted-yarns, exercised a powerful locational pull to the west and, together with the Corporate prohibition at Leicester, help to explain Coltman and Brookhouse's choice of Bromsgrove and Warwick. The needs of the Halifax and Leeds carpet industry may have been a factor in the location of the mill at Worksop.

Though the pioneers of worsted-spinning by power were scattered across the Midlands, their career patterns show striking similarities. All but one of the eleven had business or social connections with Arkwright or Cartwright, or stole their ideas, and the single exception, Sir Roger Newdegate, is probably due to lack of evidence. Their relationship, being somewhat complex, is best illustrated in the accompanying diagram before embarking on a detailed account. Five of the eleven manufacturers were Unitarians with links with Dr Joseph Priestley, the well-known scientist and political and religious Radical, and his friend, the Reverend George Walker, FRS, of Nottingham. It will be seen that the ideology of this religious connection helps to explain its interest both in new techniques and in the moral improvement of the working-classes through community building.

The earliest firm to achieve any commercial success with worsted-spinning was probably Toplis & Co. of Mansfield. It is not easy to fix a chronology because this firm, like several of its early competitors, was at first engaged in cotton-spinning. The Toplises were a family of Wirksworth and Brassington farmers whose pedigree has been traced back to the early seventeenth century. Like other Derbyshire families who subsequently became involved in the cotton industry, such as the Evans and Nightingales, the Toplis family may have been connected with lead-mining, of

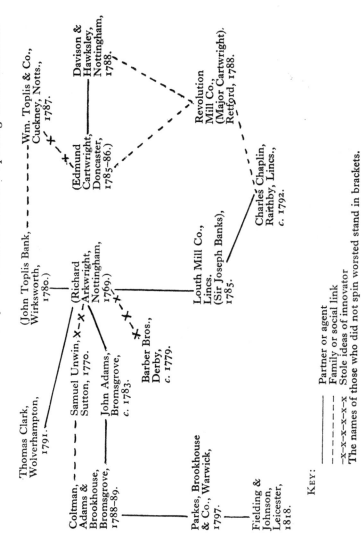

Connections between the Pioneers of Mechanized Worsted-Spinning in the Midlands

Thomas Clark,
Wolverhampton,
1791.

(John Toplis Bank,
Wirksworth,
1780.)

Wm. Toplis & Co.,
Cuckney, Notts.,
1787.

Davison &
Hawksley,
Nottingham,
1788.

Coltman,
Adams &
Brookhouse,
Bromsgrove,
1788–89.

Samuel Unwin,
Sutton, 1770.

(Richard
Arkwright,
Nottingham,
1769.)

(Edmund
Cartwright,
Doncaster,
1785–86.)

Revolution
Mill Co.,
(Major Cartwright).
Retford, 1788.

John Adams,
Bromsgrove,
c. 1783.

Barber Bros.,
Derby,
c. 1779.

Louth Mill Co.,
Lincs.
(Sir Joseph Banks),
1785.

Charles Chaplin,
Raithby, Lincs.,
c. 1792.

Parkes, Brookhouse
& Co., Warwick,
1797.

Fielding &
Johnson,
Leicester,
1818.

KEY:

――――― Partner or agent
- - - - - Family or social link
-x-x-x-x-x Stole ideas of innovator
The names of those who did not spin worsted stand in brackets.

which Wirksworth was the centre in Derbyshire. The son of the eighteenth-century heir was William Toplis (1723–1822) who, either as an apprentice or as a young man, moved from Wirksworth to Mansfield, a small market-town and a centre of the hosiery manufacture, twenty miles east of Wirksworth. The reason for his migration may have been a desire to improve trade connections between Wirksworth and the rapidly-growing hosiery manufacture of Nottinghamshire but, whatever it was, he became established in Mansfield market-place as a mercer and by 1780 he appears to have been one of the leading traders in the growing town, owning a large house and shop as well as land in the district.

In 1785, William Toplis and his second son, William II, started cotton-spinning on Arkwright's principle at Cuckney, a hamlet seven miles north of Mansfield. The termination of the Arkwright patents created something like a fever of speculation in Mansfield, for no less than eight firms sprang into existence in the decade after 1781. Half of them drew capital from Nottingham partners and a fifth firm, Samuel Unwin, had a partner who was a London banker. William Toplis was as successful as his Mansfield rivals, so that it seems very likely that he drew capital, and possibly a fund of ideas too, from his brother at Wirksworth.

Toplis's mill was soon working in association with a factory for weaving worsted smallwares, owned by Thomas Gorton & Son (of Worksop), but managed, at least initially, by William Toplis junior. Thomas Gorton's son, Richard, was among the first to attempt to follow Cartwright in the application of power to weaving; his machines sound very much like the Dutch smallware loom, which was well-known in Lancashire at this period. Gorton built a factory at Cuckney in 1787, close by a stream but powered their frames by a 14 hp Boulton & Watt 'sun and planet' engine. Judging from the correspondence with Boulton & Watt, the engine did not serve the frames very well, and was sold in 1794.

Toplis's Cuckney mill seems to have prospered until 1792, when it suffered the fate of many early mills and was burned down. The enterprise, or the main part of it, was then transferred to Worksop, five miles north of Cuckney. Drawing capital from new connections at Worksop, Toplis & Co. built two large mills on a splendid site near the centre of the town, adjoining the Chesterfield–Stockwith Canal (opened 1777) and the Mansfield–Doncaster turnpike roads. The mills were used for spinning worsted and 'weaving filleting tuban-stuff sashes etc'. The weaving of smallwares, and the location of the mills, suggests the interests of the Gortons. The spinning of cotton was also 'attempted'. The scale of the buildings, and the few known details of the products, suggest the conception of an integrated manufacture for spinning and weaving cotton and woollen goods. At the same period, William Toplis junior was experimenting with machinery for combing wool, but his 'ingenious contrivance did not obtain very wide acceptance, nor was Mr Toplis encouraged to make any attempt to improve his machine'.

Toplis's Cuckney mill survived until 1846 (when the lease ran out) but the Worksop enterprise collapsed in 1798 when the partners went bankrupt. The concern was conceived on too ambitious a scale considering that three of the main processes—combing, worsted-spinning and smallware-weaving—were still imperfectly developed by the partners. The proximity of Worksop to Doncaster and the interest of Edmund Cartwright in these three processes suggest that workmen may have been drawn from Cartwright's mill to Cuckney and Worksop. Certainly Cartwright's brother alleged that Toplis had stolen the woolcombing patent, and the failure of Cartwright's experiments was quite likely a main cause of the failure of the Worksop mills.

While the connection between Edmund Cartwright and the Worksop mills is a matter for conjecture, there is no doubt of the inspiration which the inventor gave to the entrepreneur of another north Nottinghamshire worsted-spinning factory, the 'Revolution Mill' at Retford. This mill was opened in 1788 by Major Cartwright (1740–1824), an elder brother of Dr Cartwright. Major Cartwright's letters to Boulton & Watt clearly show that he was quite ignorant of industrial techniques and relied completely upon his brother, whose early success at Doncaster had fired his imagination. Dr Cartwright had established a small factory at Doncaster in 1785 or 1786, having inherited land from his father-in-law, a Doncaster alderman. By 1788, he had prospered sufficiently to build a second mill, where his power-looms were driven by a Newcomen engine. His brother, the Major, hoped to achieve even greater success with a much more ambitious venture—success which would bring him much-needed financial relief as the Cartwright family estate at Marnham (near Retford) was heavily mortgaged. Moreover, he was at the time seeking a seat in Parliament, and Retford was in the market. The Major's political and religious connections were also important. The name of a minister, the Reverend George Walker, FRS, appears on a list of the mill's shareholders of 1794, and others were Samuel Statham (a hosier), Cartwright's in-laws (the Dashwoods, of Stamford Hall, Nottinghamshire), and other members of the gentry.

Cartwright's original intention was probably to raise £25,000 of capital but the caution of his partners soon cut this plan by half. In April 1788, four acres of land were acquired at Spittle Hill (Retford), and the mill, erected during the following summer months, was completed in time to celebrate the centenary of the Revolution of 1688, from which it derived its name of 'the Revolution Mill'. It was conveniently near to the Gainsborough Canal, which gave access to markets in the Trent valley.

While Cartwright had obviously caught the current enthusiasm for factory production, he had no precise idea of what his mill would do. Originally, he envisaged a complete unit for converting raw wool and cotton into cloth for the market, but without understanding the technical problems involved. No doubt the other shareholders were instrumental in restraining him for, in September 1788, he was advising Boulton & Watt that only half the original plan was to be proceeded with. By then he was thinking of following the example of his brother who had just started to get his looms to work with the Newcomen engine, and to rely primarily on power-looms. In the following month he was inquiring about cotton-spinning machinery that was being sold by auction in Birmingham and finally, in December, after a conversation with Edmund on the progress of his experiments with worsted-spinning, he decided to concentrate on this new branch of factory industry. He was encouraged in his decision by James Watt's advice to attend to only one branch of textile manufacture at a time. He wrote to Watt (23 December 1788); 'I am this day returned from Doncaster and Retford. Upon further consideration of our experiments on wool-spinning, that article, instead of being a secondary object, is now become the primary one, and the whole wing of the Retford Mill already built is to be appropriated thereto. . . . Each floor will contain 1,720 spindles, three will contain above 5,000 . . .'. He ordered a 30 hp engine to provide the power that Edmund estimated would be required.

It seems clear that Dr Cartwright's experiments with worsted were still only in the initial stages, for his own mill was still limited to looms in August 1788. He did not take out a patent for worsted-spinning, despite having patented his other inventions even before they were sufficiently developed to be of commercial value. Moreover, the Doncaster mill, which was not a financial success for long, prevented him from devoting much time to the Retford enterprise. Within three years, the Retford concern was suffering financial embarrassment, and lack of confidence among the partners soon brought production to a halt, probably in 1798.

There is no evidence to suggest that Edmund Cartwright ever attempted to spin worsted on a commercial scale. The letter of 23 December 1788, quoted above, reveals his experiments, but the Doncaster mill was given up in 1795, before any results could be utilized. The evidence of collusion between Dr Cartwright and Davison & Hawksley of Nottingham—who are the subject of the next few paragraphs—suggests that the latter probably obtained the benefit of any progress made at Doncaster.

It has not always been appreciated that Nottingham remained an important cotton-spinning centre after Arkwright's departure for Cromford in 1770. In the 1780s, after Arkwright's patents had terminated, several mills were built in the town with machinery driven by horse capstans, while the hosiers and tradesmen of the town were responsible for a large number of the water-spinning mills developed in Nottinghamshire, Derbyshire and Leicestershire. There was, however, no attempt to apply the new mechanical principles to worsted-spinning until Davison & Hawksley opened their first mill on the fringe of the town in 1788.

The partners were Robert Davison (1751–1807) and John Hawksley (*d.* 1815). The former was the elder son of Dr John Davison, a medical practitioner who had moved to Nottingham in about 1740. Dr Davison married a daughter of Robert Huish, a Leicester woolcomber, who became one of Nottingham's earliest successful hosiers and was Mayor in 1760. Both Robert and his brother, John, chose to follow the calling of their maternal grandfather rather than their father's profession and, entering the hosiery trade at the time of its most rapid expansion, the last quarter of the eighteenth century, they both prospered for some years in the flourishing trade.

John Hawksley also belonged to a well-established Nottingham family, his ancestors having been maltsters and distillers for generations. His early business experience is not known, but it is clear from his patents and his correspondence with Boulton & Watt that he was a man of considerable mechanical genius. He might conceivably have borrowed ideas from Leicester, but the original cast of his mind makes this seem improbable. It is not difficult to recognize that Hawksley was the technical and Davison the commercial partner.

The partners' first mill was erected on the north bank of the Leen in 1788, and was at first water-powered. The Leen proved unsatisfactory as a source of power, however, because the 'numerous mills and water-works' upon it made the flow irregular. In 1789, the partners wrote to Boulton & Watt enquiring about the cost of installing a 6 or 8 hp engine, but evidently decided it was too expensive. When the small mill was accidentally burnt down in 1791, the firm moved three miles out of town, to Arnot Hill (Arnold), and built a large five-storey mill and warehouses on the banks of a small stream. But even here the reserves of water (a mill-pool of four acres) only proved adequate to drive the machinery for two days a week, and the deficiency was made good by the installation of an atmospheric rotative engine to work the plant on the other four days. Though the engine was wasteful of fuel (the two boilers burnt 5 cwt of coal an hour), coal was 'tolerably cheap' at ten shillings a ton, so that the two sources of power proved satisfactory for a few years.

Davison & Hawksley were simultaneously developing new techniques in combing and spinning worsted, as well as in the application of steam-power, and they evidently tried to diversify their interests so as to be able to sustain any possible losses. They were also ambitious, and subsequently built up a complete industrial unit at Arnold, in which both raw cotton and the fleece passed through all the processes to the complete knitted garment. All stages of manufacture except knitting were undertaken at the mill, and the framework knitters who worked for the partners appear to have been largely concentrated in Arnold. The partners' activities in worsted-spinning thus formed only a part of their interests, and the production of worsted by power seems to have been modest. A note on the back of one of the Boulton & Watt engine-drawings reveals that they had only 250 spindles at work as late as 1797, and in 1815, when the firm was sold out following Hawksley's death, they still had only a thousand spindles in production.

The nature of the machinery is a subject for speculation, but the indications are that Hawksley did more than modify Arkwright's water-frame for worsted-spinning. Edmund Cartwright observed that Davison & Hawksley's 'spinning machinery is supposed to be upon a very superior construction' and, in conjunction with his own

FIGURE 2

Davison & Hawksley's Worsted Mill, Arnold, near Nottingham (from a contemporary print)

patent combing-technique, spun yarn 'of a quality which it was thought no mill-spinning could ever have arrived at'. This certainly suggests a finer thread than No. 60, the finest that the water-frame could spin. In 1815, it was claimed that the machinery had 'been made under the direction of the best artists in worsted-spinning in the country'.

Davison and Hawksley were also pioneers of combing by mechanical power and the rights of Hawksley's first patent were assigned to Cartwright in return for a quarter share of the royalties. It seems likely that after Cartwright's Doncaster mill was given up (1795) he relied on the Arnold partners for practical experiment with his woolcombing inventions. The partners also installed cleaning tanks and machinery at Arnold for fulling and dyeing, and had a foundry and workshop for building their own machinery. It is not too much to say that Davison and Hawksley tried to establish a largely self-contained community at Arnold. The partners lived as patriarchs, 'Mr Hawksley' at Arnot Hill House, a 'delightful habitation . . . surrounded with plantations, gardens and hot-houses', and 'Mr Davison' at Arnold Hall, a three-storey mansion 'at the entrance of the village'. They had their own granary and ground corn for the village, they maintained grocers' and mercers' shops and issued their own token coinage. They also owned and farmed land and kept cows, sheep, horses and pigs.

Despite labour difficulties and the fluctuating trade conditions of the Napoleonic wars, the partnership appears to have prospered and during the life of the two partners their business was probably the most successful in the infant manufacture. Until about 1797 the Arnold mill worked day and night, and even in September 1800, when the war had caused some contraction of trade and employment, the business still employed 600 apprentices and had about 1,400 other workers dependent on it. Correspondence with Boulton & Watt in 1797 indicates that Davison & Hawksley expected to expand considerably as soon as war-time conditions were over, but other circumstances were to prevent this further growth.

H

The decline of the firm began in 1804, when Alderman John Davison was dragged into bankruptcy and died 'in the prime of life, of a broken heart'. His brother, Robert, was almost certainly involved in this disaster and it was observed that 'though one of the most accomplished tradesmen of his day . . . he expired of an apoplexy in 1807, leaving his affairs in a state of insolvency'. Hawksley struggled on, selling the Arnold mill and property to open a new mill near the site of the first, in 1810. But 'pecuniary difficulties . . . bore heavy upon him' and, when he died suddenly in January 1815, the mill was closed down, the machinery auctioned off, and the premises converted to use as Nottingham's first gasworks.

Turning now to the origins of the Coltman & Adams enterprise, when the development of worsted-spinning at Leicester was frustrated by mob violence and the Corporate prohibition, Coltman moved to Bromsgrove, in Worcestershire, where the nucleus of his business was provided by a small cotton-spinning mill which his nephew, John Adams, owned on the fringe of the town. The origin of John Adams' business at Bromsgrove is obscure but, according to the *Universal British Directory*, the mill was opened about 1783 and soon appeared under the style of 'Adams & Co.'. The other partners were not named, but a letter of January 1785 in the Boulton & Watt manuscripts shows that Arkwright had interests in Bromsgrove, and as this was the only spinning-mill in the county, Adams may well have been one of Arkwright's local partners. Certainly it would have taken a man of Arkwright's status and connections to establish a mill in a country town so far distant from the main centres of the cotton industry. The spinning machinery was driven by a stream which runs through the town, the Spadesbourne Brook, but the water-wheel had to be augmented by a Newcomen engine. The mill was a small one, as befitted the limited local market for yarn, and even in 1795 an engine of 4–8 hp was apparently adequate to work all the machinery, and to provide for future expansion.

Brookhouse quitted Leicester for Bromsgove, no doubt glad to supervise the building of machines in conditions of safety. The Bromsgrove mill was turned over from cotton to worsted-spinning and changed its title to Coltman, Adams & Co., worsted and yarn manufacturers. Presently, we hear of the firm carding, and experimenting with combing by power. Such progress was made, indeed, that the local poet declared that there was 'No better yarn in all England', and predicted that soon the water-wheel would be driving the stocking-frames too.

The partnership was not destined to last, however. Adams cheated Coltman in some way, possibly by selling machines to other manufacturers, for he shortly (1794) appears as a worsted machine-maker in Leicester. At any rate, Brookhouse left Bromsgrove and moved to Warwick, where he joined partnership with W. and J. Parkes, who shortly began to compete with Adams for the Leicester market. Quite possibly, the embittered Coltman introduced Brookhouse to the brothers, with whom he shared common religious, political and literary interests.

William Parkes (1757–1806) and John Parkes (1763–1851) were linen-drapers and bankers in Warwick Market Place. Their father, John Parkes senior, came of a family of wealthy nailers at Dudley, Worcestershire, but his own business connections appear to have been with Nottingham, rather than the Black Country. He is said to to have settled in Warwick in 1750 and to have been a banker as well as draper; this is not difficult to accept in view of Dr Pressnell's findings on the origins of country bankers. His will reveals that he acquired considerable property and land in Warwick, including one parcel 'at the top of the Saltisford Rock, near the New Bridge', a site later to be exploited by his sons. The Parkes brothers continued their father's business after his death, and also inherited his position in the trading *élite* of the town. They were Whig-Radicals and members of the Unitarian chapel at Warwick, bitter opponents of the entrenched Tory Corporation of the town. They were probably closely connected with the Birmingham Unitarians, for John Parkes' son, Joseph, married a daughter of Dr Priestley.

By the beginning of the last decade of the eighteenth century, the brothers had prospered sufficiently to buy substantial town-houses and additional land on the north side of the town. On part of this land they built warehouses, apparently in anticipation of the cutting of the Warwick–Birmingham Canal, which was surveyed in 1792 and passed through Parliament as a Private Act the following year, the names of William Parkes and John Parkes appearing among the proprietors. Shortly afterwards, Joseph Brookhouse moved to Warwick.

The main warehouse was later extended as a cotton and worsted mill and in March 1797 the firm began production in the new buildings under the title of Parkes, Brookhouse & Crompton. A 30 hp Boulton & Watt engine was purchased to drive the machinery erected under Brookhouse's supervision. Coal was brought from Bimingham at a cost of two shillings and ninepence a ton when the canal opened in 1799, and unloaded at the company's 'extensive range of wharfs'. The mill was planned to conduct 'every process in the conversion of raw wool into fine worsted for hosiery and into coarse yarn for carpets'. One account says that 500 hands were employed, another that there were nearly a thousand workpeople. The output was stated (in 1823) to be twenty packs of yarn (i.e., 4,800 lb) per week. The main markets were at Leicester (hosiery-yarn), Worcester and Kidderminster (carpet-yarn) and London, and Brookhouse is reputed to have made a fortune from the enterprise. So large a mill would have to draw much of its combed wool for fine spinning from a very wide area, perhaps from as far as Leicester. (For the first forty years of the nineteenth century, the hand-comber was still able to produce better combings than any machine.) By 1805, the firm had already opened a warehouse in Leicester to secure closer contact with the centre of the worsted hosiery industry.

A number of other country worsted mills were opened before the end of the eighteenth century, at Wolverhampton, Bedworth (near Coventry), and Louth and Raithby in Lincolnshire. A study of their origins shows something of the diversity of factory enterprise at the time.

The building of the mill at Wolverhampton, a town which had only a vestigeal interest in the woollen industry and was distant from the main centres of the Midlands textile industry, highlights the vigour and versatility of a group of Birmingham and Black Country industrialists of this period. The central figure appears to have been Thomas Clark (*c.* 1767–1847), a leading Birmingham industrialist and political figure of the early decades of the nineteenth century. Clark was brought up as a ribbon-weaver at Coventry but, making his way to the metropolis of Midland manufacturing with only the traditional shilling in his pocket, he somehow found his way into the staple toy-making industry of the town, manufacturing chains for Coventry watches and selling them in the United States. From this, in about 1790, he moved into the iron-founding business, the newest branch of which was then the manufacture of hollow-ware, which was migrating from Birmingham to the South Staffordshire coalfield. Having opened a foundry at Wolverhampton, which is still in operation, Clark then became interested in the manufacture of webbing and braces (perhaps as a complement to the production of the metal attachments), and contrived a machine for winding cotton into balls, so saving the labour of rewinding from the hanks. 'Mr Clark told me once he was almost ashamed of the profit he got on his balls of cotton', his biographer records. 'For years no cotton was sold for ladies and women in any other shape', and the device brought Clark into business association with Arkwright and Strutt. It is also interesting to note that Clark was a member of the Birmingham New Meeting (having attended Dr Priestley's Sunday classes as a young man), and that this could have brought him into contact with other Unitarian manufacturers such as W. and J. Parkes, Coltman and Davison.

Clark thus had the capital and the knowledge of the textile industry necessary for a new venture. When George and James Scott, his neighbours at Horseley Field, Wolverhampton, con-

verted a large house into a steam mill in 1791, he was ready to become one of the eight partners in the enterprise. He used part of the
mill to open a small worsted-spinning and carpet-manufacturing
plant. The Scott brothers were brassfounders, but as neither they
nor Clark used the whole of the space or power available in the
factory, they advertised a part of it for hire to other manufacturers.
The details of the advertisement in the *Wolverhampton Chronicle*
(20 June 1792) are worth quoting:

> STEAM-ENGINE MILL, WOLVERHAMPTON
>
> A report having been circulated that the whole of the power of the
> above engine and mill is let for the carpet business, George and
> James Scott take this method of informing . . . the public that they
> have only let one-third of such power and have still remaining con-
> venient room and power for employing more than a hundred pairs
> of hands in grinding on laps, polishing, turning or brushing lathes, or
> any other trades that the power of the steam-engine can be applied
> to; which they will let in separate parts, or in whole apartments as
> may be wanted. . . .

The hiring of workshop-space was a long-established practice in
the Black Country, but the offer of power with it was novel, and
helped to establish a precedent which encouraged the continuation
of the many small manufacturing firms characteristic of the area.
Despite its small beginnings the worsted-spinning plant enjoyed a
longer life than most of the pioneers, though Clark sold out his
interest within a few years.

The worsted mill at Bedworth is a good illustration of the interest
of the country gentry in reviving the declining worsted industry.
Sir Roger Newdegate had extensive estates at Collyhurst, near Bedworth, a few miles to the north of Coventry. The coal seams there
were being exploited in the seventeenth century, but towards the
end of the eighteenth century the trade was given a fillip by connecting Griff colliery with the Coventry canal by means of a network of canals and railroads. It was probably at this time that
Newdegate's old Newcomen engine was replaced by one of larger
power, and a water-wheel (originally built by Smeaton) became
redundant for pumping water out of the mine. However that may
be, Sir Roger advertised the old wheel and a supply of water for the

purposes of a factory in 1787, and the following year a worsted-spinner named Henry Lane secured a twenty-one-year lease of the site. Unfortunately, the Newdegate manuscripts contain no information on this entrepreneur, though the number of plans, elevations and engravings of the mill illustrate Newdegate's personal interest in the enterprise. Both spinning and weaving were carried on in the mill, but the fate of the enterprise is not known.

The surviving records of a mill at Louth (Lincolnshire) throw further light on the attitude of the gentry and the enterprise of which they were capable. The Louth Quarter Sessions of Michaelmas 1783 took 'into their most serious consideration the alarming increase of parish rates and the want of regard to the employment of the poor in general, and of the infant poor in particular . . .'. The concern expressed at this meeting directed attention to a scheme, which seems to have originated with the Rev. R. G. Bouyer, the energetic secretary of The Society for the Promotion of Industry among the Poor, to establish mechanized worsted-spinning on a commercial scale in Lincolnshire.

A small and languishing manufacture of 'wildbore tammies' had been established in Louth 'many years ago', and it was hoped to revive and extend this industry. The support of Sir Joseph Banks, whose ancestral estates were at Revesby Abbey in the south of the county, was recruited. Banks approached Arkwright with a proposal to open a mill in the county on the most generous terms, but the project fell through, probably (as was suggested in Chapter Four) because Arkwright had been unable to make a commercial success of his experiments with worsted-spinning. Nevertheless a committee was formed in 1783, to go ahead with the project, and issued a handbill entitled 'Proposals for Establishing a Manufactory of Sheep's Wool, at or near Louth in Lincolnshire, by Subscription of the Gentry, Proprietors and Occupiers of Lands'.

It is worth quoting some details from the handbill, for they show the committee's aims, and its naïveté, very clearly. 'It is a known and received maxim', the paper begins, 'that the riches of every

country are in proportion to the number of its people well-employed
. . . therefore it is humbly hoped that an attempt to establish a
manufactory, by which the value of lands and consequently their
rents may be preserved . . . will meet with the general approbation of
. . . the Nobility, Gentry, Proprietors and occupiers of lands'. 'Lincolnshire', the bill claimed, 'is in no respect inferior, or less constituted for manufacturing industry than the neighbouring counties of
Yorkshire and Norfolk.' The committee went on to propose their
scheme for 'spinning long and short wool, by the force of water, and
completely manufacturing it into cloths, both for home consumption and exportation, by an improved method . . .'. They proposed
that £10,000 should be raised by subscription 'for the necessary
mills, buildings, engines, etc'. Louth was chosen as the site for the
first mills, partly, no doubt, because of the existing manufacture of
cloth, but also because as the committee wrote, 'it has a communica-
tion with the German Ocean by a navigation, and consequently will
procure a more ready trade with Germany and Holland, the best
marts for woollen cloths . . .'.

In March 1784 an account was opened at the Lincoln bank
(Smith, Ellison and Brown), in the name of 'the manufactory at
Louth'. The subscription list ultimately reached £1,540 through
the personal support of Sir Joseph Banks and the Warden of Louth.
The problem of recruiting a competent manager with adequate
technical knowledge proved just as difficult as that of raising
capital, but a Mr Thomas Clarke was eventually appointed when an
engineer from 'Messrs Girdle, Pears & Co. at Calver, near Bakewell . . . gave his opinion that Mr. Clarke's machine is constructed
exactly upon the principle of a machine erected by Mr. Arkwright'.
The mill buildings were completed by the summer of 1785, but
evidently Clarke failed to have 500 spindles at work by Lady Day
1787, as he had covenanted to do, for the mill was then leased for
seven years to Richard Brumfitt of Leeds, carpet manufacturer. He,
too, evidently failed to fulfil the terms of his agreement and withdrew in 1790. A year later, it was taken over by Messrs Eve, Cook-

son & Fawcett, a partnership between Adam Eve, a Louth shop-keeper who had a connection with the old cloth industry of Louth, and Cookson and Fawcett, Leeds merchants. However, the new management clearly had very little more success than their predecessors, for the mill was advertised for sale in the *Nottingham Journal* at the close of 1793. Unfortunately, nothing more is heard of the Louth mill, and it is to be doubted whether it ever had another tenant.

For all its failures, the Louth mill helped to inspire the establishment of another spinning-mill in the vicinity. Charles Chaplin was a considerable landowner in Lincolnshire and well-known as an improving landlord. Some of his estates adjoined those of Major Cartwright, who had a similar reputation, and he was 'indefatigable' in recruiting subscriptions for the Louth project. Chaplin opened a mill at Raithby, near Louth, about 1792, perhaps at the time that the earlier mill seemed destined to failure. The fact that he employed Edmund Cartwright's 'Big Ben' combing-machine and a steam-engine strongly suggests Cartwright's enthusiastic support. However, by 1797, all was 'gone and done with', and a year later Cartwright's own mill at Retford had collapsed. The Lincolnshire gentry proved too ignorant to understand what was involved in establishing a manufacturing industry.

Mechanized worsted-spinning was slow to return to Leicester. The hosiers and worsted manufacturers of the town were loth to incur the further wrath of the woolcombers' union, and if they did risk the introduction of new machinery, they took good care to carry on the manufacture in secret. It is perhaps for this reason that there are very few clues to the sequence of events which led to the return of the industry to Leicester. In 1794, John Adams appears in the *Universal British Directory* as a worsted machine-maker. There was no patent on Brookhouse's invention and Adams was legally free to build and sell machines on the pattern developed by his former partners. However, directories of 1805 and 1815 merely list Adams as a worsted-spinner, so it is doubtful whether he remained in this business for long.

It is only possible to identify with any certainty one Leicester firm that opened before the end of the century. In 1799, John Rawson, a Leicester hosier who had acted as agent to J. L. Thacker & Co., cotton-spinners of Wilne Mills, joined with other manufacturers to open a worsted mill on the River Soar. But in 1811 it contained only five spinning-frames (value £375) and employed only ten girls, clearly a very small affair. If there were other spinners in the town they were also operating on a diminutive scale, for several of the large country spinners maintained agencies in Leicester for long after this time. Davison & Hawksley had agents in Leicester by 1794, and as late as 1815 worsted mills at Bromsgrove, Warwick, Bedworth, Mansfield and Bristol had warehouses in the town. Coltman and Gardiner's stock-books (1792–1814) show substantial debts to the spinners at these places.

Fortunately, some records of one of the leading Leicester worsted-spinning firms, Fielding & Johnson have survived. Thomas Fielding (1768–1830) was a Leicester woolcomber who obtained the valuable Leicester agency for Parkes, Brookhouse & Crompton of Warwick. His sales ledgers (1816–34) show that he continued to supply Leicester hosiers with yarn from Warwick until May 1819, when the connection ceased abruptly as the result of a lawsuit. Very likely, this was connected with the fact that, in the previous year, Fielding had begun to build a factory in Leicester, which was powered by steam from 1822, and there are indications that he may have been financed by the Leicester banking-house of Mansfield & Co. The following year Parkes' mill was sold for a paltry sum, so clearly the vital Leicester market had collapsed, so far as the Warwick firm was concerned. One cannot be certain that Fieldings were the first to build a worsted-spinning factory in Leicester, but they were obviously in the vanguard of this development. The *Leicester Directory* of 1827 does not mention any country spinners, so it is reasonable to suppose that the industry returned to the home of the worsted hosiery industry in the early 1820s, and very likely during the building boom of 1823–24.

The only other clue to the history of mechanized spinning in Leicester is the comment by a contemporary authority, that the worsted-spinners of the town 'revived' the spinning-jenny in the depression of 1828–29. Hargreaves' jenny could not spin worsted, so clearly this writer had some later development of the machine in mind. He is almost certainly referring to the 'throstle', a machine which represented the successful adaptation of the mule to worsted-spinning. Developed in the West Riding and first demonstrated in public in Bradford in 1794, it at first contained only eighteen to twenty-four spindles and could be worked by hand. It could thus be operated in the traditional domestic environment of the industry. The throstle was similar in principle to the modern worsted-spinning machine, and manual-power later gave way to water- and steam-power.[3]

The fragments of evidence summarized in the last three paragraphs offer the basis for an interpretation of the transition to the factory system in the Leicester worsted-spinning industry. Arkwright's technique of spinning cotton by rollers was first adapted to worsted-spinning in Leicester, but intimidation of the hosiers by the combers' union drove the new industry to distant parts of the Midlands. Several worsted mills established in the 1780s and 1790s maintained their hold on the Leicester market until after 1815. The competitiveness of these country mills is suggested by the fact that Amatt & Co. of Bristol—a mill opened about 1799 by a Tiverton woolcomber—had an agency and secured substantial orders in Leicester through this period. In the meantime, however, the invention of the throstle in Bradford offered opportunity for men of small capital to secure some of the economies of the new techniques. Conceivably, the throstle gave combers the opportunity of establishing themselves as independent spinners, as it was doing in the West Riding. If this is so, the throstle would serve to mollify the combers' opposition to the new methods, and to inaugurate a more gradual transition to factory production. As the number of spindles on the throstle continued to multiply, and the machine grew in size, it became necessary to adapt it to steam-power. Fielding, possessing the market connections necessary to justify a substantial investment in new plant, seized the initiative in the teeth of the opposition of his principals at Warwick. His enterprise was paralleled or shortly followed by numbers of other Leicester woolcombers and hosiers, forty of whose names appear in the local directory of 1828.

CHAPTER SEVEN

Capital Requirements and Recruitment

1. Capital Requirements

UNFORTUNATELY the surviving business records of spinning firms in the Midlands are meagre, and only those of Oldknow, Cowpe & Co. of Pleasley Mills, near Mansfield, provide enough information for an analysis of the financial structure. However, the records of the Royal Exchange and Sun Insurance companies provide some useful details on the value of the fixed capital of a number of firms, and these help to extend some conclusions reached from a study of Oldknow, Cowpe & Co's records.

The financial structure of Oldknow, Cowpe & Co. is calculated in Table 5, and the analysis is based on the balance-sheets which have survived in the hands of the firm, now William Hollins & Co. Ltd, of Nottingham. The various qualifications that must be made in presenting the figures are noted in the footnotes to the table, and the analysis throws some light on two hypotheses which seem to be widely accepted among economic historians. The first suggests that the transition from the domestic to the factory system involved a shift of resources from circulating to fixed capital. That is to say that, whereas a merchant hosier like John Coltman might have over eighty per cent of his capital tied up in stock and money owing to him and less than twenty per cent in buildings and machinery, cotton- and worsted-spinning firms would have a much higher percentage of their resources invested in fixed capital such as a mill, warehouse, dam, water-wheel and machinery. The financial structure of Oldknow, Cowpe & Co. exemplifies this hypothesis for the first four years of the company's existence, when no profits were made and the enterprise was clearly struggling for survival. However, from 1790 to 1795, fixed capital was hardly more than half the

TABLE 5

Financial Structure of Oldknowe, Cowpe & Co., Pleasley Mills, near Mansfield, Nottinghamshire, 1786-1799

	1786	1787	1788	1789	1790	1791	1792	1794	1795	1796	1797	1798	1799
	£	£	£	£	£	£	£	£	£	£	£	£	£
Credit extended to firm's customers	68	448	2,110	2,082	3,845	4,036	5,030	4,137	4,412	7,208	8,730	11,250	10,170
Less credit received	309	743	2,724	2,161	2,997	1,983	2,025	2,540	3,310	1,722	1,656	1,003	1,333
Net Credit position	241	295	614	79	848	2,053	3,005	1,597	902	5,486	7,074	10,247	8,837
Stock	652	1,787	1,582	1,584	2,341	2,700	3,134	4,841	5,689	8,167	7,970	5,712	6,451
Stock plus net credit, i.e., total circulating capital	411	1,492	968	1,505	3,189	4,753	6,139	6,438	6,591	13,653	15,055	15,959	15,288
Fixed capital net of depreciation	3,789	3,943	4,227	3,916	4,422	5,082	6,163	7,567	7,409	7,410	7,801	8,992	10,223
Total capital, i.e., fixed plus circulating capital	4,200	5,435	5,195	5,421	7,611	9,835	12,302	14,005	14,000	21,063	22,845	24,951	25,511
Fixed capital as a percentage of total capital	90	73	67	72	58	52	50	54	53	35	34	36	60

Source: Book of Yearly Account Statements and Partnership Settlements, 1786-1813 (1793 omitted). MSS in possession of William Hollins & Co. Ltd, Nottingham. No analysis can be made for 1800, as machinery and stock are valued together.

company's capital, and for three years after that it dropped to little more than a third. In other words, after a decade of life, the firm's financial position was not strikingly different from that of John Coltman. Of course, it might be argued that Oldknow, Cowpe & Co. were not typical of their kind, but the evidence presented below suggests that, on the contrary, the firm was typical of numbers of others started by mercers and hosiers, and differed only in that it has survived much longer than the great majority of others started in the Region at that period.

The other hypothesis on which the financial analysis may serve to throw some light is the idea that the fixed capital required by industrial and mining concerns in the eighteenth century was, in absolute terms, quite modest. The recruitment of capital was not a serious problem because circulating capital could be fairly readily obtained on credit from banks and supplier-merchants or traders. This contention has most recently been advanced by Professor S. Pollard who suggests, principally on the evidence of the accounts of Fountain, Wormold & Gott, of Leeds, so far as the textile industry is concerned, that the fixed capital required for industrial development was only a small proportion of the total capital held by a merchant.[1] The Oldknow Cowpe accounts lend some credence to this idea, and would probably give it even more if the resources of the partners as merchants were known. The initial fixed capital requirements of the firm were certainly modest, but it would not have proved difficult for merchants of the status of Thomas Oldknow and Henry Hollins, the senior partners, to have obtained credit to support the business during the first four difficult years of its life.

The original fixed capital at Pleasley Works consisted of the mill, warehouses, dam, head of water and water-channel, valued at £2,472, the water-wheel, pit-wheel and penstock, valued at £400, the machinery at £621 and utensils at £296, totalling £3,789. The total stock at the mill, including raw materials, work in progress and stocks of yarn, was £406, so that the total value of assets of all kinds at Pleasley was £4,195. This figure is strikingly similar to the fixed capital and stock of a number of other contemporary firms, according to the insurance records. The Royal Exchange Assurance Company insured several of the mills belonging to Arkwright and his partners. The valuation figures are disclosed in Table 6 and, though obviously only approximate, this hardly detracts from their

TABLE 6

Valuation of several of the Mills of Arkwright and his Partners by the Royal Exchange Assurance Co., 1778–1783

Location of Mill		Valuation of:			Total
		Mill	Machinery	Stock	
		£	£	£	£
Cromford Upper	1771	—	—	—	1,500
Cromford Lower	1777	1,000	1,000	1,000	3,000
Bakewell	1778	1,000	1,000	1,000	3,000
Belper	1779	1,000	1,000	1,000	3,000
Manchester	1784		3,000	1,000	4,000

Sources: Fire Policy Registers, IV, 75,060–1, 75,867; VII, 84,787, 86,104–5; VIII, 87,827. (Guildhall Library, E.C.2.)

value for the present purpose. Similarly, the mill buildings, machinery and stock at Robinson's first mill at Linby were valued at £3,600 shortly after it was opened in 1778. The fixed capital of a typical Nottinghamshire country mill, built by Benjamin Chambers at Fiskerton, was insured for £2,000 and Evans' mill and machinery at Darley Abbey (near Derby) were insured for the same sum. Evidence from outside the region tends to confirm the impression of similiarity of mills built in the 1770s and 1780s. Thus David Dale's enterprise at New Lanark was insured for £4,800 in 1786— the figure included some of his earliest houses—and Samuel Gregg's first mill and machinery at Styall were insured for £3,500.[2] The similarity of the early mills is to be expected, as many of the early spinners were Arkwright's licencees and appear to have been restricted to a thousand spindles each by the terms of the licence. Moreover, all the early spinners imitated Arkwright's buildings as well as his techniques. As Sir Robert Peel put it, 'Arkwright

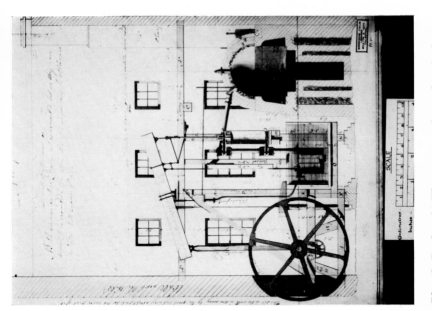

*Plate 8. Boulton & Watt steam engine and engine house,
designed for Major John Cartwright's worsted mill at
Retford, Nottinghamshire, in 1788*

*Plate 7. Sluice gates at the Darley Abbey cotton mills
of Thomas Evans & Sons. The mills stand on the River
Derwent near Derby*

Plate 9. Robinson's Forge Mill (1784) at Bestwood, near Nottingham. The River Leen flows under the centre of the mill and under the approach road

Plate 10. Brick Row, Darley Abbey, near Derby. One of the terraces built by Thomas Evans & Sons for their workers at the Darley Abbey Mills

originated the buildings; we all looked up to him and imitated his mode of building'.[3] It is reasonable to suppose that the pattern of financial development at Pleasley was paralleled in numerous other small mills built at the period on the same scale and owned by mercers, hosiers and other established traders in the centres of the hosiery industry.

The application of rotative steam-engines to warp-spinning did not necessarily make any important difference to the cost of entering the manufacture. For instance, John Bacon's mill at Sutton-in-Ashfield was insured as follows in 1795:

	£
Building used as cotton factory	800
Steam-engine therein	200
Millwright's work, including going gears, clockmaker's work carding and breaking engines and all moveable utensils	900
Stock in trade therein	500
	2,500

The steam-engine, an improved 16 hp Newcomen engine, was built by Francis Thompson and provided rotary motion.[4] Boulton & Watt engines were, of course, more expensive, but the balance-sheet figures for Pleasley for 1798–1804 included a 10 hp Watt engine, and show that such a mill could be built and filled with machinery for little more than £4,000. Another example occurs at Ilkeston, where an initial capital of £4,200 was apparently adequate in 1792 to open a mill of a thousand spindles supported by a rotative steam-engine.[5]

During the 1790s, the insurance records show much greater diversity in the valuations of warp-spinning mills, for the Cromford prototype mill was no longer the object of slavish imitation. In Lancashire and the adjacent parts of Cheshire, and in the West Riding, a large number of mills are recorded at £1,000 to £2,000 and a few at less than this, the valuation covering buildings, machinery and stock.[6] In the Midlands there are a few corresponding examples, most of which occur in Derbyshire, that part of the

I

Region closest to Lancashire, and appear to reflect the transition from domestic to factory industry within the framework of rural society. The most interesting example occurs at Peak Forest, near Tideswell (Derbyshire) in 1792,[7] and is worth quoting in full:

William Keeling junior, Peak Forest—Cotton Manufacturer

	£
Cotton mill and machinery therein	150
Utensils therein	100
Store and warehouse	30
Utensils therein	30
Total	310

More details are available for another Derbyshire mill at Edale,[8] opened by four partners whose interests were primarily in farming:

	£
Cotton mill at Edale	333
Water-wheel, millwright's work and going gears	67
Clockmaker's work, carding and breaking engines and all moveable utensils	433
Stock in trade in same	167
	1,000

Clearly the valuation is somewhat conventional, but it probably approximates to the facts. John Dalley's cotton-spinning business at Wirksworth was also insured for £1,000 as was Hardcastle & Co's at Newark and Willoughby's at Nottingham, all in 1791–92.[9] The total capital of these marginal producers is unknown, but it may well be that these men of slender capital were most dependent on the credit offered by the merchants and wholesalers in the major centres of the cotton industry. When the Midlands industry began to contract about the turn of the century, they were the first to disappear.

The earliest cotton-spinner to enlarge on the patterns prescribed at Nottingham and Cromford was probably Samuel Unwin. His four-storeyed, castellated factory, surmounted by a windmill to

pump water back into the nine-acre mill reservoir, was enlarged
from the 1771 mill sometime before 1784. The factory is said to
have cost £6,000 to build, and in May 1784, when a fire occurred,
contained stock worth at least £2,000. Arkwright's Masson mill at
Cromford, familiar to travellers along the A 6 road to Matlock,
also belongs to the early 1780s but the evidence suggests that it was
first built and used as a paper mill and only later—probably in
1790—as a cotton mill.[10] Both the Sutton and Masson mills were
powered by water, and Robinson's Linby mill, celebrated as the
first cotton mill to employ rotary steam-power, was a small building
intended to use water-power. The modern multi-storey factory,
designed to employ only steam-power, did not appear in the Midlands until 1788, the first being Major Cartwright's Revolution
Mill at Retford.

The evidence from insurance valuations and other scattered
sources gives the impression that steam-powered mills like Cartwright's cost three or four times as much to build as the early water
mills. The Sun Insurance Company's valuation is available for the
Revolution Mill,[11] and includes the value of the land occupied by
the factory and the workers' housings:

	£
Mill building	2,700
Stock, machinery, steam-engine	8,000
Manager's house, counting-house, porter's lodge	350
Row of 12 tenements	350
Two warehouses	600
Sun Insurance valuation	12,000
Site (10 acres)	1,000
	13,000

The mill contained close on 6,000 spindles and 23,000 sq ft of floor
space. The machinery was powered by a 30 hp Boulton & Watt
engine, which would have cost about £1,500.

A comparison between the cost of the Revolution Mill and the
early mills of Arkwright and Strutt illustrates the economy of scale

FIGURE 3

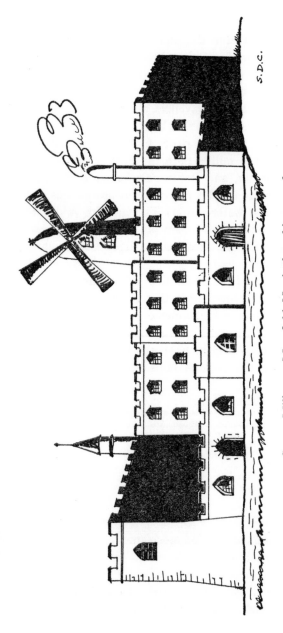

Sutton Mill, near Mansfield, Nottinghamshire, *c.* 1784
(From an engraving on Samuel Unwin's promissory notes)

introduced by steam-power and larger buildings. The scale of enterprise introduced by Cartwright was not a fortuitous development, for he had studied the established factory technique at his brother's mill at Doncaster. Edmund Cartwright's mill was built on similar proportions to the first Cromford mill, but with the addition of a Newcomen engine.[12] Arkwright's mill-buildings represented a third (£1,000) of the total value (£3,000) of the initial cost of the enterprise. Cartwright's building (£2,700) represented between a quarter and a fifth of the total cost of the production unit, if this is taken as £11,300. Thus most of the extra cost of establishing a factory lay in the purchase of machinery and stock. The Revolution Mill was not a financial success but between 1791 and 1792 it was followed by numerous other factories on a similar scale.

Examples from other parts of the Midland region illustrate the same economy of scale. For instance, Bradley & Co's New Mills, on the River Dove at Mayfield, near Ashbourne (Derbyshire) were valued as follows in 1795:

	£
Cotton mill at Ashbourne, Derbys.	1,500
Millwright's work, including going gears	1,000
Clockmakers' work, carding and breaking engines; smiths', joiners' and all moveable utensils	6,000
Stock in trade therein	1,500
	10,000

The scale of operations at this mill is illustrated by the statement that the enterprise 'returned upwards of £500 weekly', i.e., probably employed a thousand workpeople. Some seventy per cent of the capital outlay was devoted to machinery, compared with thirty per cent for the early Arkwright mills. Benjamin Wilson, an original partner in this mill, was prepared to lay out £10,000 in purchasing cotton for a similar mill at Alrewas.[13]

Fragmentary evidence from other sources lends support to the insurance valuations, so far as the total fixed capital and stock outlay are concerned. Denison's Nottingham mill, which employed a

30 hp Boulton & Watt engine and at half-capacity gave employment to 300 people, cost 'something like £15,000' to build; and Hall's Basford mill was insured for 'a nominal £10,000'. Strutt's Belper West mill (1793–95) cost £6,793 to erect, and the machinery must have cost at least as much again.[14] The size of bank overdrafts of several firms discussed in the next section point to a similar scale of operations.

The new scale of factory enterprise invariably found its location along the banks of canals, as the raw cotton was imported along these and the country's natural waterways. Major Cartwright's mill at Retford was built near the Chesterfield Canal, as were the mills of Toplis & Co. at Worksop. Other multi-storey factory blocks built at Belper (Strutt), Tamworth (Peel), Warwick (W. & J. Parkes), Newcastle-under-Lyme (Thompson), Alrewas (Dicken), and Measham (Wilkes) were all adjacent to canals. The calculations of economy of scale just made do not, of course, take into account the expense of promoting a canal scheme, purchasing shares and building wharves. In general, the canal schemes were not initiated by cotton- and worsted-spinners, though there appear to be four or five exceptions to this while other spinners who were not canal promoters invested extensively in the new form of transport. The part which spinners played in the development of the canal network may be regarded, in part at least, as a hidden cost of the new mills.

Unfortunately, we have no precise figures to indicate the extent of the circulating capital of the largest firms covered by this study. However, it is interesting to notice that William Toplis junior, the managing partner of one of the largest cotton- and worsted-spinning firms, maintained in 1794 that he had 'expended upwards of £50,000' in 'the erection and completion of . . . his spinning-mills and other manufacturing establishments'.[15] Toplis & Co. owned a small mill at Cuckney (Nottinghamshire), and two multi-storey mills at Worksop (Nottinghamshire), adjoining the Chesterfield–Stockwith Canal. All three buildings survive and comparison with insured buildings whose dimensions are known leads one to guess that Toplis's mills and their contents could hardly have been valued at more than £25,000. That is to suppose that the credit of the firm was worth at least as much again as the value of the capital assets and stock and work in progress. The proportion of fixed to circulating capital would be similar to that established by Oldknow, Cowpe & Co. between 1790 and 1795.

2. The Cost of Community Building

Unfortunately, the Arkwright and Strutt insurance records give almost no indication of the cost of building community facilities such as workers' houses, schools, markets and churches. The only buildings insured apart from the cotton mills and a paper mill at Matlock were the 'Greyhound Inn' at Cromford (£500) and the 'stables and chaisehouses belonging' (£200). More precise information is, however, available for Robinson's Linby Mill, which was a more typical community that that at Cromford, in that it consisted of only a few houses close to the water-mill. The insurance valuation[16] is worth quoting in full:

25 November 1778

George Robinson of Bulwell in Notts. and James Robinson of Linby, Cotton Manufacturers.

£

On their cotton mill, stone-built and slated, turned by water and on the mills (machines) therein together with the running tackle and other parts of the machinery belonging thereto and situated in Linby	3,000
Trade therein	300
On the building, brick and slated, situated at the south of . . . mill (counting-house)	200
Furniture therein	80
Utensils of trade in the same	20
On ten houses in one building, brick-built and tiled, situated on the north-east side of the . . . mill, not exceeding £40 on each	400
On goods in trade in a (ware) house, brick-built and tiled, situated in Mary Gate . . . Nottingham, in occupation of themselves and servants	600
	4,600

Thus at Linby, the building of the first workers' houses (for £400) represented less than nine per cent of the investment on fixed capital and stock. Moreover, this percentage would probably decline as the firm built up the value of its stock and machinery. Clearly, too, the growing total capital of the firm must be taken into account in making these calculations. Eventually '40 or 50' additional workers' cottages were built by Robinsons, but as the firm had six mills before the end of the century, it seems probable that the financial burden of erecting this property did not increase more than proportionately. At Retford, the cost of workers' houses (£350) was less than three per cent of the initial outlay (£13,000), which might be an indication of the economy of the larger mill.

Some more detailed figures available in Oldknow, Cowpe & Co's balance-sheets are of particular interest because Pleasley mills were sited away from the centre of any existing settlement. The investment in community facilities is remarkably small as a proportion of the whole investment. The details from the balance-sheets for the first fifteen years are as follows:

		£
1792	Cowhouse	9
	New house, school-house, brewhouse	171
	Road and bridge	40
	A 'necessary' at mills and Mrs Wood's kitchen	15
	Expended in building ten houses	500
		735
1794	Land in the North Field for housing	1,000
	Manager's house	200
		1,945
1799	Expenses in Mr Webster's house	15
		1,960

This expenditure can be shown as a percentage of the total capital of the firms:

	Community Expenditure	Total Capital	Percentage
	£	£	£
1792	735	12,302	6
1794	1,945	14,005	14
1799	1,960	25,521	8

After 1799, it became difficult to draw valid conclusions as mill and community property are lumped together in the balance-sheets. In the first few years the mill-workers must have been garnered from surrounding farms and villages, and it was not until October 1789, four years after the mill had commenced working, that Oldknow, Cowpe advertised for a matron for 12–16 boys and girls, no doubt the first of the pauper apprentices. By 1818, the firm had given up taking parish apprentices since they were able to secure all the 'free hands' on indenture that they required.[17] Thus, within a generation, a modest expenditure had secured a resident labour force quite sufficient for the firm's needs, a very fruitful investment.

3. The Role of the Banks

It is clear from the survey of the rise of the merchant hosiers in Chapter One that, while the resources of the hosiers and mercers varied considerably, many traded on a very modest capital. Some, of course, had other resources to call on; not a few were recruited from landed families, and the substantial numbers of hosiers who succeeded (according to the local press) in marrying young ladies with 'a genteel fortune' is truly remarkable. Others inherited wealth from 'in-laws' and at least one succeeded in marrying his sister to wealth. A similar impression of varied resources is given in the surveys of some of the careers of cotton-spinning entrepreneurs in Chapter Five.

The earliest manuscript connecting country banking with the cotton-spinning industry is the day-book of Samuel Crompton of the 'old Derby Bank'. During the short period covered by this volume, December 1776 to July 1779, Crompton's best customer appears to have been the proprietors of the Nottingham and first Cromford cotton mills, recorded here as 'Need, Strutt & Co.' or 'Strutt & Co'. Need was a customer of Smith's bank at Nottingham, so that the account at Derby probably refers only to the Cromford mill, but perhaps also to the first Belper mill. Most of Crompton's business consisted of discounting bills of exchange and this was the main service provided for the Cromford partners. Bills of exchange were the common form of mercantile payment at this period, and discounting them was a method of providing short-term credit, since the bill invariably bore a payment date which was three or six months, or even longer, after the cotton-yarn had been received by the customer.

The 'Old Derby Bank' also provided short-term credit on security; thus, on 1 August 1777, Crompton lent Need, Strutt & Co. £670. The loan was redeemed three days later when the firm brought in twenty-one bills whose total discounted value was £971. The years of 1777–78 were a period of vigorous building activity, both at Cromford and Belper, but Crompton's support was clearly confined to the provision of short-term credit and this is consistent with what is known about another bank that Arkwright used for a time. When he first came to Nottingham, he is said to have obtained some financial support from Ichabod Wright, whose bank was opened about 1760, the first in the town after Smith's. The advertised aim of Wright's bank was to offer only short-term loans to its customers 'on an emergency', and it was probably for this reason that Wright passed Arkwright over to Samuel Need, a fellow member of Castle Gate Chapel.[18] It is interesting that several future cotton-spinners can be identified among Crompton's customers: Wilkes of Measham; the Evanses of Darley Abbey; William Stretton, who was a builder's merchant in Derby as well as Nottingham, and Peter Nightingale of Lea, the lead merchant. All of these firms were in regular commercial intercourse with London before they became mill-owners.

During the last three decades of the eighteenth century there was a rapid extension of banking in the provinces, and the banker's conception of his functions may then have widened to something larger. Certainly the surviving records of Smith's bank at Nottingham show more direct involvement in industrial development than the smaller banks of Crompton and Wright.

During the period covered by the summary accounts from 1780 to 1797, twelve cotton-spinning firms had accounts with Smith's bank. Only four of these, Davison & Hawksley, Killingley, Green & Co., Pearson & Huthwaite, and Charles Morley had mills in Nottingham. The remaining eight were country spinners in Nottinghamshire, Derbyshire and Leicestershire. In Nottinghamshire, there was George, Richard & Alexander Burden at Mansfield, Samuel Unwin & Son at Sutton, George Robinson & Sons at Bulwell and Papplewick, and Toplis & Co. at Cuckney and Worksop. In Derbyshire, Jedediah Strutt & Sons had an account, as had Gardom, Pares & Co. of Calver Mill, and Robert Sykes, who bought Arkwright's Wirksworth mill. Smith & Joseph Churchill of Shepshed (Loughborough, Leicestershire) also had an account. In addition to these twelve, five individuals or firms who were partners in cotton- or worsted-spinning concerns had accounts, and two of them, Samuel Oates (Denison's partner) and Samuel Statham (a partner in the Revolution Mill at Retford) may have used their extensive overdrafts to finance their interests in spinning. It is noticeable that this list includes some of the earliest and largest firms in the Midlands industry, and that there are no small firms in it, with the possible exception of Pearson & Huthwaite.

Of the twelve cotton-spinning firms who banked at Smith's, nine may be said to have had active accounts, and in several cases the history of the account can be correlated with the known development of the firm. The clearest example is the account of Davison & Hawksley, whose original mill was opened in Nottingham in 1788. When this small mill was accidentally burnt down in 1791, the firm moved to Arnold and built a large five-storey mill and warehouses on the banks of a small stream. Davison & Hawksley's account at Smith's bank shows two overdrafts. The first, covering the period 1786–91, is no doubt in connection with the early mill; the second, covering 1792–93, is almost certainly for the second mill, as the £4,500 overdraft is described as 'on mortgage'. The details are as follows:

The Early Factory Masters

	Credit Balance £	Overdraft £
31 December 1780	1,114	
1786		569
1787		421
1788		2,794
1790		2,209
1791		3,416
1792	649	4,500 'on mortgage'
1793		358
1794	37	
1795	515	
1796		85
1797	93	

The largest overdraft held at Smith's bank at this period was allowed to Killingley, Green & Co., who had already borrowed £800 on bond in 1788 and had an overdraft of £90. When the firm built its Broadmarsh (Nottingham) mill in 1790–92, the total debt to the bank rose rapidly to £9,318 by the end of 1792. It is interesting that Green negotiated the bank loans under three separate names, Killingley, Green & Sons, Killingley, Green & Co., and Henry Green & Co. The loan was reduced to £7,470 by the end of 1795 but stood at £10,133 a year later. Shortly afterwards, Green became bankrupt. Other firms with substantial overdrafts at one time or another were Smith Churchill (£3,215 at the end of 1795) and Burdens (£4,352 in 1794). The firms built up substantial credit balances with Smith's bank before investing in new extensions of their business.

Jedediah Strutt & Sons had £7,840 in the bank before the building operations of 1792 reduced their account to £1,654, and Strutt's and Woollatt's to a £2,973 overdraft. This cautious approach to investment is even more apparent in the case of the Robinsons. Though they built six mills between 1778 and 1791, the account shows only small and obviously temporary overdrafts, £239 in 1787 and £186 in 1792.

Smith's accounts also reflect fluctuations in trade. Thus, a credit balance of £8,459 held by Robinsons in 1795 was reduced to £595 the following year, probably as a result of the falling off in trade. James Robinson wrote hopefully in the summer of 1797 that 'Our trade appears to be in a reviving state and if we should succeed in obtaining peace, I have little doubt of an increased demand an encouragement to carry on my works in their former extent . . .'.[19] At any rate he could console himself that, unlike Green, his cautious policy had saved his firm from possible bankruptcy.

The extent of Smith's support of the cotton- and worsted-spinning industry can be gauged from a study of overdrafts granted to cotton- and worsted-spinners and their partners in the peak building year of 1792:

	£
Burden	2,713
Churchill	2,624
Davison & Hawksley	45,00
Robinson	186
Oates	1,259
Morley	340
Strutt and Woollatt	2,973
Killingley, Green & Co.	9,318
Statham, Martin & Co.	5,756
Pearson & Huthwaite	252
	29,921

This total, £29,921, represents thirty per cent of Smith's total advances to its customers from the Nottingham office.

The surviving records of the country banks of this period are meagre and hardly anything can be said about the activities of other banking-houses. At Leicester, John Coltman had an account with Bentley & Buxton, bankers in the Market Place, and in some years he had an overdraft.[20] There is no evidence to show that he had the support of this bank in establishing the worsted-spinning plant at Bromsgrove, though this seems more than likely. The sole surviving file of bankruptcy papers for a Midlands cotton-spinning firm, that of Timothy Harris of Nottingham, shows that Staples & Co., Bankers, Cornhill, had advanced him £9,065 and Stephen Hall & Co., Fenchurch St, £839, before he became bankrupt in 1797. These loans, however, may have been linked with his hosiery warehouse in the City or his wire mill at Waltham Abbey as much as his business in Nottingham.[21] It is worth noticing here that some other Midland spinners banked with City firms, Richard Arkwright junior with Smith, Paine & Smith, and Benjamin Wilson, after a period with Wilkes of Measham, with Robarts, Curtis & Co. in the City.[22]

The close association between the banks and the development of the Midlands cotton- and worsted-spinning industry is also high-lighted by partnerships and family connections overlapping the two. It is possible to identify no less than fifteen spinning firms that enjoyed such close identity with banking-houses. Four bankers— Wilkes of Measham, Evans of Derby, W. & J. Parkes of Warwick, and William Harding of Tamworth—became cotton- or worsted-spinners. Five other spinners had partners or relatives who were bankers, two of them outside the Midlands. Buszard of Lutter-worth, 'surgeon and banker', has already been noticed. Samuel Unwin went into partnership with his son-in-law, James Heygate, a London hosier and banker. William Toplis was uncle to the foun-der of the Wirksworth banking-house of Toplis & Co. (later Ark-wright, Toplis & Co.), and himself opened a bank at Mansfield. William Handley (of Handley, Sketchley & Co. of Newark) was uncle to Benjamin Handley of Sleaford, who Dr Pressnell describes as a 'typical country attorney banker'. In 1807, Oldknow, Cowpe & Co. took the Paget brothers, Loughborough hosiers and bankers, into partnership; William Strutt, son of Arkwright's partner, Jedediah, was a partner in the Evans enterprises at Derby including, no doubt, the bank.

Five other Midland spinners are known to have moved into banking. Two Leicester hosiery firms engaged in spinning (Pares & Heygate, and Mill, Rowe & Co.) had become bankers before the end of the eighteenth century, as had Dakeynes of Darley Dale and Daintry Ryle & Co. of Macclesfield. Robert Peel became a banker in Manchester about the time he moved his residence to Tamworth. Here he joined with Wilkes and two Birmingham men to open the

London house of Peel, Wilkes, Dickenson & Goodall in 1790. Wilkes already had banks at Ashby, Measham and Burton. The Peel and Wilkes partnership appears to have raised the money for the purchase of the Thynne estate and thus initiated the development of Tamworth as a centre of the cotton-spinning industry.

The firms listed here as having direct interests in banking-houses were among the largest and most successful in the Region, and ten are known to have built steam-powered, multi-storey factories. The banks almost certainly played a crucial role in the supply of funds for these developments.

4. The Cycle of Mill Building

In concluding this chapter on the finance of factory development, it is important to notice the extent to which the Midland factories were built at the peaks of the building cycle. The limited number of mills for which information is available appears to represent a fairly random sample of the whole, except perhaps for the first years of the nineteenth century.

TABLE 7

Spinning-Mills completed in the Midlands year by year from 1769–1802

1769	1	1776	—	1783	7	1790	1	1797	2
1770	1	1777	2	1784	11	1791	6	1798	2
1771	1	1778	3	1785	2	1792	7	1799	1
1772	—	1779	3	1786	2	1793	4	1800	1
1773	—	1780	1	1787	1	1794	1	1801	—
1774	—	1781	2	1788	7	1795	—	1802	1
1775	—	1782	4	1789	1	1796	—		

Information given for 75 mills, i.e., 61 per cent of total known to have been erected.   *Source:* Appendix A.

The peak years for mill-building were also the years of greatest expansion in hosiery and lace, so that mechanized spinning had to compete with the staple industries of the east Midlands for capital. Even when allowance is made for lack of information, Table 7 suggests that it was less able to sustain its demand for scarce resources after the boom of 1791–92. Thus the contraction of the Midlands industry was already evident in the 1790s, and clearly the capital was flowing to the lace industry, which was by then growing rapidly. An analysis of this switch in the direction of investment is made in the final chapter of this study.

Plate 11. Cottages built for mill workers at Toplis' worsted mill at Cuckney, near Mansfield, Nottinghamshire. Some of the cottages probably served as the apprentice house

Plate 12. The image of the peasant proprietor: Toplis' workers' cottages at Cuckney, near Mansfield, Nottinghamshire

Plate 13. Terrace of cottages at Mile Ash Lane, Darley Abbey, built by Thomas Evans & Sons for the workers at their Darley Abbey Mills

Plate 14. Bedworth worsted mill, near Coventry, c. 1800, showing the different tasks on which 50 workers were engaged

CHAPTER EIGHT

The Influence of Mechanized Spinning on the Development of other Industries

1. Hosiery

DURING the period covered by this study there was a considerable growth in the hosiery industry in the east Midlands. Estimates of the total number of frames working in Nottinghamshire, Derbyshire and Leicestershire are available for the years 1782 and 1812 and in the intervening thirty years the number of frames rose from 16,750 to 25,168, while the number of villages and hamlets in which frames were worked also increased.[1] This growth and spread of the industry might be considered merely as a response to the growth of population and the decline of the Derbyshire mining industry, for the hosiery industry was notoriously an employer of cheap labour, and indeed the number of stocking-frames continued to increase after the Midlands cotton industry had begun to decline. However, there are two reasons for supposing that cotton-spinning acted as a stimulant to the growth of the hosiery industry.

The first must be explained by reference to the location pattern of the hosiery industry, particularly in Derbyshire. The impression given by Pilkington's *Derbyshire* (1789) is that there were still relatively few stocking-frames in the county when he wrote. It is true that he did not set out to make a census of frames, but his survey of every settlement in the county contains a comment on the nature of employment in each, and few frames could have escaped his notice. Pilkington's work points to the existence of three centres of the hosiery industry in Derbyshire in the 1780s. The largest concentration of frames was in and around Derby, the town itself and a string of villages stretching out towards Nottingham containing

1,170 frames. Chesterfield and Alfreton formed the second centre, stretching southwards into Nottinghamshire, and probably containing no more than 500 frames. A third centre, at Bakewell, had very few frames.

By 1812, the domestic industry was much more widely dispersed in the county; 82 small towns and villages averaged 52 frames each, not counting Derby, where the numbers had increased from 170 in 1788 to nearly 400 in 1812.[2] A new centre of the hosiery industry began to develop at Belper which, in 1788, had only 'a few stocking-frames chiefly employed by the hosiers in Derby'. About 1795 Ward, Brettle & Ward, a City firm of merchant hosiers, opened a warehouse near Strutt's mills and expanded rapidly until they became the largest employers of frames in the Region. By 1833, Belper had eclipsed both Derby and Chesterfield as a centre of the hosiery industry.[3]

In Nottinghamshire and Leicestershire there is no evidence of dispersion of the industry in this period, probably because the industry had reached a more advanced stage of growth than had Derbyshire at the opening of our period. However, it is noteworthy that the largest rural centres of the village industry coincided with the locations of large spinning-mills. In 1812, some of the largest village centres were Shepshed, which contained 900 frames, Arnold (640 frames), Mansfield (400 frames), Radford (350 frames), Ilkeston (350 frames) and Shirland (about 100 frames).[4] Unfortunately, no figures are available for Sutton-in-Ashfield, Linby and Bulwell, where the presence of Unwin's and Robinson's mills encouraged the growth of a very large hosiery industry.[5] It might be contended that the site of spinning-mills could have been chosen by reference to the existence of a concentration of frames, but the case histories of some of the firms demonstrates that it was energetic hosiers and mercers who built up the hosiery and spinning industries side by side.

The second reason for supposing that the growth of the spinning industry was a factor in the growth of the hosiery industry is that in

1812, there were already more frames employing cotton than either silk, worsted or any other material. The figures can be calculated from Blackner's 'Statistical Account of the Framework-Knitting Trade':[6]

Frames using cotton	11,804
Frames using worsted	11,170
Frames using silk	3,161
Other fibres	380
Unclassified or unknown	3,160
Total	29,675

Every stocking-frame was built specifically for one kind of fibre, so that the number of cotton-frames reflected the growth of the branch of the industry after cotton was adapted to the frame in 1730. Until about 1770, the cotton-thread for hosiery was all imported from India, and the expense of the material limited the growth of the industry. The growth of the cotton branch of the hosiery industry, that is to say, was largely a consequence of mechanized spinning.

2. The Iron Industry

For most of the eighteenth century, the old Midlands iron industry, based on the more remote forested areas of the Region, was declining. Most spinning-mills appear to have been built on the site of corn mills or fulling mills, but a few took over forge sites. Declining forges provided sites for Strutt at Milford (1777), Robinson at Bulwell (1783–84), Oldknow, Cowpe & Co. at Pleasley (1784) and for Toplis at Cuckney (1786). Wilne Mills, near Draycott, also appear to have been used for the iron industry before the cotton industry. Belper and Uttoxeter were old centres of the iron industry and may have provided other sites for cotton mills. Most early mills built their own machinery, and the workshops and equipment of a forge would have been great assets to the millwrights and smiths employed by the cotton spinners.

The established Derbyshire ironmasters responded to the boom in the cotton industry in different ways. We have already noticed families like the Evanses, the Nightingales and the Simpsons diverting their capital from iron to cotton. Two further instances, drawn from other connections of the Strutts and the Arkwrights, serve to illustrate contrasting responses within the context of the industry. The Hurt family came to wealth as lead merchants at Ashbourne, but the eighteenth-century heir to the family business, Francis Hurt, followed the movement of the trade to Wirksworth. He became a lead merchant there and an iron manufacturer and merchant at Alderwasley on the Derwent, ten miles north of Derby. His earlier trade consisted of supplying the Belper nailers with rod-iron and the rural smithies with bar-iron and share-moulds for ploughshares. When Arkwright came to Cromford he seems to have made a close connection with Hurt, for his daughter Susanna was shortly married to Hurt's son. Under the stimulus of the growing cotton industry, Hurt turned to the regular production of castings for cotton-mill machinery.[7] Walter Mather, of Derby, was another member of the Arkwright social circle, and he had foundries on the Leen at Bulwell (near Nottingham) and on the Derwent at New Mills and Makeney, near Belper. The former was leased to Robinson (the cotton-spinner) in 1783 to build Forge Mill, and the latter was sold to the Strutts in 1777 to build Milford Mill. In their place, Mather built Staveley Furnace by the newly-opened Chesterfield Canal.[8]

The later decades of the eighteenth century saw the rise of a new Midlands iron industry based on coal and ironstone seams whose exploitation was made economic by the development of natural waterways and the building of canals. These new developments in the iron industry exercised a significant influence over the location of the textile industry, and probably increased its prosperity through cheaper castings. The earliest example of this influence comes from the era before the canals were built. The lease of the Trent Navigation, from Wilden Ferry to Burton-on-Trent, was acquired by Samuel Lloyd, the Birmingham ironmaster, and Joseph Wilkes in 1763, and renewed in 1784 and 1803. Lloyd erected a forge at Burton and ironmasters like Walter Mather of Derby began to trade up to Burton.[9] Wilkes of Measham began to build iron barges and wrought-iron boilers for steam-engines. These developments no doubt were a contributory factor in the establishment of the cotton industry at Burton by 'Parsley' Peel and at Measham by Wilkes, and of the major development of the spinning industry in this area.

Other developments in the iron industry in this Region were connected with the cutting of two canals, the Chesterfield–Stockwith Canal (1771) and the Erewash Canal (1776). The Chesterfield Canal cut through formations of coal, iron and limestone, and at least twelve major furnaces were built along its banks.[10] The first and most celebrated firm to be established near this canal was Ebenezer Smith & Co. of the Griffin Foundry, Chesterfield. They started in 1777, and built steam-engines for the well-known mining engineer, Francis Thompson of Ashover, as well as other machinery. Robinsons of Bulwell, in their correspondence with Boulton & Watt in 1785, mention Smith's foundry as being the nearest to them (though it was eighteen miles to the north), and it is known that the firm sold castings to Gotts when they were building the first steam-powered woollen mill at Leeds in 1793. Robinsons, who employed the engineer Rennie, reported that Smiths 'are frequently casting wheels for us of a pretty large size'. Other Midland spinners refer to Smith's foundry, and it seems likely that they were the principal suppliers of castings to the early cotton-spinning industry, apart from those for steam-engines supplied through Boulton & Watt.[11] In the circumstances, it is not surprising that three of the earliest multi-storey spinning-mills were built near the banks of the Chesterfield Canal, these being Major Cartwright's Revolution Mill at Retford and the two built by Toplises alongside the canal at Worksop.

The cutting of the Erewash Canal and its extension, the Cromford Canal (1794), linked the principal foci of the Midlands cotton industry at Nottingham and Cromford. The Erewash Canal led to the building of two foundries near Ilkeston. The Cossall Foundry Co. (one of whose four partners was William Stretton, the architect and cotton-spinner) advertised that they made 'large engine gear' and machinery for mill work of every description, 'in brass or iron, to models'. (The advertisement is a reminder that, in an age when few mechanics were accustomed to work to scale-drawings, it was common to build machinery from working-models, often erected in the first instance to convince capitalists of the value of a design.) The Dale Abbey Ironworks (1788) made 'engine-castings', 'mill work and all sorts of machine-castings', and 'square and round stoves for cotton-mills &c'.[12] The Cromford Canal extension led to the erection of two other large works, those of the Butterley Company at Ripley (1792) and Codnor Park (1794); and of James Oakes at Riddings (Alfreton) in 1801. One of the four partners in the Butterley Company was John Wright, a grandson of Ichabod Wright, the Baltic merchant who carried iron and timber up the Trent and later opened Wright's bank in Nottingham. The company became well-known for its machine-castings and steam-engines.[13]

The South Staffordshire and Shropshire iron-smelting districts fall within the Midland regions, but they do not appear to have made any important contribution to the spinning industry, except in so far as Wilkinson's and Coalbrookdale cylinders and boilers were sold for Boulton & Watt steam-engines. The extent of Boulton & Watt's sales to the Midland spinners is discussed in the next section. The Coalbrookdale Company made Newcomen engines, and there is a record of one of their boilers being sold at Measham.[14] However, the distance of the east Midlands market suggests that this was probably a rarity.

Thus, the building of a canal network through the Nottingham-shire–Derbyshire coalfield created the necessary market for a new iron industry in the last three decades of the eighteenth century.

Although the most important shareholders of these canals were local landowners, the bulk of the capital for them was subscribed by industrialists, merchants, clergy and lawyers. Cotton- and worsted-spinners figure among the industrialists. Sir Richard Arkwright was a leading shareholder in the Cromford Canal, Edward Fox, Joseph Wilkes and William Evans in the Derby Canal, and several Nottingham spinners in the Nottingham Canal. John Coltman was the leading promoter of the Leicester Canal and Joseph Wilkes of the Grand Junction Canal.[15] All these waterways provided a wider market for the iron industry of the Nottinghamshire–Derbyshire borders.

The east Midlands cotton and iron industries thus developed during the same period and fed on each other, the iron industry providing disused sites and local supplies of quality machine- and engine-castings, while the cotton industry provided a market for the products of the iron industry, initiative and some of the capital needed for canal development. The cotton-spinners and iron-masters moved in the same social circle and, indeed, a few outstanding entrepreneurs, notably Joseph Wilkes, William Stretton and the Evanses, were active in both industries.

3. The Manufacture of Steam-Engines

Something like half the firms covered by this study of the Midlands cotton- and worsted-spinning industry installed steam-engines at one time or another between 1785 and 1815, and by no means all were built by Boulton & Watt of Soho, Birmingham, the patentees of the superior, separate-condenser engine. The figures for all the firms in the Region for which there is a record are given in Table 8, but as the records for 'Other Makers' are incomplete, the total is almost certainly deficient.

There were at least five firms making engines in the Region apart from Boulton & Watt, and although few of the engines they built can be identified, it is possible to surmise who the makers were. According to Farey's *Treatise on the Steam-Engine* 'About the years

1790 to 1793, when steam-mills began to be introduced into all the large manufacturing towns . . . great numbers of atmospheric engines were also made for turning mills [i.e., machines], particularly in the districts where coals were cheap. The principal makers of these engines were Messrs Bateman & Sherratt of Manchester . . . and . . . Mr Francis Thompson, of Ashover in Derbyshire, who made engines for that district and for Sheffield and Leeds'. Thompson, for whom Smiths of Chesterfield made castings, took out a patent in 1792 for a double-acting, atmospheric, rotative engine, some of which were installed for Davison & Hawksley at their Arnold mill and for John Bacon at Sutton. Thompson first distinguished himself in building engines for pumping coal and lead-mines, and it seems likely that the other steam-engines built by him for textile mills were used for pumping water back into a reservoir, so as to give more power to the water-wheel.[16]

TABLE 8

Stram-Engines installed at Cotton and Worsted Mills in the Midlands,
1785–1815

	For Boulton & Watt	For other Makers
Nottingham	11	0
Nottinghamshire	6	7
Leicestershire	4	0
Derbyshire	3	5
Staffordshire	1	2
Warwickshire	1	2
Northamptonshire	1	0
Lincolnshire	0	2
Worcestershire	0	1
	27	19

Source: See Appendix B.

The other steam-engine builders in the east Midlands, the Dale Abbey and Butterley companies, came in later than Smiths, and their contribution was probably only a marginal one. The role of the principal west Midland builders, the Coalbrookdale Company and Wilkinson is not known, but the distance between them and the major centres of the Midlands textile industry suggests that it was not an important one. In fact, the only record of an atmospheric engine built in the west Midlands for a textile mill relates to Bromsgrove mill, for which Stead of Birmingham erected an engine in about 1785.[17]

The Boulton & Watt engine was, of course, demonstrably superior to all other kinds, and it may therefore appear strange that so many atmospheric engines were sold. The answer lies in the high initial cost of the Watt engines compared with the 'common' engines. For instance, John Bacon's 16 hp Thompson rotative engine was insured for only £200 in 1795, presumably its approximate value, whereas an engine of similar horse-power from Boulton & Watt would have cost about £850 at this time. The Watt engine would have been more economical on coal, but this was mined in Sutton and could be bought for 5s 6d a ton.[18]

Another striking example of the cotton-spinner's reluctance to place complete reliance on steam-power is provided by the Robinsons of Bulwell and Linby, a firm which has enjoyed some fame as having been the first to install a Watt engine to drive machinery in a cotton mill. The engine was purchased from Soho in 1785 as a result of a legal contest between Robinson and his neighbour, Lord Byron, over water which was being taken for a new fish-pond at Byron's Newstead Abbey home. This engine, and a larger one purchased from Boulton & Watt in 1791, were used to augment the power of the water-wheels at Grange Mill, but Robinson's five other mills continued to depend on the power provided by the sluggish River Leen.[19] Several of the leading manufacturers, such as Samuel Unwin and Davison & Hawksley, enquired about engines from Boulton & Watt but turned to atmospheric engines when the patentees' terms were disclosed.

Other manufacturers, lacking the discretion of the more experienced spinners, were caught unawares. Thus Pearson & Grimshaw, a small Nottingham firm, wrote to Boulton & Watt: 'The engine works quite to our satisfaction but must confess the expense is far greater than we expected, the whole amount being about

£800 . . .' for a 5 hp engine. This firm, and several others, were forced to sell their Watt engines at a fairly early date. Yet others, having purchased Watt engines, sent pleading letters to the patentees asking for the premiums to be reduced. Thus, Smith Churchill of Shepshed wrote in 1794 that 'the same circumstances still exist without any alleviation whatever as was the inducement for you to make a reduction of part of the premium last year, (and we) hope you will not object to accept the same terms for the present year as cotton-spinning is a very unprofitable business at this time'. The following year they pleaded that the engine 'is not employed at more than half its power, and as long as the war continues we feel no inclination to increase it'.[20]

The main disadvantage of the Newcomen engine, its high consumption of coal, did not weigh seriously with the majority of the spinners, whose mills stood on or very close to the coalfield. Not only was coal very cheap, but spinners with mills in the country only needed to use a steam-engine for a few months in the year to return water to their reservoir and make good temporary deficiencies in the supply. As Unwins explained to Boulton & Watt, their atmospheric pumping-engine had proved 'less expensive than a rotative one because we had only to pay for the coals consumed in proportion to the power wanted to make up temporary deficiencies in the reservoir or stream'. After a further exchange of letters, Unwins were 'still at a loss to discover how any advantage could arise to us from one of your engines, taking the additional expense and circumstances into consideration . . .'.[21] Richard Gorton of Cuckney, whose smallware factory had close links with Toplises, complained to Boulton & Watt, after having one of their engines installed, that 'at present we are paying a premium for using more coal than the old engine'. Experience with Watt engines in the Midlands varied so markedly that, when Robert Denison was planning the erection of his mill in Nottingham, the accounts were so conflicting that he could not make up his mind what principle to proceed upon.[22]

If, indeed, Watt engines were more widely-used than the cheaper Newcomen types—and the figures in Table 8 are only tentative for makers other than Boulton & Watt—it was not for reasons of fuel economy alone. In Nottingham, which was still considered an attractive town before the end of the eighteenth century, there was much opposition to common engines on account of their smokiness. Harris instructed Boulton & Watt in 1785: 'the fire-engine . . . must be upon that particular plan which consumes the smoke, as my neighbours at Nottingham have already made application to the Mayor of the town to prevent it being erected, they at the same time supposing it to be built upon the old principle'.[23] It was probably this opposition to the Newcomen engine that resulted in the unusually high concentration of Watt engines in Nottingham. In the country districts, many of the spinners were also bleachers, and the common engines were disliked because of the smuts they spread over the hose and cloths in the bleach-fields. No doubt it was for this reason that Unwins first tried to make up the shortage of water in their eight-acre reservoir by erecting a windmill over the top of their mill, for when they enquired about an engine from Boulton & Watt, their expressed need was to avoid dirty fumes, rather than save fuel[24].

In Derbyshire, and in the adjacent parts of Staffordshire, relatively few steam-engines were installed until modern times. The swift Pennine streams provided a copious supply of water at all seasons, so that there was no need for supplementary power. Thus in the Midlands, as in Lancashire,[25] the Boulton & Watt engine played a less-prominent role than was at one time supposed. The erection of the multi-storey mills showed that the future lay with the improved engine, but this was not necessarily an economic proposition for small country mills.

CHAPTER NINE

Recruitment of Labour for the Mills

1. Incentives to Enter the Mills

ONE of the most difficult problems which entrepreneurs in the early cotton- and worsted-spinning industry had to face was the recruitment and retention of a labour force. The problem was, in part, a consequence of the well-known reluctance of the working-classes to enter the factories, and certainly the domestic framework knitters and weavers of the Region were not easily persuaded to exchange their freedom for factory discipline. The scarcity of labour was also a reflection of the general shortage in the manufacturing districts. The hosiery and lace industries were growing very rapidly, and their expansion coincided with that of the spinning industry. Wages appear to have been higher in hosiery and lace than for similar grades of workers (skilled, semi-skilled and unskilled) in the mills. In the rural areas, there was a steady drain of good workers to the towns and large manufacturing villages, where the best-paid work was to be found. The French wars also aggravated the labour shortage after 1792 by drawing large numbers of men into the Army.

It has already been noted that the wages paid in the spinning-mills were not sufficiently high to attract workers from regular employment in the towns. Farey points out that Derbyshire mill-workers earned higher wages than farm labourers in the county and White records that, in Bakewell, 'wages were raised immediately' after Arkwright's mill began production there. Fitton and Wadsworth suggest that Arkwright and Strutt did not employ parish apprentices, and that their labour force was probably recruited in the villages within a four- or five-mile radius of the factories. This explanation is not very convincing since other evidence, overlooked by these two authors, shows that even juvenile and female labour had to be brought into Derbyshire from the main centres of the cotton industry at Manchester and Nottingham.

Watson records that, when Arkwright's Bakewell mill was opened, 'good-natured girls' were brought from Manchester. When he opened his second mill at Cromford, Arkwright advertised for both indentured juvenile and skilled labour in the *Nottingham Journal* before doing so in the *Derby Mercury*, so presumably he had had some previous success in recruiting labour from the Nottingham area. And if Arkwright, the innovating entrepreneur, could not scrape together a labour force in Derbyshire, it is difficult to imagine other firms having any more success, unless perhaps their concerns were very small. The labour recruited in Nottingham and Manchester would not have been in regular employment—'the restless and migratory workers' mentioned in the Evans' correspondence—and since it was difficult enough to obtain even unskilled workers, how much more difficult it must have been to attract artisans from the main centres of the cotton industry.[1]

Apart from wages and bonus payment, various incentives were used by entrepreneurs in the spinning industry to attract and retain a labour force, the most common being the provision of housing at low rentals. In a much-quoted passage, Farey says that 'the vast numbers of neat and comfortable cottages . . . erected by the late Sir Richard and by the present Mr Richard Arkwright, by Messrs Strutts, Mr Samuel Oldknow and numerous others of the cotton-spinners and manufacturers' were far superior to the cottages erected in the northern counties of England.[2] The quotation is important in so far as it illustrates the prosperity which manufacturing brought to Derbyshire, but it does not help very much with the question of recruitment of labour since no 'cottagers' were drawn from the southern counties to work in the Derbyshire mills.

The quality and rentals of factory-colony housing must be compared with those in Nottingham and other centres of the cotton industry in order to assess the value of this housing as a means of

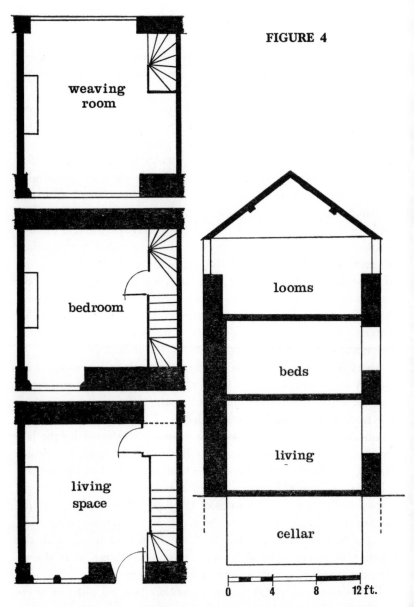

FIGURE 4

weaving
room

bedroom

living
space

looms

beds

living

cellar

0   4   8   12 ft.

No. 8 North Street, Cromford, one of a double row of cottages built by Arkwright for his workers about 1777. (From a survey made by the Ancient Monuments Society, the present owners of the property) recruiting labour, particularly skilled labour. On this point, no categorical statement can be made, but it is possible to make an estimate of the position. While very few of the factory masters attempted to build up communities on the scale of Cromford and Belper, most country mills built a row of cottages near the factory. Mill-workers' houses have survived to the present day, not only at Cromford and Belper, but also at Curbar (Calver Mill), Darley Abbey (Derby), Papplewick, Cuckney and Southwell in Nottinghamshire, and Mayfield, Staffordshire, and their standards can be compared with those illustrated in Chapter Two. The quality of the surviving factory-colony housing is altogether superior to that built at Nottingham during the period covered by this book, though built on a similar pattern. Arkwright's cottages at Cromford no doubt set the standard, the earliest being those in North Street, whose design and planning are shown in the accompanying drawing. The cottages were set behind a broad avenue of trees (Figure 4.) with lawn borders and allotment gardens nearby, and must have been very attractive to migrants from the towns.

Even so, it was not easy to secure skilled labour and some of the manufacturers found it necessary to hold out other incentives. Evans' factory-colony well illustrates this point, for in 1787 they advertised for labour in the following terms:

> Darley Cotton Mill. Wanted, Families, particularly women and children to work at the said mill. They may be provided with comfortable houses and every necessary convenience either at Darley or Allestry; particularly a milking-cow to each family. It is a very good neighbourhood for the men getting work who are not employed in the manufactory.

The rents of Evans' houses at Darley were subsidized, and varied from 3d to 1s 6d weekly. A large proportion were built of three storeys, and each had a small garden attached. Additions to the cottages were made periodically, first pig-sties then privies and ovens. Already in 1795, twelve years after the first mill opened, Evans owned forty-one houses at Darley.[4] At Belper and Milford, many of the Strutts' houses had large gardens, as did Robinson's

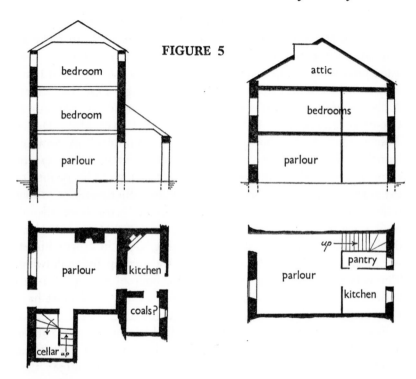

FIGURE 5

Two types of houses built by Strutts for their workers at Belper and Milford. On the left is No. 7 Long Row, Belper; on the right No. 2 Hopping Hill, Milford. (Reproduced from M. W. Barley's 'Industrial Monuments at Milford and Belper: Housing', *Archaeological Journal*, CXVIII (1961), p. 238)

cottages at Papplewick, and a number of Strutt's workpeople rented additional land known as 'Potatoe lots' at 1d a week. The impression thus given is that these firms tried to attract workers not only by providing houses but by endeavouring to reproduce the comfortable homestead of the independent peasant-proprietor. In 1783, Arkwright gave 'twenty-seven fine milch-cows, worth from £8 to £10 each' to twenty-seven of his principal workmen, perhaps another attempt to appeal to the workers' yearning for rural life.[5]

There is no evidence of other firms following this initiative, but few successful ideas were the prerogative of one manufacturer for long, as evidenced by the popularity of another kind of incentive, subsidizing the cost of provisions and coal sold to the mill-workers. Strutts, Evans, Peter Nightingale and Davison & Hawksley are all known to have supported their workers in this way, and Nightingale, in particular, advertised that both coal and provisions were 'reasonable' at his Lea Mill. Another form of subsidy were the workers' sick-clubs and provident societies, which provided cheap or free medical attention and some kind of payment during illness. Such clubs were sponsored by Arkwright—there were no less than eight in and about Cromford in 1790—by the Strutts,[6] the Evanses, Major Cartwright and Parkes, Brookhouse & Crompton at Warwick. The encouragement of providence was a catching idea among the late eighteenth-century manufacturers, and there were probably many other such clubs attached to cotton mills in different parts of the Region.

Readers of Professor G. Unwin's *Samuel Oldknow and the Arkwrights* will recall that Oldknow's attempts to maintain his labour force were centred on his efforts to find employment for the fathers and husbands of the main part of his cotton-mill labour force. This was not too difficult for cotton manufactuers who, like Oldknow, owned large estates, or who had other manufacturing interests. Several manufacturers in the Midland Region fall fairly readily into this category—Arkwright with his Cromford paper mill and £20,000 Willersley Castle to build, the Evanses, with extensive Derbyshire estates and land and ironworks, and Wilkes with his multifarious agricultural, transport and manufacturing schemes. Some other manufacturers, such as the Dakeynes of Darley Abbey, Ellis Needham of Litton Mill and Oldknow, Cowpe & Co. of Pleasley maintained farms and may well have found limited employment for men there.

Again, the growth of colonies of stocking-knitters around the mills may well have originated as a conscious response to this

L

employment problem; as appears to have been the case with Arkwright and Adams, who transported the domestic industry to Cromford and Bromsgrove. Some of the larger manufacturers, like Davison & Hawksley and Toplis & Co. were evidently anxious to build up large integrated concerns, in which all the processes from sheep-farming to the sale of knitted and woven worsted could be undertaken. This conception may have sprung less from a conviction of the value of integration as such than from a desire to achieve a 'balanced' labour force, which would provide equal employment opportunities for the whole family. Whatever the truth of these propositions, it is clear that the manufacturer with the larger capital had the greater opportunity of attracting and maintaining a labour force.

The same is also true of the community facilities provided by a few manufacturers. Clearly, only the larger manufacturer could erect public-houses, churches, markets and schools to meet the needs of a swollen local population, and even then religious motives seem to have overlaid the economic one of attracting labour. Only Arkwright responded to what the workers wanted, instead of trying to give them what was good for their souls. His initiative in building an inn (in 1779) and a market (in 1790) at Cromford was almost unique; the only other entrepreneur known to have provided this kind of facility was Wilkes, who built a coaching-inn and a covered market at Measham.[7] By contrast, several spinners built chapels or churches, and not a few opened Sunday-schools. Here the evangelical motive was mixed, in varying proportions, with the attempt to imbue virtues of subordination, regularity, providence, sobriety and other attributes of the good factory-worker. In the course of a generation the attempt could be strikingly successful, if the experience of the Strutts and the Robinsons can be trusted.[8]

The manufacturers themselves gave most publicity to another advantage of factory employment, that of security. The student of economic history would anticipate this claim, pointing to the expectation that the manufacturer would have a larger investment in fixed capital than the merchant, and hence a greater incentive to maintain his labour force in full employment. The regularity of factory labour was emphasized in advertisements for workers and enlarged upon in the public pronouncements of the manufacturers. The point was strikingly illustrated by Alderman William Howitt, a Nottingham hosier who became a later partner in the Pleasley mills. During the slump in trade in 1816, he maintained that there were some 1,500–1,600 workers in the domestic hosiery industry of Mansfield out of work, but none unemployed in the eleven mills in the district.[9] Howitt's position on the Corporation, an oligarchy to which numbers of other spinners belonged, suggests that his views were current among the manufacturing class, and the widespread use of apprenticeship and indentures for both juvenile and adult workers seems to reinforce his point.

Nevertheless, there are some important qualifications to be borne in mind. The cotton- and worsted-spinning industry was necessarily dependent on the domestic hosiery industry and was by no means immune from trade fluctuations. In 1794, for instance, hands were laid off and, towards the end of that decade, the disruption of the hosiery trade by war was partly the cause of a contraction in factory spinning.[10] During the years of the French wars there were at least twenty cases of bankruptcy among spinners in the Region, with consequent loss of employment.[11] The possible consequences of a bankruptcy may be judged from the following extract from a letter which followed the insolvency of Timothy Harris in Nottingham in 1797. A Mr Josiah Eburne wrote to the Commissioners in Bankruptcy:[12]

> I am confident that upon serious investigation . . . the Commissioners and Assignees will liberally conclude in my favour inasmuch as by my paying off the *enraged discharged* hands out of my own pocket I . . . did preserve . . . the property and all the buildings from being destroyed as it was not the first time Mr Harris had decoyed hands from other mills in regular work and then in a few days or weeks . . . dismissed them, so that they and their families were almost perishing for want and despised by their former employers.

Similarly, when Ellis Needham of Litton Mill became bankrupt in 1814, eighty apprentices were immediately turned away.

Another cause of unemployment among mill-workers was the destruction of so many buildings by fire, and sometimes by flood. A dozen mills in the Region are known to have suffered from one or the other, and there were probably others. When Unwins had a serious fire at their Sutton mill in 1784, 120 people lost their employment, though these could 'rely on the beneficient hand of their humane employers'. Moreover, the early mills were often subject to mob violence, and riot and arson led to the temporary or permanent closure of others. The Anti-Jacobin riots in Nottingham resulted in the closing of Denison's mill (300 workers) and damage to the property of other spinners. The insurance companies regarded the mills as a 'hazardous risk', and though this may not have been altogether the fault of the manufacturers, the worker might easily have taken a similar view of employment in them.

2. Terms of Employment

There were, of course, usually two and sometimes three stages in the factory spinner's recruitment of labour. The first to be engaged were the skilled workers to build the mill and construct the plant; the erection of a number of the larger mill buildings can be traced through a sequence of advertisements in the local press. For instance, when Jedediah Strutt was building at Milford, he first advertised in the *Derby Mercury* for 'eight to ten good labourers' (11 July 1782), then for 'several stonemasons and bricklayers' (29 May 1783), for 'two or three good carpenters' (11 September 1783), and finally for 'one or two millwrights' and 'one or two joiners'. The design and erection of the water-wheel and water-courses was supervised by a consulting engineer, in this instance John Smeaton. (The cast-iron wheel is said to have been the first erected after that at the famous Carron ironworks.) Sometimes private contractors were engaged for particular tasks, such as the woodwork or brickwork, or excavating the water channels. These workers or contractors would be accustomed to moving about a district to find employment, and there would be no unusual problem here.[13]

The second stage was the acquisition of skilled workers to build the machinery. A few firms may have purchased their spinning machinery from specialist builders, but most appear to have built their own up to about 1795. Skilled machine–builders were not easy to acquire, particularly away from the centre of the industry, and in the last two decades of the eighteenth century the *Nottingham Journal* and *Derby Mercury* carried a large number of advertisements from cotton- and worsted-spinners who required joiners, smiths, turners, clockmakers, whitesmiths and millwrights. So scarce were these artisans that it was not only mills in remote country districts like Pleasley, Cuckney, Retford, Lea or Ashbourne which advertised, but also those in (or very close to) the large towns, like Denison's Nottingham mill, and the mills at Radford and Arnold, near Nottingham.

It was Arkwright himself who initiated this spate of advertising in 1771, when he was building the machinery for his first Cromford mill, and in subsequent years both he and Strutt were constantly advertising for skilled labour. Some of the advertisements are interesting because they catalogue the whole range of machine-building and supervisory staffs required by the factory. Thus, in 1791, John Need, Denison's manager, advertised for 'Several hands for preparing machinery materials (i.e., components), as filers, iron-turners, wood-turners, clockmakers, etc. Also . . . two card-makers, two spinning-masters, a looker-over for the reeling and finishing; (and) an experienced hand in turning and clothing the cylinders . . .'. In the following year Need advertised for a millwright and two overlookers.[14]

Once the mill building was completed and the machinery built most of the labour force required were unskilled women and children. Only a few men were required to maintain the plant, and, in some mills, operate weaving-looms or knitting-machines. The proportion of male to female and juvenile labour is illustrated by the situation at Arkwright's Cromford mills where, in 1789, there were 150 men in a total labour force of 1,150, thirteen per cent of the total.[15] A more precise analysis of a mill labour-force can be achieved by examining Lequesne's engravings of Bedworth worsted mill, which were made about the end of the eighteenth century. Fifty people altogether are shown in the engraving, of whom only nine are men, the rest being women and children. The men are employed as weavers, in the supervision of materials, as a clerk, an overseer and a dyer. Judging from the size of the mill building, the Bedworth enterprise probably employed about 300 people, so these figures should be multiplied by six.

The recruitment of juvenile and unskilled labour presented peculiar problems and various approaches were tried. At first, the entrepreneurs were able to find a fair number of hands from among the wives and children of the skilled workers who built the mills and furnished them with machinery, and on the basis of this experience Arkwright and a number of other employers advertised for artisans with large families. A typical advertisement is Peter Nightingale's announcement in the *Derby Mercury*:

> Lea Cotton Mill. Good calico-weavers may be employed and if they have large families may be accommodated with houses and have employment for their children.

The appeals for families were not limited to the mills in rural Derbyshire, Robinsons of Papplewick were advertising in the *Nottingham Journal* as early as 1780, and in the 1790s three of the largest Nottingham firms were constantly advertising. At Radford mill Ald. Smith & Co. advertised that . . .

> a number of families are wanted; whether they have been accustomed or not to the business will be no object; houses are now ready for their reception.

Clearly, there was a regular migration of families from the countryside in periods of good trade, and Denison's manager noted in one of his advertisements that 'such persons who wish to remove their families from country villages or other places may be treated with by letter or personal application'.[16]

Several small mills, particularly those employing calico- or worsted-cloth weavers, may conceivably have recruited all their unskilled labour from the families of their adult male workers. However, it is clear that many of the larger ones did not, and had to have immediate recourse to recruitment of the local juvenile population. If Arkwright made any serious calculations of the economic value of the Cromford site, he must have been thinking primarily of the potential supply of both cheap and skilled labour provided by the declining mining industry of the locality.

The decline of the Derbyshire lead-mining industry towards the end of the eighteenth century is a well-attested fact. Pilkington refers to the contraction of the industry in his *Derbyshire* (1789), mentioning several villages whose prosperity had declined with the industry. Farey lists nineteen villages and hamlets in the county which, up to 1811, were decreasing or nearly stationary in population, and says that twelve of these were suffering wholly or partly from a decline of the lead-mines. The advent of the jenny produced further deterioration in the standard of living of the miner's household.

The newspaper advertisements of the period leave little doubt that a cheap supply of juvenile and female labour was considered an economic asset of the mining area. Thus the advertiser of a plot of land for sale at Hope in 1785 points to the possibility of developing the site for cotton-spinning and adds that the village is in 'a populous neighbourhood where children of proper ages for that business may be hired on very reasonable terms'. Similarly, a proposal to establish a cotton mill at Eyam in 1791 was supported by a reference to the abundance of child labour and to the distress among the adult population due to 'the impaired state of the mines'. At Winster, would-be manufacturers were assured that there were 'plenty of hands', and at Ashbourne they could obtain 'any number of hands'.[17]

But, in practice, the experience of the manufacturers proved very different from Arkwright's hopes and the optimistic assertions of the advertisers of vacant mills and sites. Arkwright scoured the villages around Cromford and had to draw 'poor people' from Winster, four long miles over the moors.[18] Most of his labour force

had to be brought from Nottingham and Manchester, hired on indenture. Evidence of the lead-miners' hostility to Arkwright has
already been noted, and when he built his second mill at Cromford
they sabotaged his water-supply from the Cromford Moor Sough.
Judging by the large number of Derbyshire manufacturers who
employed parish apprentices or indentured labour out of the district, few enjoyed any more success than did the innovating entrepreneurs.

In Nottingham and the hosiery districts, recruitment of unskilled
labour was probably less of a problem. Certainly Arkwright did not
have to advertise for the 300 workers for his Nottingham mill, nor
was there any shortage of labour for his Manchester mill. The only
convincing explanation for this is the continuous migration of
workers from the countryside to the towns and manufacturing
villages, numbers of which (to judge from Denison's advertisement)
were absorbed into the labour force of the cotton mills.[19]

The reason for the employment of parish apprentices is explained in Farey's *Agriculture of Derbyshire*. In 'most newly-
erected cotton-spinning mills of this and adjacent counties the
demand for children's labour . . . exceeds even the inordinately ex-
cited increase of population in the place, and children are not only
sought for through the adjoining districts, but in many instances
have been imported by scores at a time . . . from London, Bristol
and other great towns . . .'.[20] Clearly, the employment of pauper
labour was a last resort, after the local labour supply had dried up.
There is no record of any spinners at Nottingham, Mansfield,
Derby or Leicester employing apprentices; presumably they could
recruit a juvenile labour force without the trouble and expense of
boarding apprentices. Parish apprentices are known to have been
employed by at least twenty firms included in this study, and nearly
all had mills in remote or thinly-populated parts of the Region, the
only exceptions being four firms with an unusually large labour
force—Sir Robert Peel, Davison & Hawksley, Robinsons, and
Bradley & Co. of Ashbourne.[21]

Comprehensive information on the number and geographical distribution of parishes which sent apprentices to mills in the Region is not available, but a complete record of all the apprentices taken on by one firm, William Toplis & Co. of Cuckney, has survived. Toplises drew their apprentices from many parts of the country, but the places of origin fall into a simple pattern. The Cuckney Apprentice Register records the names and origins, with some other details, of 780 apprentices who arrived at Cuckney between October 1786 and April 1805. Table 9 summarizes the main sources from which they were drawn. Boys and girls were taken on

TABLE 9
Origins of Apprentices at Cuckney Mill, 1786–1805

24 parishes in Notts. and the adjacent parts of Derbyshire and Yorkshire	63
26 parishes in London and the adjacent parts of Middlesex and Essex	498
4 other parishes	44
Total sent by parishes	605
3 philanthropic organizations	98
Parents, relatives and private individuals	77
	780

Sources: Toplis & Co.'s Cuckney Apprentice Register. (MS. in custody of Mr B. Johnson, Headmaster of Cuckney Primary School, Nottinghamshire).

at ages from seven to fourteen, but most were aged eight, nine or ten years. Their contracts lasted from one to eight years, depending on the age at which they were taken on at the mill. A large number of parishes in the vicinity of Cuckney sent boys and girls to be apprentices, but mostly only in ones and twos. Some parents and relatives in the area also sent children, while others again were recruited through local trading connections, like Thomas Gadsby, a Sutton 'bag hosier', Mr J. Brown, a Chesterfield surgeon, and Mr Scrimshaw, a Mansfield baker.

When the total recruitment from these sources proved inadequate, Toplises had recourse to the London parishes. Apart from the

district of Cuckney, nearly all their juvenile labour force was drawn
from the London area, the contacts no doubt being made through
the firm's London agents, or by one of the partners visiting London
for general business purposes. The largest number of apprentices
(106) was obtained from St Margaret's, Westminster, one consign-
ment of fifty apprentices being sent up in a single week in October
1794. Other major suppliers were St Marylebone (102 apprentices),
Hackney (69), Lambeth (63) and St Saviour's, Southwark (48). In
London, as in the locality of Cuckney, every available source of
juvenile labour was tapped, and children were obtained from
parents or through trading connections, from the Foundling
Hospital and from 'Mr Houlston, Chancery Lane, visitor to the
Philanthropic Society'. Mr Houlston's children came from all over
London and were probably vagrants taken off the streets. A 'Mr T.
Royle' who sent consignments of children from the Halifax and
Wakefield area probably worked for another philanthropic society.
The parish overseers of Birmingham, Hereford and Leicester also
sent children, but were not regular suppliers.

The impression conveyed by a careful study of the Register is of
an acute shortage of child labour, and the problem was further
accentuated by a high degree of wastage. More than a third of the
apprentices recruited died, absconded, or had to be returned to the
overseers, parents, or the connections that sent them. The details
are summarized in Table 10.

TABLE 10

Wastage of Apprentices at Cuckney Mill, 1786–1805

	Number of Apprentices	% of total Apprentices
Ran away	119	15·2
Died	65	8·3
Returned to Overseers	51	6·5
Returned to parents or other senders	45	5·7
	280	36
Total number of apprentices	780	100

The high mortality-rate and the large number of apprentices who ran away is not necessarily evidence of ill-treatment. A visitor to Cuckney about 1794 wrote that the children 'employed at the respective mills . . . are kept in excellent order. They live in cottages built for the purpose, under the care of superintendents; boys under one roof and girls under another; an apothecary attends them at stated times to preserve health. They are trained to the duties of religion and are fed plentifully . . .'. An Anglican clergyman was advertised for to take a full-time appointment at the Cuckney Mills.[22]

A more convincing explanation of the loss of so many children is that they were collected from the unhealthy dregs of society. If the quotation is a fair commentary on the management of the apprentices, they died in spite of, and not because of their treatment at Cuckney. Taken far from their homes, it is not surprising that many should seek to return to their families or home town, and that others should be reclaimed by relatives. A number of consignments from the workhouses were clearly without profit. To take an example at random, seven apprentices were acquired from the Hackney Overseers in June 1794. Of this number, three ran away, two had to be returned, one died and the other left (for some unrecorded reason) a year after arriving at Cuckney.

In view of the expense of maintaining apprentices, and the high rate of wastage, it is not surprising that Toplises, like many other firms, soon abandoned the system. In the difficult trading conditions of 1805, the firm decided to divest itself of most of its apprentices, and nearly 200 were turned over to a handful of large firms in the area. Only two apprentices out of 780 are recorded as being taken on as adult workers by Toplis.

This problem of wastage was not, of course, confined to the juvenile labour force. The surviving records of Evans' mill at Darley Abbey, near Derby, show an exchange of letters between Evans and a number of other firms in the Region expressing their concern about the 'restless and migratory spirit' common among workers at this time. Strutts, Evans, Robinsons, Botts of Tutbury, John Flint of Uttoxeter, and no doubt other firms, agreed not to take on workpeople who were unable to produce a satisfactory testimonial from their previous employer. Even so, if Strutts' experience was typical, the rate of labour turnover was very high.[23]

The relation between the manufacturer and the local parish which supplied him with pauper children is illustrated by accounts of the Overseers of the Poor at Hayton, near Retford. This parish sent children to Cuckney worsted mill in 1788 and 1789, and the Overseers of these years were unusually assiduous in recording the details:

1788		£	s	d
June 1	Let John Bacon have a shilling to bear his expenses with going with his children to the Cotton Mill		1	0
June 2	For myself and Mr Dixon meeting John Bacon and his children at Norton Worsted Mill, etc. our expenses		4	0
	Ditto for my day		1	6
June 14	Both John Bacon's children 2 pairs of shoes		4	6
	A pair of stays cost		5	0
	A pair of breeches cost		2	6
	Cloth for shorts cost		3	0
	Gown cost		2	4
	A hat cost		2	0
	Paid Sarah Cooper for one week's pay for John Bacon's children		2	6
	Paid Elizabeth Pettinger for one week's board for John Bacon's children		4	0
July 23	Paid Robert Taylor for going to Norton two times with children and his expenses etc.		5	0
August 9	Paid Thos. Barthrop for going with the children to Cuckney		2	6
Sept. 11	Paid Mary Lister for keeping Hempstalk's children and Ann Swinforn when they ran away from the Worsted Mill and ale		2	0
1789				
Jan. 21	Paid Mr Toplis of Cuckney for three children bound to him	3	3	0
	Paid to the bond making		5	0
	Gave to the children			6
	My expense			8
	For my day's journey		1	6
Feb. 8	Bacon's children, 25 weeks pay	3	2	6
	Bacon's children, 3 weeks pay		3	9

The number of children involved is not stated, but it must have been at least five. Only three were apprenticed, so presumably the others were allowed to return, probably those who ran away. The interval of seven months between the journey to the mill and the 'bond making' suggests some sort of probationary period, during which the parish provided the children with clothes and paid for their board and lodging. The Overseer's entries show a responsible interest in the children's welfare, and the trial periods must at least point to Toplis's willingness to see that the children were suited. Certainly, the Overseers of the Poor were not all like Mr Bumble; even in the case of the notorious Litton mills, at least one beadle travelled from London to inspect the apprentices' condition.[24]

The Midland records confirm the opinion that the apprentice-ship system hardly lasted for a generation in most places. When the first returns were made under Peel's Factory Act (1802) a number of Derbyshire mills had already given up their apprentices. As the rural factories declined in number and the population around the surviving ones grew, there was no need to import young labour. Arkwright never employed parish apprentices, apparently prefer-ring indentured labour, and before the end of the century others were following his example. The general view was probably ex-pressed by Alderman Howitt, when he said that, at Pleasley, his firm had given up parish apprentices as 'We find it so much trouble having them in the House'. In their place, the firm engaged young people on an indenture for seven years, and adult hands for a specific number of years 'some five, some seven, some ten, and some twelve years, to work for certain wages for twelve hours a day'. By this means Pleasley Mills, and no doubt other concerns too, ob-tained the advantages of a stable labour force without the cares and responsibilities of maintaining a large number of young children, though engagement on such terms did not necessarily lead to any more humane treatment of children than under the earlier appren-ticeship system.

CHAPTER TEN

Labour Relations

1. The Scarcity of Reliable Evidence

MOST of the writing and discussion of the conditions of work in the early cotton and worsted mills has centred on the alleged sufferings of child apprentices, and particularly apprentices recruited from the parishes. But although this subject has interested professional and amateur historians for four or five generations now, research has not been very productive. It is true that the existence of a number of model employers has been established, but examples are scarce and, in the Midlands, only the Strutts have been shown to be 'good' employers. Over all other firms, whether allegedly good or bad, a question-mark lies for lack of historical evidence.

Toplises, the Cuckney and Worksop worsted-spinners, have been deemed benevolent employers, in view of Throsby's frequently-quoted remarks after visiting the mills, but a reader of the surviving Cuckney Apprentice Register is not quite so sure. Did Throsby know that fifteen per cent of the 780 apprentices ran away and that eight per cent died? Similarly, it has been supposed, very largely on the basis of a surviving 'Book of Housekeeping Expenses at Pleasley Works Apprentice-House, 1794–99', that Oldknow, Cowpe & Co. were kind employers. It is certainly true that the firm provided an elementary education and regular medical attention for their apprentices (as Toplises did), but an emphatic local protest about contracts at Pleasley Mills in 1839 brought to light legal arrangements which lead the student to question what has been written about a tradition of enlightened management at this mill.[1]

The Cromford community presents a fascinating first essay at personnel management and, as Fitton and Wadsworth show, Arkwright certainly succeeded in 'creating a spectacle'. The inns and the market-place, and perhaps the church, chapel and Sunday-schools too, provided a full measure of social opportunities. This is the side that has been most noticed, but there is another. Even in 1816, not more than one in five of the factory-hands got a tea-break in their thirteen-hour day. And for something like twenty-two years, from the establishment of the first Cromford mill to the death of Arkwright, a large number of boys—at one time there were 164 of them—were employed on night shifts, and though they were paid 'extravagant wages' they 'were extremely dissipated'. More evidence is necessary before any conclusions can be drawn, and the best that can be said for Arkwright in this context is that many other cotton mills, including those of Sir Robert Peel, worked their machinery twenty-four hours a day up to about 1796.[2]

While there is only one firm that can be said to have been model employers, there is also only one that can certainly be said to have been bad, and even here it is possible to find extenuating circumstances. The only spinner in the Region convicted under Peel's Factory Act was George Wood, a machine-smith who began to operate a few machines in 1796 and bought Morley's old mill—formerly the Nottingham pottery—in 1798. The pottery was an old building which had stood on the site for a century or more. According to the Justices' Reports:

> Mr Wood, who owns the Mill at Beck Barns, has not complied with the Act of Parliament, the lower room not being either drawn or pointed, the upper rooms very dirty and so very confined that the health of those employed in them must be very much injured; neither did the proprietor seem disposed to admit fresh air, lest his works should be damaged. . . .

Wood's attempt to spin worsted seems to have failed, just as his attempts to build mules had done. His resources were probably slender, and his partner went bankrupt a few years later. It could be argued that Wood was lacking in means, rather than in humanity.[3]

The uncertainties are even more persistent when the record of a number of 'bad' employers is investigated. The Robinsons of Bulwell and Papplewick have been castigated for ill-treatment of their

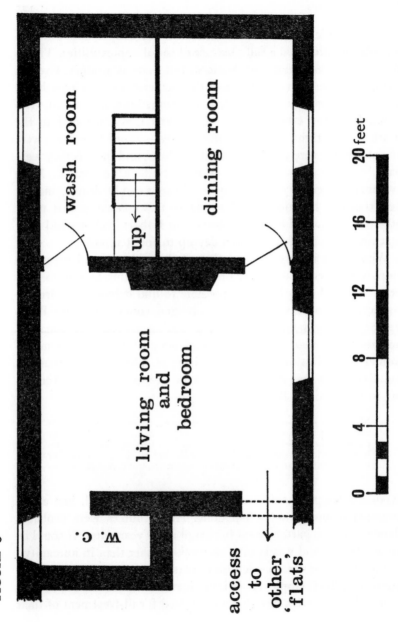

FIGURE 6

wash room

dining room

living room
and
bedroom

up ↓

w. c.

access
to
other
'flats'

0   4   8   12   16   20 feet

One of the eight 'flats' of the Apprentice House at Robinson's Grange Mill, Papplewick, built about 1785. Each 'flat' accommodated about a dozen children. The stone building is now known as Grange Cottages apprentices but, as Professor Chambers has recently shown, the high mortality rates at the mills occurred in the opening years of the nineteenth century when there was a smallpox epidemic raging in the district. Moreover, John Robinson 'formulated a plan by which employees (of his firm) were to share profits', hardly the idea of a Gridgrind.[4] Another mill where conditions were supposed to be bad was that of Alderman William Wilson at Radford, near Nottingham. According to the Factory Inquiry of 1833, Wilson's mill was 'reported in the town as the worst-conducted in Nottingham', yet an inspecting medical practitioner reported that 'After examining the state of the drains, water-closets, and several of the working-people on oath, I was pretty well convinced that the accusations against the management of this mill were in great degree unfounded'. As in the case of the Robinsons, the known character of the proprietor seems at variance with popular report on conditions at his mill. Alderman Wilson was an Evangelical nonconformist and a Radical, the only supporter on Nottingham Corporation of Lord Rancliffe, who became MP for the town through the support of 'poor working-men'. Radford mill never worked nights, and Wilson's son ran a mission-hall and Sunday-school at Radford, which his father probably opened.[5]

Among the Nottinghamshire mills, the heaviest indictment is against Lamberts, the Nottingham hosiers who opened a mill at Gonalston. Here, again, the case is less conclusive than appears at first sight. The firm were the first employers of Robert Blincoe, a pauper apprentice from St Pancras workhouse, whose *Memoir* will be examined in some detail later. In this case, the only witness for the prosecution, namely Blincoe, is inconsistent, and towards the end of his statement seems to be suggesting that Lamberts were quite humane employers, certainly after the management problems had been sorted out. Lowdham mill was recalled by Blincoe as 'a large and lofty edifice' with a separate apprentice-house half a mile away. The apprentices:

M

were kept decently clad, had a bettermost suit reserved for Sundays
and holidays, were occasionally allowed a little time for play in the
open air, and upon Goose Fair day . . . were conveyed in carts to that
celebrated place, and regaled with furmety, and 6d in money was
allowed to the very youngest! They went pretty regularly to
Lowdham Church on Sundays. . . . They were worked hard; but not
hard as to distort their limbs, nor occasion declines [in health] or
deaths. Their food latterly was good, and cleanly cooked. Their
bedding, though coarse, was clean. [Altogether] they were
humanely treated.[6]

The proprietors of the mill, Almond and Lambert, were (according
to other sources) prominent High–Church Anglicans.

Taken together, these half-dozen examples indicate that many of
the conclusions reached have been based on insecure foundations.
They suggest interpretations based on preconceived notions of the
truth or calumnious reports. Clearly, to make a more exact historical
assessment, it is necessary to study not only favourable and critical
reports on mill conditions, but also the contexts in which the reports were made and the personalities of those who left the records.
The main difficulty is, of course, lack of evidence, since so few
business records have survived. However, it is possible to make a
detailed study without business archives, using instead a variety of
local sources, and this has been attempted in the following pages for
two firms which are generally supposed to have ill-treated their
pauper apprentices.

One firm, Davison & Hawksley, was located at the centre of the
Midlands cotton industry at Nottingham, and two of its partners,
Robert and John Davison, were merchant hosiers, Presbyterian
dissenters and members of the *élite* of Nottingham society, the
Corporation. The other firm was Needham, Frith & Co. of Litton,
near Tideswell, in the High Peak of Derbyshire. Here the partners
were farmers and Churchmen, combining their interest in textiles
with that of farming in a district remote from the centres of the industry at Nottingham and Manchester. In many respects the two
firms provide a contrast, and a number of general conclusions can
be drawn from an intensive study of them.

It is the writer's contention that the heat generated in the debate over the factory apprentices has—with one or two scholarly exceptions—diverted too much attention from general questions of personnel management, labour relations and the motives of leaders of industry in this period. The treatment of juvenile labour is, after all, only part of the more general question of industrial conditions, and it is hoped that, by focussing attention on the general question, the details of the parts will come into better perspective.

2. Davison & Hawksley's Arnold Mill

The case against Davison & Hawksley, proprietors of Arnold Mill, was originally recorded by William Stumbles, a local working-class preacher, in 1859. He wrote:

> There was no Factory Act in those days and the hands at [Arnold Mill] were accustomed to work night and day and, as the result, there was great mortality among the apprentices. These were mostly obtained from Bristol and London, out of the workhouse. . . . The mortality was so great among them that as many as six or seven some weeks were buried at Arnold Church. This shameful waste of human life was thought to have resulted partly from overwork, and partly from the crowded state of their lodging rooms.[8]

Stumbles' essay is a mixture of reminiscence, local legend, and material borrowed from earlier local histories. One of the local authors, writing in 1815, gives an outline of the history of Arnold Mill, but has only praise for the benevolent and humane acts of the proprietors.[9] Nevertheless, later writers have reflected Stumbles' views.

It is certainly true that the Arnold mill employed parish apprentices and worked day and night shifts up to about 1797.[10] Moreover, Arnold burial-registers contain a large number of entries for Davison & Hawkesley's mill just after the turn of the century: 27 deaths in 1801, 12 in 1802, 8 in 1803, 12 in 1804, and 4 in 1805. This, however, is not necessarily an endorsement of the local historian's conclusion that the apprentice mortality was the result of overwork, neglect and overcrowding. 'This was notoriously a period of famine and fever', Professor Chambers points out, 'in all the parishes concerned (in cotton-spinning) and in Nottingham the burials in 1801 were among the highest in the whole series; and Messrs Davison & Hawksley made their name at this time by buying corn wherever they could get it, having it ground by their own steam mill and offering it for sale at a price lower than cost at Week Day Cross at Nottingham. Were they feeding the people of Nottingham and starving their apprentices at Arnold? Or were the apprentices at Arnold . . . victims of the epidemic of smallpox that was raging outside? . . .'[11]

There is other evidence to uphold Davison & Hawksley as benevolent employers. In their advertisements for juvenile labour, the firm promised that boys and girls in their employ 'will be well-clothed, lodged and boarded; they will attend church every Sabbath, and have proper masters appointed for their instruction'. Another advertisement maintained that boys apprenticed to the firm would be taught 'a very good trade . . . at a proper age' and reminded parents and others that 'apprentices will be taught to read and write'.

The boys wore a uniform of leather jacket and breeches with white, homespun, worsted stockings; very likely the girls had a distinctive dress, too.[12] In 1800, Davison & Hawksley recorded that they had no less than '600 apprentices to feed daily in our house',[13] which shows that (like most spinners who employed apprentices) they had a separate apprentice-house. The apprentice-house, now a row of fifteen cottages, still survives, and the accommodation appears to have consisted of three 'flats' in each cottage, with the overseer's house at the end of the row (Figure 7). The plan suggests the division of the apprentice labour force into 'family' groups, with a dozen or so children in each.

If their own statements are anything to go by, the partners in the Arnold mill were kind and considerate to the people of Arnold. In 1798, Davison declared 'I have now lived amongst you nearly twelve years, and I challenge malice itself to prove one single act of mine of oppression, injury or even unkindness to any one individual

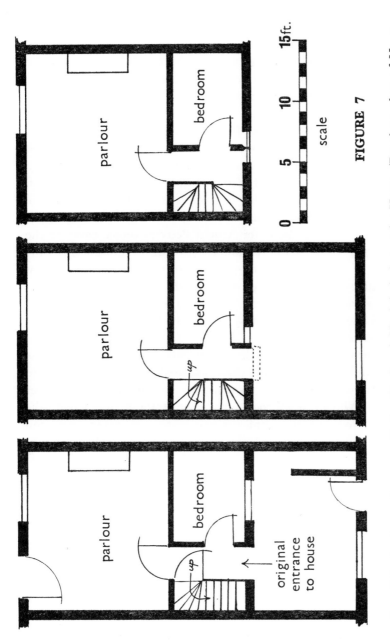

One of the fourteen cottages constituting Davison & Hawksley's Apprentice-House. (Based on plans of No. 3 Cottage Row, Arnold, prepared by Mr M. W. Spick.) The present kitchen and back bedroom are additions to the original property

FIGURE 7

during that period. Many of you have I relieved and assisted in
various ways in your distresses. . . .' John Hawksley presented the
villagers with a piece of land on which they could build their own
corn mill, union flour mills being a popular measure of self-help
among the working-classes at this period.[14]

One of the worst aspects of factory employment at this period,
according to the contemporary reformers, was the payment of
workers in 'truck' or kind. It is true that Davison & Hawksley ran
their own farm, maintained their own grocer's and mercer's shops,
employed a miller and a baker to grind corn and bake bread for the
community, and issued their own token coinage.[15] However, the
Justice's Clerk's fee-book for Arnold Petty Sessions, covering the
years 1794–1802, shows a number of workers appealing to the
Justices of the Peace for non-payment of wages, but none against
payment by truck. Other evidence leaves no doubt that this ob-
noxious practice was commonly resorted to by the 'bag' hosiers of
villages like Arnold, but not by 'gentlemen hosiers' like Robert and
John Davison.[16]

Another alleged abuse of the factory system was the excessive use
of corporal punishment, and though several attempts were made to
take Davison & Hawksley to court for assault, no case was ever
proved. William Sherbrooke, the magistrate before whom the
workers brought their complaints, was known for his humanity, and
his failure to institute proceedings must not be assumed to be a con-
spiracy between him and the Arnold Mill partners.[17] Something is
known of the lives and character of the mill managers, two of
whom were Methodist preachers of some local celebrity, while the
third was the son of a Nottingham hosier who (like the Davisons)
was a member of High Pavement Chapel and the Corporation. The
first two were men of unusual energy and ability, the third came of
an outstanding family,[18] and it is unlikely that any of them would
have been callous or indifferent to the welfare of the Arnold mill-
workers. Davison himself was only prepared to allow corporal
punishment when absolutely necessary, and once told his frame-

work knitters 'you . . . know that correction may be occasionally necessary. . . . If your own apprentices were week after week (to) destroy or waste the work they had made, or that (which) was entrusted to their care, and by which you are to be enabled to maintain them, I believe you would take the liberty of correcting them. . . .'[19]

The evidence so far might be deemed inconclusive; conceivably Davison & Hawksley could have been exercising some kind of deceit. Fortunately, other evidence has survived. In a handbill, written in July 1798 to protest against an attack on his house following reports that his firm was ill-treating their apprentices, Davison declared:

> We owe a serious duty to those who have placed those children under our care, and therefore I hope you will excuse me saying a few words upon that subject—I declare to you in the most solemn manner, that neither my partner nor myself would conduct our business at the expense of humanity, or otherwise, than by a kind and generous conduct towards those children. The best way of repelling this groundless and malicious charge (made against the partners) is to offer to you, and to the surrounding country, nay to request it of you, to come in a proper and peacable manner, and view their treatment in every respect both as to food, raiment, lodging, morals, medicines for the sick, and in every other point. However troublesome it may be to us, we will permit you to make this examination at any time, and if you really believe, as calumnious reports state them to be, it is your duty to accept the offer I now make you, and which my partner wishes you to accept as much as myself.[20]

Thus the evidence suggests that Davison & Hawksley were benevolent employers. However, there is a further difficulty, for although the firm may be exonerated from the charge of ill-treating their juvenile labour force, how does one explain the poor labour relations which undoubtedly existed at Arnold? 'The large number of cases brought by the agent of Davison & Hawksley for riotous behaviour of labourers, for absconding from work, for spoiling and neglecting it, and for threatening to set the mill of fire, points to an alarming state of indiscipline among the adult labour force (only one apprentice to be found among them); and the numerous informations laid by the labourers themselves against the poor-law officers for refusal to grant relief are far from suggesting that they were cowed by an oppressive exercise of authority'.[21] The problem of labour relations at Arnold can be considered under four headings. The well-known reluctance of domestic workers to enter the mills, coupled with the scarcity of labour in the last decade of the eighteenth century, provides one approach for the analysis. Other factors to be examined are the depressed condition of most of the framework knitters at Arnold, the unpopularity (in and after 1791) of the Jacobin political ideas of Robert and John Davison, and the collision of the firm with the powerful woolcombers' trade-unions when Hawksley introduced Cartwright's 'Big Ben' combing-machine at Arnold.

The difficulty of recruiting labour was, as we have seen, common to all cotton and worsted mills in the Midlands, but was particularly acute at Arnold. The village was only four miles from Nottingham and must have suffered a constant drain of its best workers to the centre of the cotton-hosiery industry where the best-paid employment was to be found. Arnold Mill was growing rapidly between 1793 and 1800; over these seven years the number of apprentices increased from 50 to 600, while the domestic and adult labour force was built up from modest numbers—perhaps 650—to 1,200.[22] The acute shortage of workers is reflected in Davison & Hawksley's series of advertisements for labour, and in the wording of these advertisements. Two of them call for 'young women, and a quantity of either boys or girls as apprentices, *from any parish or otherwise,* nine years old or upwards'.[23]

The strict discipline and regular hours of the factories were anathema to the local population of framework knitters and their families, and the Arnold Overseers' account-books show that the workhouse was a regular source of labour for the firm, workers being drawn from places as far away as Leicester (25 miles) and Wirksworth (35 miles). With such a force, there was bound to be management problems. 'In so great a number of apprentices', Robert Davison pointed out, 'there will be some base and refractory ones; you who are framework knitters and keep but few know this by experience . . .'.[24] The kind of problems which the Arnold

Mill management had to contend with are illustrated in Table 11.

Labour Problems at Davison & Hawksley's Arnold Mill. Analysis of Cases brought before Arnold Petty Sessions, 1794–1802

Year	Absconded	Rioting, Assault	Disobedience and Spoiling work	Theft and fraud	Other
Dec. 1794	3	1	—	—	—
1795	13	—	—	—	—
1796	19	—	1	1	—
1797	—	—	3	—	—
1798	8	6	4	1	1
1799	3	2	—	1	1
1800	2	3	1	3	—
1801	—	—	—	—	—
Jan.-Mar. 1802	1	7	—	—	—
	49	19	9	6	2

Most of the offences were fairly trivial and show a tendency to diminish as the firm established itself at Arnold. The riots of 1802 were over Davison's attempt to change the course of a road in the village, and may be taken as an exception to the general trend. Nonetheless, two things suggest that industrial relations were in particular bad odour in the village, and the first is a comparison with two other firms for which detailed information has survived. Unfortunately, there is no precise information on the size of the labour force employed by Robinsons at Bulwell and Papplewick, but as they had six mills, at least five of which were modelled on the Arkwright enterprises, the firm probably had at least 1,500 factory workers and no doubt employed a large number of framework knitters as well. Their total work-force was very likely comparable with the 2,000 employed by Davison & Hawksley in 1800. Nevertheless, the number of cases which Robinsons' brought before Arnold Petty Sessions were much smaller:

TABLE 12

Labour Problems at Robinsons' Mills. Analysis of Cases brought before Arnold Petty Sessions, 1794–1802

Year	Absconded	Riot	Disobedience and Spoiling work	Theft	Other
Dec. 1794	—	—	—	—	—
1795	3	—	—	—	—
1796	2	—	—	—	—
1797	—	—	5	—	—
1798	—	—	—	1	—
1799	4	6	—	—	—
1800	—	—	—	—	—
1801	—	—	—	1	—
1802	—	—	—	—	—
TOTAL	9	6	6	2	0

Toplis & Co. had nearly 600 apprentices at Cuckney in 1800 and, as previously noticed, the development of this firm parallels that of Davison & Hawksley. In all, 119 Toplis apprentices absconded over a period of nineteen years—an average of 6·25 a year—of which only one was sent to the Southwell House of Correction. Most of Davison & Hawksley's fifty-nine cases, some adult and some children, were sent there. Either Toplises' and Robinsons' were more lax in the treatment of their apprentices and workpeople or, more likely, labour relations were more difficult at Arnold Mill.

Fragments of information suggest a more or less continuous hostility to the firm, William Stumbles' remarks being a second-generation echo of the odium in which the firm was held. Two or three incidents call for particular attention. A handbill issued during a bread famine in the autumn of 1800 infers that the Arnold Mill proprietors were popularly regarded as a kind of Bishop Hatto, whose barns were full while the poor starved outside, whereas their correspondence with Nottingham Corporation show that, on the contrary, they were offering to alleviate the shortage of grain by grinding corn free at their own steam mill.[25] In March 1802, the Petty Sessional records note 'five men reported for riotous behaviour at *their* licensed Methodist chapel at Arnold'. The chapel was the Old Meadows Chapel which was started by William Huddlestone and George Wall, two preachers who were managers at Arnold Mill and whose names appear frequently in the Petty Sessional records reporting workers to the Justices. It seems that the tension between villagers and the management at the mill had grown to such a pitch that the members of the Methodist chapel had revolted against their leaders.[26]

In 1798 and again in June 1802, riots broke out in Arnold, ostensibly because of Davison's attempt to close a footpath, and a military detachment had to be called from Nottingham to quell the demonstrators. The multitude, according to the *Nottingham Journal*, were 'deluded by a few designing men'. These incidents, together with reports of threatening letters, attacks on Davison's house and garden (1794, 1798, 1800, 1802) and his carriage (1799), contrast with the evident care of Davison & Hawksley for their employees.[27] Clearly there were other factors at work in the situation, and to these we now turn.

During the second half of the eighteenth century the framework knitters in the common branches (i.e., those engaged on the plain, unskilled work) gradually deteriorated into a depressed class as their wage-rates remained static while prices rose. A minority of the knitters engaged in the fancy hosiery and lace branches earned good wages (20s to 50s weekly), but the majority (about two-thirds of the whole number) could earn no more than 12s weekly. The skilled branches of the industry were concentrated in Nottingham, where the lucrative fashion work was undertaken under the supervision of merchant hosiers, and where a coterie of framesmiths and knitters in intimate daily contact with each other were constantly contriving new meshes and new garments on the versatile stocking-frame. The surrounding villages were the home of the less-skilled knitters, and any villager with mechanical ability found it necessary to move to

Nottingham to have his talent properly rewarded, or to find patronage for some innovation.

In Nottingham itself, the competition for workshop space and for employment by the gentlemen-hosiers of the town forced the common branches into the rural environs, the umbra of the manufacturing area. Thus a continual process of selective migration removed the talent and energy from the periphery to the centre, robbing villages like Arnold of any share in the prosperity which the hosiery industry's growth might have brought them. Already, in 1790, the knitters in these villages were complaining that it was impossible for a man to maintain himself and his family with 'honesty and decency'; and over the next two decades a highly-charged atmosphere developed which finally exploded into the era of Luddite machine smashing.[28] Davison & Hawksley employed a large number of outworkers—probably over a thousand—on the manufacture of plain cotton- and worsted-stockings, the most poorly-paid products of the hosiery manufacture.[29] The discontents of these workers, and others in Arnold, provided fertile ground in which agitations over minor issues grew to major proportions and threatened to strangle the whole enterprise.

The plight of the framework knitters and their families was clearly a cause of discontent and resentment among the Arnold villagers, but it is not sufficient to explain Davison & Hawksley's labour problems, since other firms with a better labour record (notably Robinsons') also had framework knitters in the common branches working for them and living around their mills. It is necessary to consider other factors in the situation, and the Radical political ideas of the Davison brothers suggest another possible approach.

Robert Davison was a member of High Pavement Presbyterian Chapel, Nottingham, and probably his partner was too. In the last quarter of the eighteenth century, under the leadership of its outstanding minister, the Rev George Walker, FRS, the chapel became a centre of progressive political as well as theological thought.

Walker became the voice of Radicalism in the east Midlands, ably supported by his friend, Major John Cartwright, and carried many of his wealthy congregation with him. A 'violent party spirit' had existed in Nottingham from the era of the Civil Wars, and this spirit quickly revived when the French Revolution broke out.[30] In the reaction that set in in 1792, the democrats or Jacobins, as the Radicals were called, were marked out as victims of popular fury, and the properties of several High Pavement spinners suffered. In April 1792, the Nottingham mill of Benjamin & Charles Morley and a house of Alderman William Smith were attacked and damaged. In August 1793 the house of Joseph Oldknow, a partner in the Pleasley mill, was assailed by a mob, and was only saved when the owner discharged a blunderbus into the crowd. Less than a year later, when there were uncontrolled riots in Nottingham, an attempt was made to fire Denison's newly-built cotton mill in the town, and some tenements and the mill workshops were burned down. (Writing soon afterwards to Boulton & Watt, Denison said that he planned to sail to America with his family to seek 'a retreat from this scene of profligacy and persecution.'[31]) There is no record of attacks on the industrial or private property of those who conformed with the Established Church and orthodox political mood.

In spite of these attacks on the property of his friends, and difficult labour relations at Arnold, Robert Davison continued to play a prominent role in the violent politics of Nottingham. In 1795 he appears as spokesman of a group of Radical dissenters, closely connected with the Corporation and calling themselves the 'New Society'. The Society made themselves unpopular by opposing Pitt's proposals to change the law of treason and sedition, and they particularly objected to the threat to limit 'the rights of political discussion and remonstrance, individually or in popular meetings'. In 1797, both Davison and Hawksley played leading parts in public meetings in Nottingham calling for the resignation of Pitt's ministry and, in the riotous election of 1803, Davison was one of the most prominent figures in the controversy.[32] Nottingham was a parliamentary borough with a large electorate, many of whom lived in Arnold and other surrounding villages. But not all the framework knitters who had a vote supported the Radical cause, and an analysis of the poll-books shows that in the three elections of 1796, 1803 and 1806 their support was almost evenly divided between the Whig and Tory candidates:

Election Year	Whig Votes	Tory Votes
1796	333	467
1803	615	454
1806	717	587

Arnold politics were unusually volatile; an unpopular hosier's house had been attacked there in 1778, fifteen years before Davison & Hawksley had moved to the village. One of the firm's managers wrote to a friend that the local people 'are more earnest after news than any I know of. They are either mad with joy, or half-dead with disappointment'.[33] The country workers, no less than those in the town, had not yet learned the tolerance which Davison espoused and, entering into the full turmoil of local politics, he could hardly expect to escape some of the buffets. An idealist, he risked the safety of his business for the political cause in which he believed.

The only other member of Davison's group with a mill in or near Nottingham was Denison, whose £15,000 factory was closed down after the riots of 1794. Most cotton-spinners in the locality did not share Davison's advanced views; the Robinsons and Elliots, for instance, were Anglicans, and Robert Hall of Basford was a Methodist for whom the local people had a special affection. The other cotton-spinners who were members of the 'New Society'—John Hancock, Thomas Wakefield and Joseph Oldknow—had mills in the Mansfield area, fourteen miles to the north of Nottingham so that, by a coincidence of geography and politics, Davison & Hawksley were marked out as scapegoats of popular ebullience. However, popular contempt for the firm was not only founded on their performance in the local political arena. After the collapse of Edmund Cartwright's pioneer enterprise at Doncaster, Davison & Hawksley assumed the role of innovating entrepreneurs in mechanised combing, and quickly ran head-on into the vested interests of the wool-combers' union.

The centre of the Midlands worsted industry was at Leicester, where the woolcombers are said to have been responsible for the organization of their fellow-craftsmen in the adjacent parts of the Midlands. The Leicester woolcombers were behind the riots of 1787 which resulted in the expulsion of mechanized worsted-spinning from the town and, encouraged by this success, they planned to promote a Bill in Parliament to ban the new machines from use in their trade. Though this plan failed, they did petition Parliament, calling attention to the alarming tendency of the machines to create unemployment among 15,500 spinners, many of whom would be members of their own families. Combers, on the average, gave employment to about ten domestic spinners each.[34]

Some interesting details of the woolcombers' organization emerged from an inquiry in 1794. The combers had trade clubs or societies in most of the Midlands centres of the worsted industry, the organization being centred on Leicester, a town from which Davison & Hawksley drew a large number of their combers. The clubs were linked by a 'house of call' system, whereby combers travelling to seek employment could obtain hospitality with other combers in different parts of the country. According to one witness before the Commons inquiry, nine out of ten woolcombers belonged to one or other of these clubs. William Toplis maintained that the clubs were 'governed by laws or rules of their own, by which they (the combers) are restrained from taking apprentices (except their eldest sons) or extending their number by instructing the apprentices or servants of their employers . . .'.

The combers' solidarity is supposed to have been complete: 'if a body of woolcombers disagree with their employers, no other set of woolcombers dare to succeed them until the difference is done away with'. And though the combers were employed in large numbers by the masters of the new worsted mills (Toplis, for instance,

said he had employed 100 to 150 of them 'for several years'), they
refused to be subjected to factory discipline. Toplis insisted that his
woolcombers could 'upon an average, earn from 25s to 28s per week,
when they chose to work every day, whereas the average wages paid
to them seldom exceed 10s per week, and this difference arises solely
from their refusing to do more work and not from it being withheld
from them'.[35] It is interesting to conjecture that the 'alarming state
of indiscipline' which Professor Chambers identified at Davison &
Hawksley's Arnold Mill may have been encouraged by the habits
of the combers working there.

During the trade boom of 1792–93, worsted-spinners like Davison & Hawksley and Toplis & Co. experienced considerable difficulty in recruiting a sufficient number of combers to meet the needs
of their growing business, and both opened new, multi-storey,
steam-powered mills at this time. Their desperate need of combers
is reflected in advertisements in the local press:

> To Woolcombers. Wm. Toplis & Co. have opened a free shop, at
> Mansfield . . . for Combers from any part of the kingdom. The prices
> given are equal to any society, and steady good workmen may make
> very handsome wages.
> TO WOOLCOMBERS. WANTED, ANY NUMBER AT ARNOLD MILL.

In spite of these appeals they were unable to recruit the numbers
they needed, and turned to the possibility of mechanized combing.[36]

In 1793, the only combing-machine was the 'Big Ben' invented
and patented by Edmund Cartwright and still in an early stage of
development when he had to give up his mill at Doncaster. At
Arnold, Hawksley made some improvements to 'Big Ben' (in return
for a quarter of the royalties) and in 1794 six sets of combers were
built which made an annual profit of £6,600 for the next seven
years. Thus, in effect, Davison & Hawksley were the innovating
entrepreneurs in mechanized combing, though Cartwright's invention was shortly pirated by Toplis and John Adams at Bromsgrove.[37]

Although Cartwright's machine was not capable of producing the
finest combings, it did save labour in preparing the coarser yarns.

According to the combers, 'one machine only, with the assistance of one person and four or five children, will perform as much labour as thirty men in the customary manual manner'. The 'Big Ben' machines also had an important advantage over hand-combing in that they produced 'one continued even flux' of combed fibres, whilst the product of the hand-comber was 'in short lengths with irregular ends, subject to both loss and imperfection in uniting them for the purpose of spinning'.[38] Together, the combing and roller-spinning machines enabled the worsted-spinner to make a continuous mechanized process of the whole process from the fleece to the yarn.

Needless to say, the combing-machines met with uncompromising opposition from the woolcombers' unions, which resorted to every kind of stratagem to prevent the use of the machines.[39] Davison & Hawksley did little to appease the combers, and when they refused to teach their trade to apprentices and other workers, the firm advertised for young men to be taught the trade. The advertisement does not actually say that the firm was looking for men to train as combers, but a subsequent announcement in the local press confirms the reader's suspicions.

> Wanted at Arnold Mill, A number of young men from 16 to 30 years old who would hire for a term of years to learn a good and comfortable trade; at which they may work in all weathers and earn the first week 8s and every following week one shilling more, till they can readily get 21s or more. . . .

> Wanted, 20 young men to comb wool by which they will very soon earn a clear guinea or more weekly.[40]

Toplises managed to get a few of their parish apprentices transferred to Worksop woolcombers, and very likely Davison & Hawksley did the same in their locality.

When the woolcombers failed to check this contravention of their apprenticeship regulations, their union tried to bring about a strike at the Arnold mill. A letter sent by the Bromsgrove branch of the union to Arnold is worth quoting in full, even though the meaning of some phrases is obscure:

N

10 August 1795
Gentlemen,
    Knowing that Big Bens are a destruction to our trade, it is our
opinion, with many more Societies, that you should turn out and
leave Ben to hack for himself; and inform the apprentices that they
will have no right to their trades, and we hope that Curtes and
Grastick will turn out with you, and there will be no notice of their
learning the apprentices.
    Gentlemen, if we tamely set down to hack for machines, in a little
time we may do nothing else.
                                Done by order, WM. NOON, B.R.

Davison & Hawksley retaliated by calling a meeting of worsted
mill-owners and announcing in the *Nottingham Journal* that members of the meeting would 'post the names of the members of the
Society from whence the letter was sent at the different comb-shops,
where they cannot expect to be employed'. They threatened to
prosecute any future workman's combination, and made good their
threat in 1800 when they secured the conviction of one of their
workmen for trying to organize a strike.[41]

In 1796, 'Cartwright's patent combing-machines' were advertised extensively in the local press, and Robert Davison was listed
as one of the four agents. The advertisements claimed that the
machines produced 'a superior article' (which was not strictly true)
and that they secured to the manufacturer 'an absolute command
of his necessary supply of combed wool at critical seasons without
advancement of price', an oblique reference to the irregular working
habits of the woolcombers which would have aggravated relations
between the Arnold Mill proprietors and the combers even further,
if indeed that were possible.[42]

The subsequent tactics of the woolcombers are obscure, but it
seems possible that the demonstrations which took place at Arnold
in February 1798 and in March and June 1802 may have had angry
woolcombers at their centre. However, by and large, the impression
left is that, in view of the unpopularity of the firm with large sectors
of the local population (framework knitters, anti-Jacobins and
woolcombers) the partners emerged comparatively unmolested.
And while it is not surprising that a woman employee should have

threatened to set fire to the mill, it is remarkable that some of her male contemporaries did not actually do so. The history of Luddism shows that there were enough people in Arnold who were not afraid to take the law into their own hands, and it may be fair to conclude that Davison & Hawksley suffered less trouble than they might have done because they treated their apprentices and workpeople well— a claim they certainly made for themselves—and built up a loyal labour force.

A popular form of criticizing the factory system in the eighteenth century was to maintain that the health and morals of the child apprentices were being neglected, so that public concern was focused on the children. Davison & Hawksley may have deserved their unpopularity, but there is no reason to suppose they neglected their juvenile labour force, and some evidence that they went to considerable lengths to win a reputation as good employers. Nevertheless, a fundamental inconsistency in the firm's behaviour is obvious. On the one hand, they were clearly anxious to be benevolent employers, and to let it be known that they were acting as Christian gentlemen in their business careers. On the other hand, the political careers of Robert and John Davison, the work regimen established by the firm, and the uncompromising attitude taken to the woolcombers all strongly suggest a doctrinaire attachment to the idea of *laissez-faire* rather than to the moral teaching of Christianity. Very likely, Davison & Hawksley did not see the two sets of principles as being at variance and it is interesting to enquire how they came to hold them with such earnestness, and whether other cotton- and worsted-spinners shared their views.

Robert and John Davison's membership of High Pavement Chapel while the Rev George Walker was minister has already been alluded to. Walker was a friend and correspondent of Joseph Priestley and a former pupil of Adam Smith at Glasgow, and though his papers have been lost, it is clear from his *Memoir* that his ideology was similar to that of Priestley and a number of other dissenting clergymen, most of whom became Unitarian in the last decade of the eighteenth century. This group of ministers and their following were Radical in politics and ideology, placing strong emphasis on the value of humanity. This stemmed from the doctrine, peculiar to Unitarians and largely fashioned by Priestley, of justification by works alone. The dissenting Radicals were characteristically upper middle-class and paternalistic in their attitude to the working-classes. However, in their economic thinking, Priestley and his following accepted the political economy of Adam Smith, without any important reservations. They were thus wedded to a belief in the necessity for freedom of initiative for the entrepreneurs. In his twenty-five years at High Pavement, Walker showed a particular interest in manufacturing industry—he was a partner and Nottingham agent for Major Cartwright's mill at Retford, and wrote one of the earliest treatises on the applications of the steam-engine—so that he could hardly avoid the implications of his ideology for the manufacturer.[43]

Davison and Hawksley were not the only followers of the Unitarian ideology, and at least seven other cotton-spinners were represented among the High Pavement membership. There were Robert Denison of Denison, Oates & Co.; all three partners in Hancock & Wakefield; Charles Morley; Thomas Oldknow and Henry Hollins of Oldknow, Cowpe & Co.; Alderman William Smith of the Radford Mill, and Elihu Samuel Fellows of Dalley, Fellows & Co. of Wirksworth. Henry Green also appears to have been a member for a period. In other centres of the Midlands cotton-worsted industry, the leading figures were Unitarians: the Strutts at Derby, Coltman and Whetstone at Leicester, John and William Parkes at Warwick, Major Cartwright at Retford, Samuel Unwin and John Bacon at Sutton-in-Ashfield, and the Churchill family at Shepshed.[44]

Although the spinning-mills were scattered and in some cases isolated, the spinners were a closely-integrated group in positions of leadership in provincial society. The High Pavement Chapel membership dominated Nottingham Corporation from 1689 to

1832, and Major Cartwright and the Rev George Walker were leaders of progressive political thought in the east Midlands. Philosophic societies were started by Coltman in Leicester (about 1780), by Jedediah Strutt and Dr Erasmus Darwin in Derby in 1784 and by the Rev George Walker and the Rev Gilbert Wakefield (another celebrated Radical) in Nottingham at about the same time.[45] Again, close links with Priestley are discernible. Dr Darwin was a founder-member of the famous Birmingham Lunar Society, Wakefield was contemporary with Priestley at Warrington Academy, and John Parkes' son married Priestley's daughter. There is no doubt that the philosophic societies discussed political and social questions as well as scientific subjects, and both in these and in the Unitarian chapels industrialists imbibed Radical political and religious ideas, and the new economic orthodoxy.

Not all spinners were Radical dissenters, of course, and a number of leaders of the industry—the Arkwrights, Peels, Evans, Robinsons and Wilkes, for instance—were Anglicans. However, it does seem that the dissenting Radicals, who were enthusiasts, exercised a decisive influence over their friends in the industry. The links of the Strutt family with the Arkwrights, the Evans, the Toplises and other Derbyshire manufacturers, are well-known. Elizabeth Strutt twice married into the Evans family, and while Thomas Evans had been 'attentive to the interests of the employees of his manufacturing concerns', his daughter-in-law took her concern further. 'The grand desideratum in politics', she wrote in 1793, 'is the diffusion of knowledge and morals among the poor. This the manufacturer has it in his power considerably to promote and is culpable in the neglect of it'.[46] However, by 1816, the Strutts maintained that they had achieved some success in civilizing the working-classes in Belper and Duffield. 'It is well-known in this neighbourhood that *before* the establishment of these works', they wrote, 'the inhabitants were notorious for vice and immorality, and many of the children were maintained by begging; now their industry, decorous behaviour, attendance on public worship, and general good conduct, compared with the neighbouring villages, where no manufactures are established, is very conspicuous'.[47]

Finally, it is important to notice how closely the class of new manufacturers were integrated, and this may be illustrated by counting the connections of Samuel Unwin of Sutton-in-Ashfield, a prominent dissenter who built the Unitarian chapel in his native village. Unwin's partner was James Heygate, the City banker, who was also in partnership with John Pares of Cardom, Pares & Co., Calver Bridge. John Pares' daughters married into the Paget family (later partners in Oldknow, Cowpe & Co. of Pleasley) and the Greg family of Styall. Two of Unwin's daughters were married to cotton-spinners, one to John White, the Chesterfield hosier who was a partner of Robert Hall in the firm of Halls & White, cotton-spinners, Basford, the other to Elihu Fellows of Dalley, Fellows & Co. of Wirksworth. Unwin's closest personal friend was John Coltman of Leicester, the pioneer of mechanized worsted-spinning and partner in Coltman & Adams of Bromsgrove. Coltman's workman and protegé, Joseph Brookhouse, became a partner in Parkes, Brook-house & Crompton of Warwick. Unwin's residence at his country house at Tansley, just above Matlock, would certainly bring him into contact with Arkwright and his circle, not least because Unwin's carriage was well-received at Welbeck Abbey, the Notting-hamshire home of the Dukes of Portland.[48] A similar circle was built up round Joseph Wilkes of Measham and Arkwright at Crom-ford, and even a small country manufacturer like Nicholas Cress-well of Edale had a brother who was a woolstapler in Huddersfield and a brother-in-law a silk merchant in Macclesfield.

It is not too much to suggest that the Unitarian teaching was not only an important influence on the old dissenting families, but also on their friends and connections. Among this whole group the welfare of workers was a moral as well as an economic concern but, for all that, their doctrinaire attachment to unpopular political views and to a free-market economy made them targets for angry resentment. Such feelings were often expressed in terms of calumnious reports about the treatment of children, but also erupted into resistance to discipline, riots, and appeals to the magistrates, and sometimes even to the central government. There was bound to be hostility to factory discipline, but this was only one cause of poor labour relations. The angry complaints about the treatment of factory children are a distant and imperfect echo of the collision between the ideology of the urban manufacturing class and the innate conservatism and resentment of the working-classes.

3. Ellis Needham and the *Memoir of Robert Blincoe*

It is now almost sixty years since Paul Mantoux in his *Industrial Revolution in the Eighteenth Century* considered the employment of pauper apprentices in the early cotton-mills and drew attention to a unique account of sadism and suffering, John Brown's *Memoir of Robert Blincoe*. Mantoux accepted this account of an apprentice's miserable life at its face value, as indeed have subsequent writers on the subject of factory apprenticeship, despite growing evidence that the 'evils' of the factory system have been much overstated.

It is worth recalling initially what is known of the author and the circumstances in which the *Memoir* was written. John Brown has been described as 'a somewhat erratic journalist' whose life ended in suicide in 1825. The pamphlet was a contribution to the literature issued in connection with the agitation against 'White Slavery', and first appeared in *The Lion*, a Radical periodical published by R. Carlile, 'a violent partisan'. The political impact was so considerable that it was reprinted in *The Poor Man's Advocate* the same year. In 1832 John Doherty, the well-known agitator for factory reform, published Brown's work as a separate *Memoir*. Seven years later Mrs Frances Trollope borrowed material from the *Memoir* for her novel, *The Life and Adventures of Michael Armstrong, the Factory Boy*, which purports to be an exposure of the worst horrors of the Industrial Revolution in the expanding textile districts. Several historians have recognized this melodrama as a valid commentary on the subject of juvenile labour in cotton mills.[49]

Robert Blincoe, who supplied the original material in 1822, became a moderately successful cotton manufacturer in Stockport.[50] (His early experience under factory masters does not appear to have deterred him from becoming one of them.) It has perhaps been assumed too readily that the injured and innocent Blincoe could have no axe to grind and that his testimony could be trusted implicitly. In fact, the evidence available when Mantoux wrote should have made him at least suspicious for, in a final section of the book, Brown castigated Samuel Oldknow's mills at Mellor. The publication of Professor Unwin's *Samuel Oldknow and the Arkwrights* (1924) demonstrated that this was a model community, and that Brown's remarks could only be interpreted as irrelevant political propaganda.

The 'villain' of the *Memoir* is a cotton manufacturer named Ellis Needham, the principal partner in a firm known as Needham, Frith & Co., which started spinning about 1782. Sufficient is known about the partners and the history of the firm to interpret its origins, rise and decline. In the *Memoir of Robert Blincoe* it is recorded that 'like most of the fraternity', Needham's 'origin was obscure'. This is not true. Needham came of a well-known local family, and his father, Ellis Needham senior, owned extensive estates in Chapel-en-le-Frith, Tideswell, Bakewell, and other parishes in the Peak District of Derbyshire. He appears to have had a successful career, for he inherited a much smaller portion from his father, a Peak Forest 'yeoman'. Needham senior shared his property between his four sons, and Ellis took freehold and leasehold estates in the vicinity of Chapel. The Jurors' Books refer to him as 'gentleman' or 'farmer' of Hargate Wall, Tideswell, but he must have sold most of his inheritance to build Litton Mill as, by 1795, his farming interests were confined to eighteen rented acres. He mixed freely with the smaller landowners and manufacturers of the district, enjoyed entertaining, and was a friend of the Vicar of Tideswell and a leading member of the town's Anglican congregation.[51]

There is no direct evidence that Ellis Needham had any experience in the textile industry before the opening of Litton Mill. However, both Chapel and Tideswell came within the outer orbit of the domestic industry based on Manchester, and Tideswell and the adjacent hamlet of Litton had a framework-knitting industry. It may well be that Ellis Needham's grandfather originated his family's rise to fortune as he had dealings with a Stockport yarn merchant. Certainly many other farmers in the district prospered as agents of Manchester and Stockport merchants. Hargreaves' jenny made an early appearance in the district, and it was ownership of these machines that first drew many manufacturers and merchants into spinning.[52]

Ellis Needham's partner was Thomas Frith, a Tideswell farmer whose family came from Chapel. No more is known about Frith's early years than about Needham's, other than that he was a land-owner and churchman. Again it is only possible to surmise an early interest in cotton, beginning with a loom or two and gradually building up as the local and Manchester markets extended.[53]

In 1779, Arkwright opened a small mill by the River Wye at Cress-brook, about two miles south-east of Tideswell and strategically placed to supply the growing domestic weaving and hosiery indus-tries of the district. When Arkwright's patent was nullified in 1781, a number of imitators came on the scene, among them Needham, Frith & Company who built a mill on the model of Arkwright's enterprise, a mile farther up the River Wye. The partnership was sufficiently early in the field to reap the unusually high profits accruing to innovating entrepreneurs and, in 1784, the power of the mill was enlarged by building a weir, probably to divert the Wye into a channel to drive the water-wheel, which had hitherto derived its power from a stream rushing off the precipitous hillside. How-ever, a sign of weakness appeared in 1786, when Needham tried unsuccessfully to sell the 900-spindle mill.[54]

In the last two or three years of the eighteenth century a contrac-tion set in in the Midlands textile industry. Firms distant from the centre of technical development in Manchester found it difficult to keep pace with the rapid progress of the industry, and Litton, according to Blincoe, was engaged only on the coarsest work. The capital required for entering warp-spinning in the earliest years had been modest; Edale Mill, near Chapel-en-le-Frith which, like Litton, was built on the model of Cressbrook, was insured for a mere £1,000 in 1795.[55] The more economic multi-storey, steam-powered factories offered incisive competition for the small country mills.

To these troubles, common to the industry of the Peak District, were added other mishaps and difficulties. Frith withdrew from the partnership in 1799, and in 1805 the mill was narrowly saved from a serious fire. Six years later the water-wheel broke and the mill was stopped for a whole month in winter. Ellis Needham's son, who by now was managing the mill, told a visiting JP that it was 'useless'. The run-down of the mill during these years is evidenced by a reduction in the number of apprentices from 160 in 1803 to 80 in 1807.[56] These were the years during which Blincoe served his time at Litton and without taking the analysis further, it is clear that this was not a normal competitive cotton-spinning mill, but an enterprise starved of capital, struggling through years of depressed trade, and probably poorly-managed as well.

The evidence of other mills leaves little doubt that the employment of parish apprentices was less and less profitable, and the system was generally abandoned in the first years of the nineteenth century. In any case, as the first generation of apprentices intermarried and produced further children, it became less necessary to bring in apprentices from outside. However, both the Litton and Cressbrook mills imported apprentices for more than thirty years. The explanation, implicit in the Blincoe *Memoir* and made quite clear by Farey, is that after completing their time the apprentices, many of them girls, were discharged from the mills, often to become a charge on the poor-rates of the Derbyshire parishes in which the mills were situated. The increasing burden of these rates made the cotton manufacturers and their mills unpopular, particularly in a parish like Tideswell where the decline of the lead-mining industry was already creating unemployment. Manufacturers were also disliked by the local landowners because of their avidity to invest their 'acquired wealth in the purchase of lands around them, at higher prices than other purchasers could be found to give'. At the close of 1814, Needham was made the conspicuous victim of his own folly. Farmers in Tideswell petitioned Lord Scarsdale with complaints about the burden on the parish of Needham's former apprentices, and he was given notice to quit. The immediate consequence was that eighty more apprentices were thrown on the parish, some of whom may have been taken on when the mill was re-opened by Robert Needham the following spring.[57]

Having sketched the history of Ellis Needham and his mill, it is now possible to examine the *Memoir of Robert Blincoe* in more detail. Blincoe's complaints can be summarized briefly. The hours of labour at the mill were said to be excessively long—occasionally 'sixteen hours without rest or food'. The food was monotonous and the apprentices so seldom washed and were so poorly clothed that they were in a 'filthy and ragged condition'. The dormitory accommodation was inadequate; fifty boys slept in a room in the apprentice-house which smelt 'from oil and filth'. Corporal punishment was frequent, the overlookers being 'fierce and brutal'. Needham himself is pictured as a beast who took a delight in the suffering of the apprentices. Medical attention was inadequate, and when 'contagious fevers rose in the mill . . . the number of deaths (was) . . . such as to require frequent supplies of parish children to fill up the vacancies'.

The most revolting part of the *Memoir* is that in which the sadism of Needham and one of his overseers is described. While this bestial behaviour cannot be condoned, it is important to relate it to the conscience of the period. Cruel punishments to children were not unusual in the eighteenth century, and two of those described in such horrific detail in the *Memoir* were, in fact, advocated by progressive educationists—notably Lancaster—at the beginning of the last century. Lancaster worked out an elaborate code of rewards and punishments, among which was 'the log', a piece of wood weighing four to six pounds, which was fixed to the neck of the child guilty of his (or her) first talking offence. On the least motion one way or another the log operated as a dead weight on the neck. Needham clearly tried to copy this progressive idea of the age. More serious offences found their appropriate punishment in the Lancastrian code; handcuffs, the 'caravan', pillory and stocks, and 'the cage'. The latter was a sack or basket in which more serious offenders were suspended from the ceiling.[58] Needham clearly borrowed this idea, too, though his children are alleged to have been suspended by their arms over the machines.

Fortunately, we are not dependent on the Blincoe *Memoir* for our information on the Litton mill. Some of the allegations made in the pamphlet are supported by the report of two county magistrates appointed to inspect mills under the provisions of Peel's Health and Morals of Apprentices Act (1802). In 1807, Joshua Denman visited the mill and reported that 'Two rooms in this mill were clean, and all the working-rooms whitewashed, and in all there was a free ventilation, but the privies (were) not well-conducted. There are about eighty apprentices, many of them I believe from the Foundling Hospital, who are kept in a lodging-house at no great distance from the mill. These apprentices work successively in the night, though this is expressly prohibited by the Act. It is by no means certain to what hours they are confined. They are not instructed during the working hours. . . . Though there are separate apartments for males and females in the lodging-house, the rooms appear crowded; one in particular, in which are lodged sixteen apprentices, though in my opinion eight ought to be the utmost number in it. Upon the whole, from the dimensions of the building it appears almost impossible to contain so many persons consistently with health and anything approaching to comfort'.

In 1811, further details were provided by M. M. Middleton, JP, 'I found the house in which the apprentices board and lodge very clean; but two of them having come to me with a complaint of being worked too hard, and of not having sufficient support, I thought it right to examine some of the apprentices upon oath as to the facts they complained of, and the substance of their deposition is as follows, viz., that they go into the mill about ten minutes before six o'clock in the morning, and stay there till from ten to fifteen minutes after nine in the evening, excepting the time allowed for dinner, which is from half to three-quarters of an hour; that they have water porridge for breakfast and supper, and generally oatcake and treacle, or oatcake and poor broth for dinner; that they are instructed in writing and reading on Sunday.'

There can be little doubt that apprentices at Litton suffered from long hours, monotonous diet and crowded living conditions. However, though they had opportunity to make their complaints, brutal treatment, inadequate clothing and filthy accommodation are not mentioned. Nor is sickness or death referred to.[59] It is fair to suspend judgment and examine further evidence.

This is provided by John Farey in the third volume of his *Agriculture of Derbyshire*. In the course of his long and detailed survey of Derbyshire in 1807–09, Farey visited Needham and commended him in his book as an agricultural improver. The reader of Farey is conscious of an unusually able mind, meticulous in observation and scrupulous in judgment. In the course of a carefully composed passage on the cotton mills of the country, Farey attempted to dispose of some apparently popular opinions about child-labour in the mills. 'I am far from intending to insinuate that great care, and even kind attention, is not bestowed on the cotton-mill apprentices in general throughout this county', he wrote. 'In several cases I have seen this to be the case, and a rather sedulous inquiry on this head from others has not disclosed even suspicious hints to the contrary in any instance, as far as I can recollect; nor am I disposed to think or represent that any very considerable or remedial degrees of vice or immorality exist in these apprentice-houses or mills, nor that their employ is as unhealthy as some have represented. . . .'[60]

Farey's proposition that the abuses of the apprenticeship system
had been much exaggerated is lent support by the records of mortality at Litton and other mills contained in the Tideswell burial-
registers. Some time after the Cressbrook mill was burned down,
the site was purchased and the mill rebuilt by a firm called Barker
Bossley & Co. The managing partner of this enterprise was William
Newton (1750–1830), a Tideswell machine-builder whose sonnets
earned him the title of 'the Minstrel of the Peak'. Newton enjoyed
the reputation of a model employer, and it is therefore instructive
to compare mortality rates among apprentices at the Litton and
Cressbrook mills over the first thirty years of their existence:

TABLE 13

*Mortality of Pauper Apprentices employed in Factories in the Parish of
Tideswell, 1780–1810*

Deaths at Litton Mill	6
Deaths at Cressbrook Mill	6
Deaths at T. Gorton's (mill?)	3
Other apprentice deaths	1
	16 deaths

Source: Bishop's Transcripts of Tideswell Parish Registers. (Lichfield Diocesan Registry).

Even if it is true that 'part of the dead were buried in Taddington
churchyard' (which came within the parish of Bakewell), the statement that the number of deaths was 'such as to require frequent
supplies of parish children to fill up the vacancies' hardly seems
justified. The apprentices were attended by 'a medical gentleman',
and the occasion when there were 'forty boys sick at once' may well
have been during the smallpox epidemic (1803), which struck down
several apprentices at Robinson's mills at Linby and Davison &
Hawksley's mill at Arnold.[61]

Is it possible to reconcile the Blincoe *Memoir* with the reports of
the county magistrates and Farey's observations? The circumstances and style in which the pamphlet was written, the character
of the author and, above all, the number of misrepresentations we
have already discovered, clearly make the remainder of the work

suspect. It is only possible to rely on that part of the *Memoir* which finds corroboration in the magistrates' reports, and these appear less inconsistent with Farey when we begin to examine the regimen established by firms recognized both by contemporaries and recent historians as model employers. It is not necessary to look beyond the Peak District for this purpose. William Newton was recognized as a model employer largely because he provided gardens for his apprentices, and ran a choir and orchestra. It is less well-known (though it appears in the magistrates' reports) that he worked his apprentices from 6 am to 8 pm six days a week, an hour shorter than the working day at Litton, but hardly justification for the contrasts that exist between the mills in the literature. A cripple child employed there in 1800 was beaten by the overlooker and ran away, and there is no reason to suppose that this instance of corporal punishment was unique. In 1807, Cressbrook was reported as being dirty and the diet reported on in 1811 does not sound less monotonous than that at Litton.

The Methodist firm of Daintry, Ryle & Co. of Macclesfield, had a factory in Eyam, a parish adjacent to Tideswell, where in 1807 they employed ninety indentured workers. 'It is a great misfortune', wrote the visiting magistrate, 'that in these works belonging to these truly respectable persons, they thought themselves under the necessity of hiring an old building . . . the weaving-rooms are very narrow, very low and very close. This is so very obvious that one can scarcely conceive how the health of the people is preserved in any reasonable degree'.[62] No such criticism was made of the machine-room at the Litton mill. This is not to condone the treatment of apprentices at Litton, but to suggest that standards there were not so different from those in other mills, and reached a level which Farey, surveying the agriculture and industries of Derbyshire as a whole, could recognize as adequate.

Recent studies of two eighteenth-century spinning-mills that became notorious in the literature of the nineteenth century show similarity in one important respect. In both cases the mills ill-deserved their reputation, which originated in the calumnious reports of individuals or small groups who had (for one reason or other), an aversion to the factory system. Conditions at Peels' Radcliffe Bridge mill (near Manchester) were supposed to have been responsible for an outbreak of typhus which caused nearly fifty deaths in 1783. A recent study of the situation led its author to conclude that the 'outbreak of fever at Radcliffe was in no way remarkable and the numbers were not excessive'.[63] The story originated with a local hand-loom weaver who was antagonistic to the mill.

Davison & Hawksley were notorious in the annals of the district for their ill-treatment of pauper apprentices, yet our research suggests that the partners were responsible and enlightened employers, and that their unfortunate record probably originated with the partners' unpopular political views and the opposition of the woolcombers' union to mechanization. In no district were the factory masters more resented than in Tideswell; landowners, farmers, weavers and knitters alike despised the new mills. After two generations, Edale and Cressbrook could still not recruit local labour.[64] Blincoe's allegations, embroidered by the reformers, would never be denied in Tideswell. It is not too fanciful to suppose that Farey, the only responsible outsider to visit the scene of Blincoe's apprenticeship, was scrupulously fair in his implication, and that Litton, like the Radcliffe Bridge and Arnold mills, was the victim of popular prejudice against the factory system.

There is, of course, no denying that at Litton Mill hours were long, work tedious, diet monotonous, punishment harsh and accommodation crowded, but such conditions were not originated by the factory masters. Ellis Needham was a member of the class, albeit one of the less successful, who were responsible (as Farey demonstrated) for notable and permanent advances in wages, housing, education, working environment, regularity of employment and productivity of the land. There can be little doubt that the *Memoir of Robert Blincoe* was written by a gullible sensationalist, whose statements must be treated with the utmost caution. Certainly, it cannot be regarded as a reliable commentary on Litton, let alone other cotton mills of the period.

At the same time, it must be recognized that working conditions at Litton and other mills in the locality, like Cressbrook, Eyam and Edale, were almost certainly inferior to those at mills owned by more substantial capitalists, such as the Strutts and Davison & Hawksley. The difference also reflects the contrasting prosperity of the districts in which the mills were situated. Litton Mill stood in a remote district where the penumbrae of the two cotton-textile regions met, and where only the coarsest and most poorly-paid work was available. As a major industry, cotton-spinning had only an ephemeral existence in this area; according to Radcliffe it rose rapidly after 1788 and disappeared almost as quickly after 1803. Litton was one of the few precursors of the short-lived prosperity, and one of the few dwindling survivors. The proper historical context of the Blincoe *Memoir* is thus a fast-declining industry. Ellis Needham, and his workers with him, were the unhappy casualties of rapid technical and economic change in a highly-competitive industry.

CHAPTER ELEVEN

The Decline of the Midlands Spinning Industry

IT remains only to consider why the Midlands and particularly the hosiery districts of Nottinghamshire, Leicestershire and Derbyshire, failed to retain the lead in factory production they were granted through the initiative of Lombe, Paul, Hargreaves, Arkwright and William Strutt. It is a striking fact that all these men chose the Midlands for the site of their important innovations and, in addition, that the associations of Edmund Cartwright were with the Midlands. Moreover, the Region had a developed mercantile organization, including some of the earliest country banks, mechanical and metallurgical skills that were renowned, and good natural resources of coal, iron and water-power. Considering all these circumstances it is surprising, on the face of it, that the Regional factory-spinning industry made such a poor showing in competition with Lancashire and the West Riding. It is clear that the Region had already lost its early leadership by the end of the eighteenth century, so that the causes of decline must have been operative within the period covered by this book. A careful reassessment of details from the foregoing chapters should highlight the various factors in this loss of leadership.

On Lombe and Paul, little more can be said. The Derby Silk Mill had no authentic successors in the Region before the end of the eighteenth century, and its importance to the transition to the factory system in cotton-spinning was limited to the precedent which the building and its organization offered to Arkwright and the Strutts. The Paul-Wyatt factories at Birmingham and Northampton were commercial failures with no direct link with the later Midland industry, so far as can be ascertained. Hargreaves' jenny was important to the evolution of the factory system where it outgrew its original cottage setting, but this importance has little relevance to the Midlands, except for the peripheral parts of the Region which felt the attractions of the Manchester market. Knitting-yarns could just as readily be produced on the water-frame as on the jenny, and the cheaper roller-spun yarns soon drove Hargreaves and his partner to dependence on Arkwright.

The crucial figure is Arkwright, and his entrepreneurial decisions were the most important single factor in the development of the Midlands cotton industry during his lifetime. Without a doubt, Arkwright's choice of Cromford for the major location of his mills cut him off from the leadership of the cotton-spinning industry by isolating him from the markets and technical progress of the major centres of the textile industry, particularly Nottingham and Manchester. The move to Cromford was made against the wishes of Need and—to judge from his choice of sites—without enthusiasm from Strutt. Yet Arkwright's early success was sufficient to draw capital from Nottingham, Leicester and Derby into the Derbyshire dales and to revive the indigenous textile industry of the Peak. A large part of the Midlands cotton industry came to be clustered around Arkwright in the remote valleys of Derbyshire and its Staffordshire border.

Quite apart from the importance of technical progress, the very isolation of these sites predestined the Derbyshire mills to an uncertain future. In the long run, the distance from Nottingham and Manchester was bound to make transport costs so high and delivery dates so uncertain as to outweigh any possible advantage conferred by ample water-power or cheap labour. Towards the end of the last decade of the eighteenth century, the cotton-spinning industry became highly competitive. Thus the original basis of the Midlands spinning industry was laid on very insecure foundations, and Arkwright's son lead the withdrawal by reducing his father's industrial empire to three mills spinning only coarse cotton-yarn.

The failure of the Midlands to keep pace was apparent when

Lancashire triumphed with the mule and the West Riding with the throstle. Nottingham was no less interested in fine spinning than Manchester: lace was just as important to the former as muslin to the latter. Why William Strutt failed to capitalize his experiments with the early mule remains a mystery, the only logical explanation being that Strutts had so much capital tied up in factory production that they were less interested in an invention which, for the time being at any rate, was a domestic machine. Strutt turned instead to the further exploitation of the established techniques of factory production, and his vital contribution to the development of iron-framed buildings enabled all the textile regions to reap new economies of scale with less risk of fire. It was not until 1804 that cotton-yarn was spun sufficiently fine to be used in the lace industry, and though this may have caused a slight revival in cotton-spinning in Nottingham, the game had already gone to Lancashire.

In worsted-spinning, developments took a different course, though the outcome was similar. The opposition of the wool-combers and Leicester Corporation to mechanized spinning dispersed the industry at its birth and delayed technical progress for a vital quarter of a century. During these years Bradford stole the lead, and by the end of the Napoleonic wars, when mechanized spinning began to creep back into Leicester, all that could be hoped for was an industry ancillary to the now stagnating hosiery manufacture.

In Nottinghamshire and its Derbyshire border, attempts to adopt the mule proved a dismal failure. Three Nottinghamshire firms that attempted to introduce the mule in turn became bankrupt, Hardcastle & Co. (Newark) in 1793, Killingley & Green (Nottingham) in 1797, and John Bacon (Sutton-in-Ashfield) in 1801. At Ilkeston (Derbyshire) another early mule-spinning firm, Wyer & Co., became bankrupt in 1799.[1] Nor were these firms marginal ones. The only specialized spinning-machine builder in Nottingham during these years was George Wood, son of Coniah Wood, Arkwright's Nottingham workman. He made several attempts to adapt Alderman Green's machinery to Crompton's principles, 'but Green, after spending considerable sums upon it, failed in the attempt, and confined spinning to Mr Arkwright's system'.[2]

The mule was certainly not a more complicated machine than the hosiery- and lace-frames that were being developed in Nottingham at this period. The failure to develop this machine is a problem, the answers to which can only be made in terms of scarce means and alternative uses. The capital and, in particular, the mechanical skills of the district, were absorbed in developments in hosiery and lace, where the greatest rewards seemed to lie. In the late eighties and nineties, the idea of imitating cushion-lace by contriving a machine to *twist* (rather than knit) lace increasingly attracted the mechanical genius of the town. So it happened that, during the critical period of technical development of cotton- and worsted-spinning, Nottingham mechanics were not primarily interested in offering competition to Lancashire and the West Riding.

To elaborate this point, it can be said that Lancashire acquired important external economies in the manufacture of cotton which the Midlands industry never managed to develop. (By 'external economies' is meant the ancillary industries and services that develop around a staple industry.) In Lancashire, the cotton industry was established in the early seventeenth century so that specialists in importing and selling cotton and providing credit facilities, as well as in building and developing the specialized machinery needed by the industry, had a long time in which to evolve. By contrast, in Nottingham and the hosiery districts of the Midlands, all the cotton-yarn used was imported from India by London merchants until about 1770, and the primary interest of merchant hosiers and workmen in the fancy hosiery and lace industries meant that ancillary services were slow to emerge. The most important Lancashire ancillary industry to develop was the engineering industry, and in particular textile-machine building, based on Manchester and Stockport. The cumulative technical progress made by the engineers and machine-builders was far more significant than the contributions of the handful of inventors who figure in the textbooks. It was the community of Manchester mechanics that rapidly outpaced the Midlands industry.

In 1777, when the machinery of James and Hargreaves' factory at Nottingham was sold up, their sixteen-spindle jennies were already obsolete in Lancashire. By 1780, machines of 120 spindles had come into general use. During the ensuing decade, Stockport-built jennies and mules were sold in places as far apart as Bulwell (Nottingham) and Chesterfield. By the boom period of 1789–92, Nottingham had capitulated to Manchester and Stockport so far as the building of spinning machinery was concerned: Denison & Oates' mill, 'the most handsome and largest manufactory ever erected in Nottingham', was modelled on the Liverpool mill of Peter Atherton, the Warrington and Manchester machine-builder and cotton-spinner.[3] In 1793, a Manchester firm of machine-builders were advertising mules for sale in the columns of the *Nottingham Journal*.

The general disinterest of the Nottingham framesmiths in exploiting the technical break-through made by Hargreaves and Arkwright is in sharp contrast with the involvement of the ironfounders of the Region in the early engineering industry. As noticed in Chapter Seven, the last two decades of the eighteenth century saw a remarkable expansion of the iron industry of the Region following the cutting of the canals. The industry was not only well-prepared to supply castings for machine parts, but also offered to build textile (and other) machinery. Furthermore, the Midlands industry provided firms both in the Region and in Lancashire with steam-engines. Smith & Co. of Chesterfield, working in partnership with Francis Thompson, built steam-engines for such leading Lancashire spinners and machine-builders as Thomas Houldsworth, James Kennedy and A. & G. Murray, and provided castings for Gott's pioneer woollen mill at Leeds. The relative proximity of Midland spinners to Boulton & Watt and John Wilkinson may also be counted to their advantage. But the iron-founders were not textile innovators, and their enterprise was no substitute for the energy of the rapidly-growing Lancashire machine-building industry.

The fact that Britain was at war for most of the years between 1792 and 1815 must not be overlooked in assessing the contrasting fortunes of different sectors of the economy and various regions of the country. Though Leicester does not appear to have suffered from the war effort (other than by losing 'a great number of hands' to the Army), the fashion trades of Nottingham suffered considerably from changes in fashion which favoured a plain military kind of dress, with less ornamentation. This loss of orders was not entirely compensated for by contracts for sailors' jackets and perhaps other clothing for the Forces. Lancashire, on the other hand, tended to be favoured by war conditions. A sharp rise in the price of wool (due to wartime shortages) induced even more people to buy the cheaper cotton clothes instead of the traditional woollen ones. The effect of this price change on the manufacturers was indicated by Robert Davison in a letter to Lord Carrington (Robert Smith, the banker) in 1802:

> . . . the high price of wool has produced a very great and alarming rivalry in cotton fabrics . . . the substitution of the latter for the former is immense, . . . large mills and factories originally destined to the working of woollens have been compelled to devote their works to cotton. My concern here [i.e. Arnold Mill], which I believe has used as much or more sheep's wool than any other of the kind, has . . . been compelled in self-defence to divert a great part of its machinery from wool to cotton, and such substitution must increase every day to the utter exclusion of sheep's wool, unless it be reduced in price.

The Midland cotton-spinners were less well placed to benefit from this change than their Lancashire rivals. The demand for cotton hosiery represented only a minor part of the cotton market, but in any case the Midlands as a whole were by 1802 already rapidly declining to an inferior, peripheral position as compared with Lancashire. The real gain was Lancashire's.[4]

It is interesting to speculate on the consequences to the Midlands spinning industry of the structure of enterprise in factory spinning

in the Region. Most of the capital and enterprise for the development of the industry were supplied by leaders of the established
textile industry and their connections. The remainder came from
outside the industry. The artisan or mechanic with a small capital
played a negligible part; Thomas James, George Wood and William
Newton are the exceptions that prove the rule. In Lancashire and
the West Riding, by contrast, much of the enterprise of the rapidly-
developing industry originated with the 'small man', who himself
worked, or had recently worked, the jenny or the loom. Both in
Lancashire and the Midlands, most of the technical innovations
came from the group of framesmiths and small masters, in daily
contact with the machinery of the trade.

The merchant hosiers and their class were generally content to be
patrons of mechanical ingenuity in others. A few, like Unwin, Hall,
Coltman and William Strutt, were interested in the application of
science to industry and were responsible for introducing some new
techniques. But the great majority were, from their education and
apprenticeship, experienced only in the commercial side of the
business, and those from other industries can hardly be expected to
have known more.

The contrast here with Lancashire is particularly striking. Several
of the most successful Manchester mule-spinners, who were already
demonstrating the superiority of Lancashire yarns in the 1790s,
were machine-builders by origin. Peter Atherton, the most successful of the earlier Lancashire spinners, M'Connel and Kennedy,
James Kennedy, and Adam and George Murray, all gained the
leadership of their industry because they combined technical ex-
pertise with the flair of the successful entrepreneur. With the exception of the Strutts, and perhaps Davison and Hawksley, this combination was alien to the Midlands spinning industry.

The early Nottingham lace industry gave mechanics the opportunity to become independent machine-owners, and the industry
was built up almost entirely on their initiative. Arkwright's selective
licensing and the high initial cost of entering warp-spinning in a

Region where there were no jenny-workshops to bridge the gap between cottage and factory industry, served to exclude this enterprise. Clearly, the absence of mechanics among the mill-owners of the industry was not solely, or even primarily responsible for the decline of the industry, since machinery could be bought in Manchester and Bradford, and managers with technical ability, though scarce, could be employed or taken into partnership. However, this social factor may be of importance in so far as able mechanics would be less willing to experiment with machinery improvement in an industry where success brought little opportunity to acquire independence. It was not only that wages were higher in the lace-machine building industry, but the opportunity to become an independent master was conspicuously better.

There is no reason to suppose that Lancashire's geographical situation was vital to her success in competition with Nottingham and its vicinity. The period of transition to factory production saw the rise of Liverpool as a cotton port, but London was by no means eclipsed. Raw cotton could be brought all the way to Nottingham and Burton by water. Moreover, the Midlands had the advantage of being nearer to the markets of London and the south.

From 1797 onwards, there was an almost continuous series of bankruptcies among the Midland spinners. Most of the firms which collapsed were small, but there was a handful of larger ones— Green & Co., Lamberts, and Dickens. Numbers of others went into voluntary liquidation, among them some of the largest in the industry—Denison, Major Cartwright, Toplis, and Davison & Hawksley. The small Nottingham firms, and the peripheral mills of Lincolnshire and Northamptonshire, disappeared with hardly a trace. By 1833, there were only three mills in Nottingham and the adjacent villages. The industry survived mainly in two areas. In Nottinghamshire it became concentrated in and around Mansfield, making coarse yarns for the hosiery industry. A number of concerns also survived in the Derbyshire dales, spinning coarse for the Nottingham and Manchester markets. Among these, Strutts must be counted as the outstanding firm. With the success of Heathcoat's bobbin net-lace machine a few firms in the Region took to doubling lace thread. Others took up specialities for the hosiery manufacture, like angola and merino-yarns. The Burton–Tamworth area remained a minor centre of the cotton industry until the middle of the nineteenth century, when it disappeared.[5]

Where the cotton- and worsted-spinning industry collapsed, the disappearance of the industry did not result in a complete reversion to the pre-factory age. The mill buildings erected by the cotton-spinners were subsequently an important asset in the growth of other textile industries in the Region, particularly the lace manufacture of Nottingham and district.[6] The introduction of cotton-spinning also gave a permanent stimulus to parts of the Region which had previously been remote and backward, notably the Derwent valley, and Belper became a new home of the hosiery industry. But perhaps most important were the intangible benefits, the changed attitude towards economy in production. The transition to the factory system in the Midlands spinning industry was the first major breakthrough in the techniques of concentrated production by mechanical power and it created a major precedent that could not be overlooked by other industries in the Region as technical progress suggested new possibilities of production by power.

References

THE following abbreviations have been used in the references:

DM   *Derby Mercury*
DAJ   *Derbyshire Archaeological Society Journal*
NJ   *Nottingham Journal*
NR   *Nottingham Review*
NBR   The published series of *Nottingham Borough Records*. The
            volumes used in this study are: VI, 1702–60 (1914); VII,
            1760–1800 (1947); and VIII, 1800–35 (1952).
JHC   *Journal of the House of Commons*
PP   *Parliamentary Papers*
UBD   *Universal British Directory*, 5 volumes, 1790–8.

Three standard works on the Nottingham industries are referred to
constantly and abbreviated as follows:

Blackner   J. Blackner, *History of Nottingham* (1816)
Felkin   W. Felkin, *History of the Machine-Wrought Hosiery and
            Lace Manufactures* (1867)
Henson   G. Henson, *History of the Framework Knitters* (1831)

The location of manuscript sources of information is indicated by the
following initials:

A.O.L.B.   Assay Office Library, Birmingham
B.R.L.   Birmingham Reference Library
D.P.L.   Derby Public Library
N.P.L.   Nottingham Public Library
P.R.O.   Public Records Office, London
C.R.O.   County Records Office
J.R.O.   Joint Records Office (of Lichfield and Staffs.)
S.C.L.   Sheffield Central Library

The most important manuscripts used, the Boulton & Watt MSS, have
been abbreviated to B. & W. MSS. Documents in this collection are at the
Birmingham Reference Library, unless otherwise stated.

CHAPTER ONE

1 Henson, 60; J. Throsby, *History of Leicester* (1792), 402; *DAJ*, LXXIV
  (1950), 50.
2 *UBD*, II, 672; IV, 100.

3 H. Hartopp, *Register of the Freemen of Leicester*, I (1927), II (1933); parish registers of All Saints and St Warburg's, Derby.
4 *NJ*, 8 December 1792.
5 W. Gardiner, *Music and Friends*, III, 111–12.
6 Bedworth Parish Apprentice Register, 1802–21 (Warwicks. C.R.O.); *JHC*, IL (1794), 20, 280.
7 Pilkington, II, Sec. 6; W. Radcliffe, *Origin of . . . Power Loom Weaving* (1828), 9–10, 63–6.
8 Henson, *passim*.
9 Summary of statistics of frames in D. M. Smith, 'The British Hosiery Industry at the Middle of the 19th C.', *Institute of British Geographers Transactions*, No. 32, 1963. Numbers of hosiers in C. Deering, *Nottinghamia Vetus et Nova* (1751), 99–101; *NJ* 25 May 1771, Willoughby's *Nottingham Directory* (1799); Weston's *Leicester Directory* (1794); *UBD* II.
10 Blackner, 238–40; *DM*, 4 September 1783; *NJ*, 21 May 1768, 28 January 1769; *UBD*, I, II, III.
11 Blackner, 213–45; Henson *passim*.
12 J. D. Chambers, 'The Worshipful Company of Framework Knitters, 1657–1778', *Economica*, IX (1929); Henson, 96; *NBR*, V, 250; *NJ*, 16 January 1790.
13 On Samuel Unwin (1712–99) see the author's 'Sutton Old Mill', *Journal of Industrial Archaeology*, II (1965).
14 C. Deering, op. cit., 91–2; Hartopp, I, 374, 171.
15 H. Hartopp, op. cit.
16 Infra, Chapter V (A), (B), Chapter VI, (Parkes).
17 R. A. Church, *Victorian Nottingham* (1966), Ch. 2.
18 *NJ*, 17 February 1787; *JHC*, XXVI (1753), 787; *NJ*, 8 February 1794.
19 J.A.S.L., Leighton-Boyce, *Smiths the Bankers, 1658–1958*, (1958), 36, 47–8; Ledger of Samuel and Abel Smith & Co., 1748–52.
20 Henson, 304–17; *NR*, 3 June 1831; J. D. Chambers, *Notts. in the 18th Cent.* (1932), 124; Royal Exchange Registers, VI, No. 82,263.
21 Blackner, 85, 225–7; T. M. Blagg and F. A. Wadsworth, *Notts. Marriage Licences* (1935), II, 486; *NJ*, 29 June 1782; Smiths' Ledger, 1748–52.
22 *NR*, 12 June 1829; *NJ*, 29 April 1775.
23 F. A. Wells, *British Hosiery Trade* (1925), 72–3; *NJ*, 12 July 1783, 7, 28 August 1790.
24 Blackner, 234, 249.
25 *NR*, 3 June 1831; Henson 307–15; Blackner, 232–4, 244–5.
26 Blackner, 245, n.3; R. A. Church, op. cit., Ch. 3.
27 W. J. & F. Lambert (J. Brown ed., *Memoir of Robert Blincoe* (1832), 12). The other firms were Hancocks & Wakefield (Holden's *Triennial Directory*, 1805), Burnside & Watson and William Wilson (Felkin, 140).
28 F. M. Eden, *State of the Poor* (1797), II, 574; Henson, 238, 285, 416; Blackner, 222–3; Felkin, 183.

29 Arkwright Wage Books (Chesterfield Public Library), 1786–88, 1793–96, 1804–08, 1808–11; J. B. Firth, *Highways and Byeways in Derbyshire* (1908), 244–50; F. M. Eden, op. cit., Rogers Edn, 170, 172; *NJ*, 31 January 1795, 12 May 1804.
30 *NJ*, 26 December 1795; *NBR*, VI.
31 Infra, Ch. VII (4).
32 F. A. Wells, op. cit., 92–4.
33 Felkin, Ch. XIV; *NR*, 3 June 1831.
34 Felkin, 285.

CHAPTER TWO

1 T. C. Hine, *Nottingham Castle* . . . (1876), 34–5, n.1.
2 Advertisements in *NJ*, e.g. 14 March 1778, 15 September 1792, 9 April 1803, 19 May 1810.
3 S. D. Chapman, 'Working Class Housing in Nottingham in the Industrial Revolution', *Trans. Thoroton Society*, LXVII (1963).
4 A. T. Patterson, *Radical Leicester* (1954), 54–5.
5 Henson, 94–9; *High Pavement Chapel Biographical Catalogue* (1932), 25.
6 Obituary, *NJ*, 13 May 1769.
7 Henson, 94–9, 264, 279–86. For White *see infra* Ch. V (A).
8 *JHC*, XXXVI (1778), 740–2; *NJ*, 3 January 1778, 14 January, 28 February 1775.
9 W. H. Chaloner, 'Sir Thomas Lombe and the British Silk Industry', *People and Industries* (1963), Ch. I; *NJ* 12 September 1772.
10 W. Hutton, *History of Derby* (1791), 204; J. Pilkington, op. cit., II, 171; R. S. Fitton and A. P. Wadsworth, *The Strutts and the Arkwrights* (1958), 47; Report of the Select Committee on Children Employed in Manufactories, *PP*, 1816, III, 217.
11 S. D. Chapman, 'Sutton Old Mill', loc. cit., *UBD*, II; N. Pevsner, *The Buildings of England: Derbyshire* (1953), 99; Infra, Ch. V (G).
12 Infra, Ch. V (F); *High Pavement Biographical Catalogue*, 26; Blackner, 251; Willoughby's *Nottingham Directory* (1799).
13 *Birmingham Gazette*, 11 July 1748, 11 January 1768, 27 March 1809; J. Jaffray, 'Hints for a History of Birmingham' (1857), I, XVIII.
14 Wyatt MSS (B.R.L.); Henson, 364–5.

CHAPTER THREE

1 Condensed from C. Aspin and S. D. Chapman, *James Hargreaves and the Spinning Jenny* (Helmshore Historical Society, 1964).
2 *NJ*, 25 April 1778; *Manchester Mercury*, 29 August 1777.
3 Aspin and Chapman, Chs. 3, 5; W. Radcliffe, *Origin of . . . Power-Loom Weaving* (1828), 65; Blackner, 249.
4 Aspin and Chapman, Ch. 3.

5 *Manchester Mercury*, loc. cit., *NJ* 5, 12 September 1772, 4 September 1773.
6 Aspin and Chapman, 39.
7 *NJ*, 7 March 1789, 29 August, 24 October 1795.
8 *DM*, 21 March 1782, 14 June 1787.
9 R. Lowe, *Agriculture of Notts.* (1794), 171; *DM*, 6 September 1798, 31 December 1807.
10 *NJ*, 25 May 1771.
11 J. Farey, *Agriculture of Derbyshire*, III (1817), 485. The locations referred to are Bradwell, Brough, Castleton (2 'mills'), Chapel (2 'mills'), Dovehole, Netherbooth, Peak Forest and Great Longsden.
12 *DM*, 8 May 1788; J. Pilkington, II, 300, 312, 421; *DM*, 20 October 1796.
13 W. Radcliffe, 65; *DM*, 13 February 1794, 23 February 1797, 27 February 1800.
14 *DM*, 20 October 1796; *An Account of the Cotton and Woollen Mills . . . 1803–1818*, House of Lords Sessional Papers, CVIII (1819), 6–9.
15 *NJ*, 4 May 1793; *DM*, 21 September 1797.
16 *DM*, 24 December 1795.
17 For sources on Cantrell and other mill spinners, *see* alphabetical list in Appendix A.
18 Merchant contacts surmised from later partnerships between factors and merchant hosiers and yarn merchants; *see* Gardom Pares & Co., Dalley, Fellows & Co.; assignment of mortgage of Brund mill (Cantrell) to Manchester cotton dealer.
19 For Firth *see* Ch. X (3).
20 P. Gaskell, *Artizans and Machinery* (1836), 33–4; J. Kennedy, *Rise of the Cotton Manufacture* (1819); Royal Exchange Registers, XXIX, 143682.

CHAPTER FOUR

1 Fitton and Wadsworth, *The Strutts and the Arkwrights*, 60–5.
2 S. Glover, *Derbyshire Directory* (1829), xvi, 250.
3 Henson, 304–17; Castle Gate Chapel 'Church Book', January and June 1775; W. Bray, *Sketch of a Tour into Derbyshire and Yorkshire* (1777), Pinkerton's Edn., 1808, II, 375.
4 Quoted in Fitton and Wadsworth, 67.
5 Sale of mill, *NR*, 14 March 1834, *NJ*, 5, 12 September 1772.
6 W. Bray, loc. cit., *Plan of the Cromford Moor Long Sough, 1777* (Bagshawe MSS., S.C.L.); *Cromford Tithe Commutation Map, 1840* (D.P.L.).
7 *DM*, 12 April 1776; Award in Cromford Sough Proprietors *v.* Arkwright, 14 October 1785 (Bagshawe MSS.).
8 M. H. Mackenzie, 'The Bakewell Cotton Mill and the Arkwrights', *DAJ*, LXXIX; Royal Exchange Registers, VII, 86104.
9 *Plan of the Cromford Moor Long Sough, 1777*.
10 Rees *Cyclopaedia* (1819), article on 'Cotton Manufacture'.

11 M. H. Mackenzie, op. cit., 70
12 Fitton and Wadsworth, 106–7; Rocester MSS. (Staffs. C.R.O.); Ashworth MSS. (quoted Aspin and Chapman, 54); S. Chapman, 'Pioneers of Worsted Spinning', *Business History*, VII, 109; Royal Exchange Registers; IV, 75060–1, 76867.
13 Barker MSS. (S.C.L.), 60108/6.
14 Fitton and Wadsworth, 81, 93; G. M. Mitchell 'The English and Scottish Cotton Industries', *Scottish Historical Review*, XXII (1925).
15 J. Hodgson, *The Textile Manufacture in Keighley* (1879), 240.
16 Banks-Stanhope MSS. (Spalding Gentlemen's Society); *see below*, Ch. VI.
17 Wilkes to B. & W., 19 October 1783; J. T. Godfrey Ed., *The Stretton MSS.* (1910), 179.
18 Report of the Select Committee on Children Employed in Manufactories, *PP*, 1816, III, 279, 281–2; G. Unwin, *Samuel Oldknow and the Arkwrights* (1924), 16–20; J.A.S.L., Leighton-Boyce, op. cit., 110.
19 Fitton and Wadsworth, Ch. VIII, 170, 198, 215.
20 R. A. Church, op. cit., Ch. 4.
21 *The Trial of a Cause instituted by . . . His Majesty's Attorney-General . . . to Repeal a Patent granted 16 December 1775 to Mr. Richard Arkwright* (1785), 99.
22 Pares MSS. (D.P.L.), 27 letters 25 April 1782–1 June 1783. The various firms are considered below in Chs. V and VI.
23 Specification of Patent No. 1018 (11 June 1772); Henson, 370–1; Fitton and Wadsworth, op. cit., 66.

CHAPTER FIVE

1 Analysis of occupations and addresses in *Nottingham Poll Book, 1780*.
2 *NJ*, 20 December 1794.
3 In 1789 there were twelve silk mills in Derby employing 1,200 people. (J. Pilkington, II, 171). Eight years later eleven silk mills in the town were employing 1,000 people (F. M. Eden, *State of the Poor* (1797), 171). About 1809 there were seven silk mills in Derby (J. Farey, III, 482). During this period the silk point-net was developing very rapidly. Cotton stockings were 'much preferred' to silk ones (Henson, 165).
4 *Gentleman's Magazine*, LV (1785), 169–70; J. B. Firth, *Highways and Byeways in Derbyshire* (1908), 224–50; *DM*, 24 November 1785.

CHAPTER SIX

1 S. D. Chapman, 'The Pioneers of Worsted Spinning by Power', *Business History*, VII (1965); *The Humble Petition of the Poor Spinners of the Town and County of Leicester* (Leicester, 1787); Ledgers of J. and H. Hadden, 1787–1800, 1805–17 (University of Nottingham).

2 S. D. Chapman, loc. cit.
3 Quoted Aspin and Chapman, op. cit., 46. J. Hodgson, *The Textile Manufacture in Keighley*, 19, 167, 240.

CHAPTER SEVEN

 1 S. Pollard, 'Fixed Capital in the Industrial Revolution', *Journal of Economic History*, XXIV (1964).
 2 Royal Exchange Registers, IV, 73349; XXIV, 127330; XXIII, 133996; XXIV, 143468; Sun Fire Policy Registers, CCCXXXVI, 519065.
 3 Report of the Select Committee on Children employed in Manufactories, *PP*, 1816, III, 134, 141.
 4 Royal Exchange Registers, XXIX, 143655; *NJ*, 21 November 1801; J. Smeaton, *Designs, 1741–1792* (Newcomen Society, 1950), 85.
 5 S. Pigott, *Hollins, A Study of Industry* (1949), 56; *NJ*, 18 October 1800, Ilkeston Manor Court Rolls, 1791–93.
 6 Innumerable entries in Royal Exchange Registers.
 7 Royal Exchange Registers, XXIII, 130291.
 8 Ibid., XXIX, 143301.
 9 Ibid., XXIV, 127330; XVIII, 121267; XXV, 135163.
10 Royal Exchange Registers, VII, 86104; *NJ*, 11 Sepetember 1790.
11 Quoted in *East Retford Advertiser*, 1 April 1854.
12 *NJ*, 21 October 1797.
13 Royal Exchange Registers, XXIX, 143634; *UBD*, I; Allsopp MSS. (Ind Coope Ltd, Burton), Letter Book of Benjamin Wilson, 9 June 1801.
14 Blackner, 395; *NJ*, 2 September 1820; H. R. Johnson and A. W. Skempton, 'William Strutt's Cotton Mills, 1793–1812', *Trans. Newcomen Society*, XXX (1955–56), 193.
15 *JHC*, IL (1794), 565.
16 Royal Exchange Registers, IV, 73349.
17 *NJ*, 24 October 1789, House of Lords Committee on Cotton Factories, *PP*, 1818, XCVI, 197–201.
18 Ichabod Wright's Diaries (MSS. N.P.L.), *Lloyd's Evening Post*, 13/15 March 1767; Fitton and Wadsworth, 63.
19 Letter to B. & W., 29 July 1797.
20 E.g. £395 in August 1800 (Coltman's 'Stock Book No. 1').
21 P.R.O., B/3/2119.
22 J.A.S.L., Leighton-Boyce, op. cit., 110–11; Allsopp MSS., Letter Book of 1801–08, various entries.

CHAPTER EIGHT

 1 D. M. Smith, op. cit., 129; J. Pilkington, op. cit., *passim*; Blackner, 238–40.
 2 J. Pilkington, op. cit., II, 134–222, 315–32, 410; Blackner, loc. cit.

3 Pilkington, II, 237; S. Bagshaw, *Derbyshire Directory* (1846), 291;
D. M. Smith, op. cit., 134; Report of the Commissioner appointed to
inquire into the Condition of the Framework Knitters, *PP*, XV, 1845,
Evidence, Qu. 4490–6.

4 Blackner, 238; Framework Knitters' Union Papers, 1812 (MSS. N.P.L.).

5 Surmised from framework knitters' union notices in *NJ*, e.g., 28 August
1790, 28 June 1794.

6 Blackner, 242–4.

7 *DM*, 2 March 1799; Bailey; S. Glover, *History and Gazeteer of the
County of Derby* (1833), II, 5–6.

8 J. Lindsay, op. cit.; Stenton & Metcalfe MSS. (Notts. C.R.O.); Fitton
and Wadsworth, 78.

9 Benjamin Wilson's Personal Ledger, 1779–95, 70.

10 List of furnaces in Derbyshire in 1806, Farey, op. cit., I, 397.

11 F. Nixon, 'The Early Steam Engine in Derbyshire', *Trans. Newcomen
Society*, XXXI (1957–59); Robinsons to B. & W., 27 July 1785.

12 *NJ*, 6 May 1797, 6 April, 22 December 1798, 13 July 1799.

13 J. Farey, loc. cit., S. Bagshaw, op. cit., 207, 571; *DM*, 24 April 1794;
R. H. Mottram and C. Coote, *Through Five Generations, A History of the
Butterley Co.* (n.d.).

14 *DM*, 3 December 1807.

15 G. G. Hopkinson, 'Inland Navigations of the Notts and Derbys Coal
Field', *DAJ*, LXXIX (1959), 31–2; *NJ*, 30 October 1790; W. Gardiner,
op. cit., I, 83, 231, 311; C. R. Clinker and C. Hadfield, 'Ashby Canal and
its Railways', *Trans. Leices. Archaeological Society*, XXXIV (1958), 59.

16 J. Farey, *A Treatise on the Steam Engine* (1827), 422; F. Nixon, op. cit.,
J. Smeaton, *Designs, 1741–92*, 84–5.

17 John Adams to B. & W., 25 December 1795.

18 Royal Exchange Registers, XXIX, 143655; *NJ*, 21 November 1801;
E. Roll, *An Early Experiment in Industrial Organisation* (1930), 312;
S. Unwin to B. & W., 26 January 1788.

19 D. M. Smith, *Industrial Archaeology of the East Midlands* (1965), 80–90.

20 Letters to B. & W. from S. Unwin, 28 May 1788, from Davison &
Hawksley, 14 November 1789, H. Pearson, 30 January 1789, S. & B.
Churchill, 20 October 1794, 8 October 1795, B. & W. 'Engine Book'.

21 S. Unwin to B. & W., 30 January 1798, 30 March 1798.

22 R. Gorton to B. & W., 2 September 1791; P. Atherton to B. & W., 17
May 1791.

23 T. Harris to B. & W., 19 November 1785.

24 *DM*, 20 May 1784; S. Unwin to M. Boulton, 15 December 1789
(A.O.L.B.).

25 A. E. Musson and E. Robinson, 'The Early Growth of Steam Power',
Economic History Review, XI (1958–59).

P

CHAPTER NINE

1 J. Farey, op. cit., III, 499; W. Watson, 'Observations of Bakewell beginning 31 May 1774', *DAJ*, XI (1889); Fitton and Wadsworth, 104; *NJ*, 13 December 1777; *DM*, 20 September 1781; J. Lindsay, op. cit., 296–9.

2 J. Farey, II, 221.

3 *DM*, 25 January 1787.

4 J. Forrest, 'The Darley Abbey Cotton Spinning and Paper Mills', M.Sc.Econ. Thesis, London, 1957, p. 99.

5 Fitton and Wadsworth, 247, 101; *Cromford Tithe Commutation Map, 1840* (D.P.L.).

6 *DM*, 17 June 1790; Fitton and Wadsworth, 252–3.

7 Royal Exchange Registers, IV, 75060; *DM*, 17 June 1790; S. Bagshaw, op. cit., 251; T. Bulmer, *Derbyshire Directory* (1894).

8 Report of the Select Committee on Children employed in Manufactories, *PP*, 1816, III, 217, 221.

9 House of Lords' Committee on the Cotton Factories Bill, *PP*, 1818, XCVI, 199.

10 *DM*, 20 February 1794; Robinson, Churchill, Davison & Hawksley to B. & W., quoted in Chs. VII and VIII.

11 Appendix D.

12 P.R.O., B/3/2119. Italics represent underlining in the original.

13 S. Smiles, *Lives of the Engineers* (1861), II, 138; Haslam's (joiners) account book, 1751–59 (for Sutton Mill); Louth Mill 'Cash Book' (Banks-Stanhope MSS.).

14. *NJ*, 22 October 1791, 8 September, 22 December 1792.

15 J. Byng (ed. Andrews), *The Torrington Diaries, 1781–94* (1954), 251–3.

16 *DM*, 15 July 1784; *NJ*, 8 July 1780, 13, 20 December 1794, 22 December 1792.

17 J. Pilkington, op. cit., II, 412, 454; J. Farey, op. cit., III, 616–17; *DM*, 15 July 1784; 17 March 1791, 12 June 1783, 23 February 1797.

18 J. Pilkington, II, 454.

19 J. D. Chambers, 'Population Change in a Provincial Town, Nottingham, 1700–1800', in L. S. Pressnell ed. *Studies in the Industrial Revolution* (1960); F. Collier, *The Family Economy of the Working Classes in the Cotton Industry, 1784–1833* (1964), 14.

20 J. Farey, III, 501–2.

21 Appendix C.

22 J. Throsby ed., R. Thoroton, *History of Notts.* (1790), III, 376; *NJ*, 31 August 1793.

23 J. Lindsay, op. cit., 297–9; Fitton and Wadsworth, 238–40.

24 Belper MSS., 3560/6 (D.P.L.).

25 *NJ*, 13 December 1777; House of Lords Committee on Cotton Factories Bill, *PP*, 1818, XCVI, 197–200.

CHAPTER TEN

1 S. C. Pigott, op. cit., 55–6; *NR*, 21 June 1839 et seq.
2 Report of the Select Committee on Children employed in Manufactories, *PP*, 1816, III, 280, 277, 134
3 *DM*, 29 September 1796, 23 February 1797; Willoughby's *Nottingham Directory*, 1799; *NBR*, VIII, 37; J. T. Godfrey, op. cit., 175; *NJ*, 24 September 1808
4 J. D. Chambers, *Vale of Trent*, 61–2; R. Mellors, *Bulwell, Then and Now* (1914), 43.
5 Factory Inquiry, *PP*, 1833, XX, 42–6; Obituary of Wilson, *NR*, 1 November 1833; *A Report of the Evidence given before the . . . Municipal Coporations Commission* (Nottingham Constitutional Club, 1833); R. Mellors, *Old Nottingham Suburbs* (1914), 58.
6 J. Brown ed., *Memoir of Robert Blincoe* (1832), 26.
8 W. Stumbles, 'Glimpses of Arnold the last 100 years' (1859), in *Sketches of Mental Recreation after Daily Toil* (1875).
9 Blackner, 394–5.
10 *NJ*, 26 November 1796; Davison & Hawksley to B. & W., 4 May 1797.
11 J. D. Chambers, loc. cit.
12 *NJ*, 20 December 1794, 16, 23 January 1796, 26 November 1796.
13 *NBR*, VII, 397–8.
14 Handbill entitled 'To those Inhabitants of Arnold who have aided or abetted the late Riotous Proceedings', signed by Robert Davison, 18 July 1798. In possession of Mrs G. Palmer (*née* Davison) of Lambley, Notts.
15 *NJ*, 6 October 1810, 6 February 1802; R. W. King and J. Russell, *History of Arnold* (1913), 88–91.
16 *NJ*, 7, 28 August 1790; C. Erickson, *British Entrepreneurs: Steel and Hosiery* (1959), 84–7.
17 Justice's Clerk's Fee Book (Sherbrooke MSS., Notts. C.R.O.); J. D. Chambers, loc. cit.
18 King and Russell, 123, 130. George Wall subsequently became a President of the Methodist Conference.
19 Handbill on 'Riotous Proceedings . . .'.
20 Ibid.
21 J. D. Chambers, loc. cit.
22 J. Throsby, op. cit., II, 234; *NBR*, VII, 399.
23 *NJ*, 20 December 1794, 31 January 1795, 16, 23 January 1796 (quoted here), 26 November 1796, 12 May 1804.
24 Handbill on 'Riotous Proceedings . . .'.
25 Handbill headed 'To the Public', issued by Davison & Hawksley, 2 September 1800 (Smith MSS., N.P.L.); *NBR*, VII, 397–9.
26 Justice's Clerk's Fee Book, 25 March 1802 (my italics); King and Russell, loc. cit.; *Methodist New Connexion Jubilee Book, 1876*.

27 W. Stumbles, loc. cit.; *NJ*, 11 June 1802; Handbill on 'Riotous Proceedings . . .'; Justice's Clerk's Fee Book.
28 R. A. Church and S. D. Chapman, 'Gravenor Henson and the Making of the English Working Class', in G. Mingay ed., *Land, Labour and Population* (1966).
29 *NBR*, VII, loc. cit.
30 S. D. Chapman, 'Pioneers of Worsted Spinning . . .', *Business History*, VII (1965), 103–4; Henson, 383–401.
31 *NBR*, VII, 274; Blackner, 387–90; Denison to B. & W., 29 August 1794.
32 Petition to Robert Smith, M.P., 27 November 1795 (Smith MSS., N.P.L.); *NBR*, VII, 330–1; Blackner, 392; *NJ*, 1, 15 April 1797; R. Davison, *Ten Letters . . . upon the late Contested Election at Nottingham* (1803); *A Letter to Mr. Bowles . . .* (1803).
33 Henson 401–5; letter from J. Wellersley, 8 September 1808 (Enfield MSS., N.P.L.).
34 *Leicester Journal*, 1, 8, 22 December 1787; *The Humble Petition of the Poor Spinners of . . . Leicester* (1787).
35 *JHC*, IL, 395, 546; Arnold Parish Overseers Accounts, especially volume of 1816–17 (Notts. C.R.O.). Cf. W. Gardiner, op. cit., II, 149.
36 *NJ*, 10, 17 November 1792, 8 December 1792; *JHC*, IL, 565.
37 S. D. Chapman, loc. cit.; *JHC*, LVI (1801), 272, 417, 456.
38 *JHC*, IL, 280, 565, LVI, 272.
39 *JHC*, IL, 450, 571.
40 *NJ*, 31 January 1795, 12 May 1804.
41 *NJ*, 3 October 1795; K. T. Meaby, *Extracts from Notts Records of the Eighteenth Century* (1947), 235.
42 *NJ*, 2 January 1796 et seq.
43 Joseph Priestley's MS. Sermons (Manchester College, Oxford), considered by C. M. Elliott, 'The Social and Economic History of the Principal Protestant Denominations in Leeds, 1760–1844', D. Phil. Thesis, Oxford, 1962; G. Walker, *Essays, with a Memoir* (1809); G. Wakefield, *Memoirs* (1790), 227–9; *NJ*, 6 May 1797.
44 High Pavement Chapel Baptismal Register and Minute Books, I (1779–1812); Fitton and Wadsworth, 36; S. D. Chapman, op. cit., 99, 110, 104; W. Gardiner, op. cit., I, 62; *NJ*, 5, 12 January 1793.
45 High Pavement records; C. H. Beale, *Catherine Hutton and her Friends* (1895), 64–5; *DM*, 12 January 1831; G. Wakefield, *Memoirs*, loc. cit.
46 Quoted in J. Lindsay, op. cit., 279.
47 Report of the Select Committee on Children employed in Manufactories, *PP*, 1815, III, 217.
48 Pedigree of Unwin and Clay families (W. Clay Dove Esq. of Sutton); S. D. Chapman, op. cit., 98–9; C. H. Beale, op. cit., 22–3.
49 W. H. Chaloner, *People and Industries*, 43–4, and 'Mrs Trollope and the

Early Factory System', *Victorian Studies*, IV (1960–61); P. Mantoux, op. cit., 414, n.1.

50 Factory Inquiry, *PP*, 1834, XXI, 17–18.

51 *DM*, 16 May 1793, 2 May 1799; Wills of Needham family (Lichfield J.R.O.); Jurors' Books, 1784–1815 (Derbys. C.R.O.); 'Valuation of Hill and Hargate Wall Estates, 29 April 1795' (Bagshawe MSS., John Rylands Library, Manchester); diaries of Rev Thos. Brown of Tideswell, 1792–95, 1797–99 (S.C.L.).

52 W. Radcliffe, op. cit., 12; S. Bagshawe, *Derbyshire Directory* (1846), 554.

53 Will of Thomas Frith, 26 November 1812 (Lichfield J.R.O.); Land Tax Returns, Tideswell.

54 Belper MSS. 3560/38 (D.P.L.); *NJ*, 11 February 1786.

55 Blincoe *Memoir*, 27; Royal Exchange Registers, XXIX, 143301.

56 *DM*, 2 May 1799, 10 January 1805; House of Lords Account of Cotton Mills, *PP*, 1819, CVIII, 48; Blincoe *Memoir*, 31.

57 J. Farey, op. cit., II, 33; III, 504; Belper MSS. 3560/38.

58 P. J. Rooke, 'A Study of Rewards and Punishments in the Elementary Schools of England and Wales, 1800–93'. M.A. Thesis, London, 1962.

59 House of Lords Account of Cotton Mills, *PP*, 1819, 48–9.

60 J. Farey, op. cit., II, 27; III, 501.

61 Blincoe *Memoir*, 30–1; J. D. Chambers, loc. cit.

62 House of Lords Account of Cotton Mills, *PP*, 1819, loc. cit.; Belper MSS., 3560/43.

63 Anon., 'The Putrid Fever at Robert Peel's Radcliffe Mill', *Notes and Queries*, CCIII (1958), 26–35.

64 Return of Apprentices in Cotton Mills in Derbys. in 1841, Derbys. C.R.O.

CHAPTER ELEVEN

1 List of Bankrupts, Appendix D.

2 J. T. Godfrey, ed., *The Stretton MSS.*, 175

3 Blackner, 248; B. & W. MSS., 2 letters from P. Atherton, 17 May, 4 July 1791.

4 J. Nicholls, *History of Leics.*, I (ii) (1815), 568; Blackner, 228–9; R. Davison to Lord Carrington, 28 August 1802 (Smith MSS., N.P.L.).

5 List of Bankrupts, Appendix D; Factory Inquiry, *PP*, 1833, XX, 6 et seq.; Report of the Select Committee on Children employed in Manufactories, *PP*, 1816, III, 225, 281; House of Lords Committee on Cotton Factories Bill, *PP*, 1818, 135–7, 197–201; S. Bagshawe, *Derbyshire Directory* (1846), 460, 579, 630; S. C. Pigott, op. cit., 73–5.

6 Disused cotton mills were used extensively for 'stallholding' in the early days of the lace industry, *see* advertisments in *NJ*, e.g. 13 October 1833 (Green's mill).

Appendices

APPENDIX A

MILL OWNERS CONSIDERED IN THIS STUDY, WITH A SUMMARY OF SOURCES OF INFORMATION ON EACH

(A) *Cotton-Spinners*

Name of Firm   Location of Mill(s) and Date

NOTTINGHAMSHIRE

JOHN BACON   Sutton-in Ashfield 1783.
R. Lowe, *Agriculture of Notts.* (1794), 171; *UBD*, I (Alfreton), III (Mansfield); *NJ*, 26 January 1799, 21 November 1801.

A. G. and R. BURDEN   Mansfield 1785, 1788.
R. Lowe, loc. cit.; *NJ*, 12 October 1771.

BENJAMIN CHAMBERS   Fiskerton
R. Lowe, loc. cit.; *NBR*, VII, 431.

COX & HALLS   Nottingham 1791.
R. Lowe, loc. cit.; W. P. W. Phillimore, *County Pedigrees: Notts.*, I (1910), 310; *NBR*, VII, 428; *NJ*, 25 May 1771; Bailey; B. & W. MSS.: 10 letters 26 January 1791–18 November 1794.

DAVISON & HAWKSLEY   Nottingham 1788, Arnold 1792.
Numerous sources quoted in S. D. Chapman, 'The Pioneers of Worsted-Spinning by Power', *Business History*, VII (1965).

DENISON & OATES   Nottingham 1792.
R. Lowe, loc. cit.; Bailey; T. M. Blagg and F. A. Wadsworth, *Notts. Marriage Licences* (1935), II, 405; Blackner, 8, 248, 395; *NJ*, 8 November 1800; B. & W. MSS.: 14 letters from R. Denison, 23 May 1791–16 October 1794, 5 letters from P. Atherton, 17 May 1791–11 February 1796.

KILLINGLEY & GREEN   Nottingham 1792
Bailey; J. T. Godfrey, ed., *The Stretton MSS* (1910), 53, 167, 175, 181; Blackner, 390–1; *NJ*, 1 September 1801; B. & W. MSS., 12 letters 3 May, 1791–26 September 1793.

HALLS & WHITE   Basford 1787.
Nottingham Poll Book, 1780; T. M. Blagg and F. A. Wadsworth, II, 508, 538; *NBR*, VII, 3; Bailey; K. T. Meaby, *Notts. Records of the Eighteenth Century* (1947), 176; S. Woodhouse, 'Memoir of Robert Hall', *The New Methodist Magazine*, January and February 1828;

C. Hall, *Memoirs of Marshall Hall, M.D., F.R.S.* (1861), 1–4; B. & W. MSS.: letters of 13 January 1781, 23 June 1788. On White *see* Bailey; Henson, 282; *UBD*, II (Chesterfield).

HANCOCKS & WAKEFIELD   Mansfield 1789.

R. Lowe; *NJ*, 28 December 1782; Bailey; *UBD*, IV (Nott'm.); Factory Inquiry, *PP*, 1833, XX, 6.

HANDLEY, SKETCHLEY & CO.   Newark.

R. Lowe; W. Dickinson, *Antiquities of Newark* (1805), II, 291; T. M. Blagg and F. A. Wadsworth, II, 437; Handley MSS. (Notts. C.R.O.); J. T. Godfrey, ed., op. cit., 220–1; J. Sketchley, *Birmingham Directory* (1767).

HARDCASTLE & CO.   Newark 1791.

R. Lowe; Newark Poll Book, 1790 (MS., Notts. C.R.O.); *NJ*, 8 June 1793.

T. HARRIS   Nottingham.

NBR, VII, 434, 436; Bailey; *NJ*, 8 February 1794; B. & W. MSS.: 20 letters 16 June 1784–4 December 1793; P.R.O. B/3/2119.

JAMES & HARGREAVES   Nottingham 1769.

Numerous sources quoted in C. Aspin and S. D. Chapman, *James Hargreaves and the Spinning-Jenny* (1964); *see also* footnotes to Chapter III.

W., C. and F. LAMBERT   Gonalston 1784.

John Brown, *A Memoir of Robert Blincoe* (1832 Edn.), 12–26; Bailey; *UBD*, IV (Nott'm.); *NJ*, 26 January 1793, 3 May 1794, 19 May 1810; Land Tax Returns (Lowdham); inspection of surviving mill.

MARKLAND, EVISON & LITTLE   Southwell 1786.

NJ, 3 January 1789, 29 May 1790, 11 September 1790, 4 February 1797, 28 October 1797; Land Tax Returns, Southwell.

C. and B. MORLEY   Nottingham *c.* 1781.

A. Parker, 'The Nottingham Potters', *Trans. Thoroton Society*, XXXVI (1932); F. Buckley, 'Old Nottingham Glasshouses', *Trans. Society of Glass Technology*, X (1926); T. M. Blagg and F. A. Wadsworth, II, 274; *NJ*, 3 September 1774; *Nott'm Poll Book, 1780*; Bailey; Stretton's Map of Nott'm (MS., 1799–1800, N.P.L.); B. & W. MSS.: 4 letters, 18 June 1788–29 August 1799.

OLDKNOW, COWPE & CO.   Pleasley 1784, 1798.

S. C. Pigott, *Hollins, A Study of Industry* (1949); G. Unwin, *Samuel Oldknow and the Arkwrights* (1924).

PEARSON & GRIMSHAW   Nottingham.

NJ, 3 July 1790; Bailey; *UBD*, IV (Nott'm.); B. & W. MSS.: 5 letters, 12 April 1786–18 January 1792; *Trial of a Cause . . .*, 46.

G. and J. ROBINSON   6 mills, Bulwell and Papplewick; 1778, 1784, 1791; others not known.

J. D. Marshall, 'Early Applications of Steam-Power: The Cotton Mills of the Upper Leen', *Trans. Thoroton Society*, LX (1957); R. Mellors, *Old Nottingham Suburbs, Then and Now* (1914), 222–3; L. I. Butler, *Linby and Papplewick Notebook* (1950), 8; *NJ*, 22 June 1771; Bailey; B. & W. MSS.: 15 letters 3 January 1785–12 September 1797; Royal Exchange Insurance Registers, IV, 73349.

W. SMITH & CO. (RADFORD COTTON CO.)   Radford *c.* 1791.
R. Lowe; B. & W. MSS. 'Engine Book'; *UBD*, IV (Nott'm.).

STANFORD & BURNSIDE   Nottingham 1782, 1800; Mansfield 1788.
Bailey; Elliott MSS. (N.P.L.); Felkin, 75; *DM*, 19 November 1807; B. & W. MSS., 'Engine Book'; *UBD*, III (Mansfield), IV (Nott'm.); J. Throsby's edn. of Thoroton's *History of Notts.* (1797), II, 314.

C. and G. STANTON   Mansfield *c.* 1792.
R. Lowe; *NJ*, 27 August 1774, 13 February 1790; *UBD*, III (Mansfield).

STRETTON, THACKER & CO.   Wilne *c.* 1781.
J. T. Godfrey, ed., *The Stretton MSS.*, iii–v, 181; *DM*, 5 April 1787, 11 February 1796; Land Tax Returns, Wilne and Shardlow.

G. TRUEMAN   Nottingham *c.* 1791.
UBD, IV (Nott'm.); *NJ*, 26 November 1791; B. & W. MSS., 3 letters, 1790.

W. TOPLIS & CO.   Cuckney 1785, Worksop 1792.
S. D. Chapman, 'Pioneers of Worsted Spinning . . .'.

S. UNWIN & CO.   Sutton-in-Ashfield, 1770; Mansfield, 1782; Tansley.
S. D. Chapman, 'Sutton Old Mill', *Journal of Industrial Archaeology*, II (1965).

WELPDALE, COTTRELL & CO.   Mansfield.
Royal Exchange Registers, XXIII, 131581 (1792).

S. WALSH   Bulwell 1793.
R. Lowe; *NJ*, 7 March 1789, 29 August 1795, 24 October 1795.

DERBYSHIRE

R. ARKWRIGHT & CO.   10 mills ⎱
J. STRUTT & CO.   5 mills ⎰ *see* Chapter Four.

A. BRADLEY & CO.   Mayfield (Ashbourne) 1784.
UBD, I (Ashbourne); will of Anthony Bradley, 6 June 1812; containing lease of 13 February 1773 (Litchfield J.R.O.); Allsopp MSS., Benjamin Wilson's Personal Ledger 1779–95 (Ind Coope, Burton).

N. CRESSWELL & CO.   Edale *c.* 1790.
Juror's Books and Land Tax Returns, Edale (Derbys. C.R.O.); *DM*, 5 August 1802; Royal Exchange Registers, XXIX, 143301, XXI, 123234; pedigree of Cresswell of Edale (S.C.L.).

C. CALLOW   Derby.
UBD, II (Derby); *DM*, 7 September 1786; Land Tax Returns, St. Alkmund's, Derby.

J. COOPER & CO.   Woodeaves 1784, Mayfield 1793.

    DM, 11 March 1790; *UBD*, I (Ashbourne), IV (Nott'm.); B. & W.
MSS., 'Engine Book' and letter dated 21 July 1791; Land Tax Returns,
Mayfield; *NBR*, VIII, 43, 80, 86, 192. For Dale *see DAJ*, III (1881), 3.

D. DAKEYNE (OR DAKIN) & SONS (briefly A. Flint)   Darley Dale 1788.

    DM, 15 March 1787; T. N. Ince, 'Pedigrees of Families in and about
Wirksworth' (MS., *DPL*, 1860); *NJ*, 8 August 1789, 10 July 1802; *DM*,
31 December 1801; Specification of Patent No. 1,961, 16 September
1793; S. Glover, *History . . . of the County of Derby* (1833), 393–4.

DALLEY, FELLOWS & CO.   Wirksworth.

    UBD, IV (Wirksworth); W. P. W. Phillmore, *Notts. Pedigrees*, I, 56;
NJ, 26 March 1791.

T. EVANS & SONS   Darley Abbey 1783.

    J. Lindsay, 'An Early Industrial Community', *Business History Review*,
XXXIV (1960); J. Forrest (Mrs J. Lindsay), 'The Darley Abbey
Cotton Spinning and Paper Mills 1783–1810', M.Sc.Econ. Thesis,
London, 1957.

FOX & PICKFORD   Derby.

    DM, 14 June 1787, 6 September 1798, 31 December 1807. Pickford may
well have been connected with the firm of canal-carriers whose boats
brought raw cotton up the Trent to Derby at this period.

GARDOM, PARES & CO.   Calver, 1778.

    M. H. Mackenzie, 'Calver Mill and its Owners', *DAJ*, LXXXIII
(1963), LXXXIV (1964).

J. GOODDY   Hartington.

    Belper MSS. 3545/4 (D.P.L.).

GREEN & BROCKSHAW   Wingfield Park, South Wingfield, 1795.

    'House of Lords Account of Cotton and Worsted Mills . . . 1803–1818';
bankruptcy in *London Gazette*, LX (1814), 2251.

HEWITT & BUNTING   New Brampton (Chesterfield).

    UBD, II (Chesterfield); *DM*, 31 July 1800.

W. KEELING   Peak Forest

    Royal Exchange Registers, XXIII, 130291 (1792).

C. KIRK   Bamford 1783.

    J. Pilkington, II, 387; *Gentlemen's Magazine*, LXI (1791), 1054;
Bagshaw's *Derbyshire Directory* (1846), 505; Land Tax Returns, Bamford; will of Kirk 2 April 1829 (Lichfield J.R.O.).

G. & C. LOWE   Amber Mills, Shirland 1794.

    'House of Lords Account . . . 1803–1818; *NJ*, 17 February 1809;
Jurors' Books (Derbys. C.R.O.); *Reliquary*, XII, plate 34.

NEEDHAM, FRITH & CO.   Litton 1782.

    See detailed study in Chapter X (3).

P. NIGHTINGALE   Lea 1784.

    Fitton & Wadsworth, 86; Bailey; Barker MSS. D.193-4 (S.C.L.);

DM, 15 July 1784, 14 December 1786, 22 March 1787; Cromford Moor Sough Proprietors *v.* Arkwright (Bagshawe MSS., S.C.L.); J. Hunter, *Familae Minorum Gentium*, I (1894), 142–3.

RADLEY & CHAPMAN   Chesterfield.
UBD, II (Chesterfield); R. H. Oakley, 'The Mills of Holymoorside (Chesterfield)', *Derbyshire Miscellany*, II (7), July 1961.

STONE & HARRISON   Winster 1791.
DM, 20 October 1796.

J. & T. TURTON   Fritchley, Crich 1798.
Land Tax Returns, Crich, 1799; *DM*, 2 August 1802, 24 March 1803, 4 July 1805.

WOOLEY & MACQUEEN   Winster, Matlock.
'House of Lords Account . . . 1803–1818', 6–9; Juror's Books (Derbys. C.R.O.); Land Tax Returns, Winster.

T. WYER & CO.   Ilkeston 1792.
Ilkeston Manor Court Rolls and Enclosure Award Map (Ilkeston Public Library); *NBR*, VII, 438; Bailey; *NJ*, 18 April 1772, 19 March 1791, 18 October 1800; *DM*, 17 December 1801. The other partners were a farmer, a shopkeeper, a hosier and a maltster.

STAFFORDSHIRE

JOHN BOTT & CO.   Tutbury 1783.
T. L. Coxon, 'Tutbury Cotton Mills' (typescript, 1962, Staffs. C.R.O.); C. H. Underhill, *History of Tutbury*, 117–24; S. Shaw, *History of Staffordshire* (1798), I, 58; Bailey. There were five partners in the mill, John & Charles Bott described themselves as 'tammy weavers', two others as 'millers', and the fifth as 'gentleman'.

T. CANTRELL & SONS   Brund 1790.
Mortgage-deeds for Cantrell mill, Derbys. C.R.O. and Bagshawe MSS. (S.C.L.); wills of Cantrell family in Lichfield J.R.O.; J. Pilkington, II, 289; *DM*, 28 August 1794; Land Tax Returns, Brund; *NJ* 11 February 1786.

DAINTRY, RYLE & CO.   Endon (Leek), Eyam.
C. S. Davies, *A History of Macclesfield* (1961), 125–6, 141–2; 'House of Lords Account . . . 1803–1818', 48; *DM*, 2 March 1797.

DICKENS & WILSON   Alrewas 1784
P. Mathias, *The Brewing Industry in England 1700–1830* (1959), 323–4; Bailey; *DM*, 16 February 1815; Allsopp MSS. (Ind. Coope, Burton) Benjamin Wilson's Personal Ledger 1779–95 and Letter-Book 1801–08.

W., J. & J. FOWLER   Tamworth.
UBD, IV (Tamworth); 'House of Lords Account . . . 1803–1818', 30.

T. PARKES   Sudbury (Uttoxeter) 1783.
DM, 10 May 1798, 5 June 1800; Land Tax Returns, Uttoxeter.

ROBERT PEEL Snr.   Burton 1780, 1784, 1791.

Lloyd MSS. (B.R.L.); Aspin & Chapman, op. cit., Ch. I.
(Sir) ROBERT PEEL   3 mills, Tamworth, *c.* 1790.

N. Gash, *Mr. Secretary Peel* (1961), Ch. I; F. Espinasse, *Lancashire Worthies, Second Series* (1877); D. G. Stuart, 'The Parliamentary History of the Borough of Tamworth', M.A. Thesis, London, 1958, 117–18; W. Pitt, *Agriculture of Staffordshire* (1796), 171; B. & W. MSS., paper entitled '7 January 1811. Robert Peel & Thomas Yates' (Outline history of firm); J. Wheeler, *Manchester, its Political, Social & Commercial History* (1836), 529; L. H. Grindon, *Manchester Banks & Bankers* (1877), 113, 124–5.

WALKER, THOMPSON & WARD   Newcastle-under-Lyme 1797.

UBD, IV (Tamworth); B. & W. MSS., paper entitled 'Robert Peel and Thomas Yates' and five letters from Richard Thompson.

(Name not known)   Alton *c.* 1787.

DM, 30 April 1801, 16 May 1805; W. Pitt, *History of Staffordshire*, 227.

LEICESTERSHIRE

W. BUSZARD   Lutterworth *c.* 1800.

Rev. C. Holme, *History of the Midlands* (Rugby, 1891); Scholes' *Manchester Directory, 1794.*

S., J. & B. CHURCHILL   Shepshed 1779.

Henson, 403; Bailey; *DM*, 28 August 1800; B. &. W. MSS., nineteen letters 26 December 1791–8 October 1795.

MILLER, HOWE & CO.   Leicester 1791.

Leicester Journal, 5 August 1796; H. Hartopp, *Roll of the Mayors . . . of Leicester* (1935), 185; C. J. Billson, *Leicester Memoirs* (1924), 8.

J. WILKES (WILKES & JEWSBURY)   Measham 1783, 1802.

Pedigree of Wilkes family of Overseal (Leics. C.R.O.); J. Farey, *Agriculture of Derbyshire*, I, 338–9, II, 361–2, 492 etc., W. F. Crick & J. E. Wadsworth, *A Hundred Years of Joint Stock Banking* (1936), 244–5, 251; Lloyd MSS. (Trent Navigation Leases); B. & W. MSS., 'Engine Book and nine letters 19 October 1783–23 October 1798.

NORTHAMPTONSHIRE

T. BURDETT   Burton Latimer *c.* 1792.

UBD, III (Kettering); Bailey; *NBR*, VII, 443; *Northampton Mercury*, 28 June 1794, 19 April 1806; 3 June 1815; *NJ*, 19 May 1792.

R. CLARKE   Duddington (Stamford).

Royal Exchange Registers, XXIII, 129969 (1792).

HAYES & GIBSON   Northampton.

J. H. Thornton, 'The Northamptonshire Cotton Industry', *Journal of the Northants. Natural History Society*, XXIII (1959), 241–59; *DM*, 4 February 1802; B. & W. MSS., nineteen letters 1797–98.

WARWICKSHIRE

T. GILL   Birmingham 1788.
  J. Sketchley's *Birmingham Directory, 1767*; Pearson & Rollason's *Birmingham Directory, 1780*; Bailey; Pye's *Birmingham Directory, 1788*; J. Jaffray, 'Hints for a History of Birmingham' (MS., B.R.L.), Ch. 8; *Birmingham Gazette*, 20 October 1788 et seq., 7 April 1794.
PARKES, BROOKHOUSE & CROMPTON   Warwick 1797.
  S. D. Chapman, 'Pioneers of Worsted Spinning . . .'.
B. SMART   Milverton (Warwick) 1792.
  Victoria County History, Warwicks., VI, 164.

LINCOLNSHIRE

R. LOWE   Lincoln.
  DM, 27 September 1798; *Lincoln Poll Book, 1790*.
W. ROSTALL   Claypool.
  Royal Exchange Registers, XXIV, 130776 (1792).

SHROPSHIRE

(Name not known)   Isle (Shrewsbury)
  Plymley, *Agriculture of Shropshire* (1803), 341–2.

(B) *Worsted-Spinners*

NOTTINGHAMSHIRE

J. CARTWRIGHT (REVOLUTION MILL CO)   Retford 1788.
DAVISON & HAWKSLEY*   Arnold 1792.
W. TOPLIS & CO.*   Cuckney 1785; Worksop 1792.
  S. D. Chapman, 'Pioneers of Worsted-Spinning . . .'.

DERBYSHIRE

R. & T. BARBER   Derby *c.* 1778.
  S. D. Chapman, op. cit.

STAFFORDSHIRE

G. & J. SCOTT & CO. (THOMAS CLARK)   Wolverhampton 1791.
  Wolverhampton Chronicle, 20 June 1792; 'House of Lords Account . . .', 30; Wolverhampton Rate Books (MSS., W'ton Public Library); T. H. Ryland, *Reminiscences* (B'ham, 1904); Minutes of Evidence . . . on Petitions against Orders in Council, *PP*, III, 1812, 107–8.

LEICESTERSHIRE

FIELDING & JOHNSON†   Leicester 1818.
  Fielding MSS. (Leicester Museum Archives Dept.); W. R. Millmore,
  'Fielding & Johnson Ltd.', *The Wool Record*, 31 July 1952.
J. W. RAWSON & CO.   Leicester 1799.
  Victoria County History, Leics., IV, 397.

WARWICKSHIRE

HENRY LANE (Sir R. NEWDEGATE)   Bedworth 1788.
  Newdegate MSS. (Warwicks C.R.O.); 'House of Lords Account . . .
  1803–1818', 34.
PARKES, BROOKHOUSE & CROMPTON*   Warwick 1797.
  S. D. Chapman, 'Pioneers of Worsted Spinning . . .'.

LINCOLNSHIRE

LOUTH MILL CO. (Sir JOSEPH BANKS)   Louth 1784.
  Banks-Stanhope MSS. (Spalding Gentlemen's Society); *UBD*, III
  (Louth); A Young, *Agricultural Survey of Lincolnshire* (1797), 407; *NJ*,
  28 December 1793.
C. CHAPLIN   Raithby *c.* 1792.
  A Young, loc. cit., *UBD* III (Louth); Banks-Stanhope MSS.

APPENDIX B

COTTON AND WORSTED MILLS IN THE MIDLANDS IN WHICH STEAM-ENGINES WERE INSTALLED, 1785–*c.*1815.

BOULTON AND WATT ENGINES:

County	Owner and Location of Mill	Source of Information
Nottinghamshire	Arkwright, Nottingham	B. & W. 'Engine Book'
	Cox & Halls, Nottingham	,,
	Denison & Oates, Nottingham	,,
	H. Green & Co., Nottingham	,,
	Harris, Nottingham	,,
	James, Nottingham	,,

  * Already mentioned as cotton-spinners.
  † Not included in Tables 1 and 3.

	Morley, Nottingham	,,
	Pearson, Nottingham	,,
	Smith (2 engines), Nottingham	,,
	Stanford & Burnside, Nottingham	,,
	Burden, Mansfield	,,
	Cartwright, Retford	,,
	Gorton, Cuckney	,,
	Oldknow, Cowpe & Co., Pleasley	,,
	Robinson, Papplewick (2)	,,
Leicestershire	Churchill, Shepshed	,,
	Miller, Howe & Co., Leicester	*Leic. Journal*, 5 August 1796
	Wilkes, Measham (2)	B. & W. 'Engine Book'
Derbyshire	Arkwright, Cromford	Fitton & Wadsworth, 80
	Cooper, Matchitt & Co., Fenny Bentley	B. & W. 'Engine Book'
	Strutt, Derby	,,
Warwick	Parkes, Brookhouse & Crompton	,,
Northampton	Hayes & Gibson	,,
Staffordshire	Walker, Thompson & Ward, Newcastle	,,
OTHER ENGINES:		
Nottinghamshire	J. Bacon, Sutton	J. Smeaton, *Designs*, 84–5
	Davison & Hawksley, Arnold	,,
	Lambert, Gonalston	Site inspection
	Robinson, Papplewick	Royal Exchange Regs., XVIII, 119287
	Toplis, Worksop (2)	Site inspection
	Unwin, Sutton	Letters to B. & W.
Derbyshire	Fox & Pickford, Derby	*DM*, 31 December 1807
	Hewitt & Bunting, Chesterfield	*DM*, 31 July 1800
	Lowe, Shirland	*NJ*, 17 February 1809
	Stone & Harrison, Winster	*DM*, 20 October 1796
	Wyer, Ilkeston	*DM*, 17 December 1801
Staffordshire	Dickens, Wilson & Co., Alrewas	*DM*, 16 February 1815
	Scott, Wolverhampton	*WC*, 20 June 1792
Warwickshire	Gill, Birmingham	*BG*, 7 April 1794
	Lane, Bedworth	Newdegate MSS.
Worcestershire	Adams	B. & W. MSS.

| Lincolnshire | Chaplin, Raithby | A. Young, *Agriculture of Lincs.*, 407 |
| | Louth Mill Co. | *NJ*, 28 December 1793 |

Abbreviations: B. & W.—Boulton & Watt.
      BG —*Birmingham Gazette.*
      DM —*Derby Mercury.*
      NJ —*Nottingham Journal.*
      WC —*Wolverhampton Chronicle.*

APPENDIX C

COTTON AND WORSTED MILLS KNOWN TO HAVE EMPLOYED PARISH APPRENTICES
Source of Information

Nottinghamshire

Cartwright	*Manchester Mercury*, 20 November 1798.
Davison & Hawksley	*NJ*, 26 November, 1796, etc.
Lambert	*Memoir of Robert Blincoe.*
Robinsons	Linby Parish Registers.
Toplis	⎰J. Throsby, op. cit., III, 376;
Burden	⎱Cuckney Apprentice Register

Derbyshire

Bossley (Cressbrook)	*PP*, 1819, CVIII, 48.
Blackwell (Edale)	Return of Apprentices in Cotton Mills, 1841 (Derbys. C.R.O.).
Dakeyne	*NJ*, 10 July 1802.
Gardom Pares	Surmised from building of 'London Row' for the mill. (Site inspection.)
Lowe	*NJ*, 17 February 1809.
Needham	*Memoir of Robert Blincoe*
Oldknow, Cowpe	S. Pigott, op. cit., Ch. 6.

Staffordshire

Bradley	*DM*, 13 October 1796.
Bott	*DM*, 20 May 1790.
Dickens & Wilson	*DM*, 16 February 1815.
Peel	*PP*, 1816, III, 134, 138.

Leicestershire

| Wilkes | *DM*, 3 December 1807. |

Warwickshire
Bedworth   Lequesne engravings (Newdegate MSS.).
The location of the mills of these firms is given in Appendix A.

APPENDIX D

PROPRIETORS OF COTTON- AND WORSTED-SPINNING-
MILLS IN THE MIDLANDS WHO BECAME BANKRUPT,
1769–1815

Name of Firm	*Source of Information*
John Hardcastle & William Walker, Newark	*NJ*, 8 June 1793.
Benjamin Stone & Edward Harrison, Winster	*DM*, 20 October 1796.
Henry Green & Co., Nottingham	*NJ*, 12 August 1797.
Timothy Harris, London & Nottingham	*NJ*, 2 December 1797.
	P.R.O. B/3/2119.
William Gibson, Tideswell*	*DM*, 4 January 1798.
William Toplis & Co., Cuckney	*NJ*, 15 June 1798.
Thomas Wyer & Co., Ilkeston	*DM*, 27 March 1799.
Matthew Etchells, Matlock*	*DM*, 11 April 1799.
Thomas Oliver, Thomas White & James Oliver,	*DM*, 20 February 1800.
Alstonfield (Staffs.)*	
Thomas Parkes, Uttoxeter	*DM*, 5 June 1800.
Dakeyne & Co., Darley Dale	*DM*, 31 December 1801.
John Bacon, Sutton	*NJ*, 21 November 1801.
John James, Nottingham	*NJ*, 29 January 1803.
Henry Elwick & Jospeh Trueman, Nottingham	*NJ*, 16 March 1805.
Barker Bossley & Co., Cressbrook	Belper MSS., 3557/21.
William, Charles & Francis Lambert, Gonalston	*NJ*, 14 April 1809.
& Nottingham	
George Hodgkinson, Nottingham	*NJ*, 18 August 1810.
Joseph Dicken, Alrewas	*DM*, 1 December 1814.
Ellis & John Needham, Tideswell	Belper MSS. 3560/38
	(December 1814).
Thomas Green, Alfreton	*London Gazette*, LX
	(1814), 2251.

Peel, Wilkes, Dickenson and Goodall became bankrupt as merchants in 1805.
(L. S. Pressnell, op. cit., 111).
The same list of bankrupts may also be drawn from the Bankruptcy Order
Books at the Public Record Office, London.

* Not included in Appendix A; probably jenny spinners.

Bibliography of Principal Sources

MANUSCRIPT SOURCES OF INFORMATION
Assay Office Library, Birmingham.
  Boulton & Watt MSS.
Birmingham Reference Library.
  Boulton & Watt MSS.; Lloyd MSS., Wyatt MSS.
Chesterfield Public Library.
  Arkwright Wage books.
Derby Public Library.
  Belper MSS.; Pares MSS.; T. N. Ince, 'Pedigrees of Families in and
    about Wirksworth, (1860).
Derbyshire County Records Office, Matlock.
  Land Tax Returns; Jurors' Books; Miscellaneous deeds.
Guildhall Library, City of London.
  Royal Exchange Fire Policy Registers.
Ilkeston Public Library.
  Ilkeston Manor Court Rolls; Ilkeston Enclosure Award.
Leicester Museums Archives Dept.
  Coltman MSS.; Fielding and Johnson MSS.
Leicestershire County Records Office.
  Pedigree of Wilkes Family.
Lichfield Diocesan Registry.
  Bishops' Transcripts of Parish Records.
Lichfield & Staffordshire Joint Records Office.
  Wills.
Manchester, John Rylands Library.
  Bagshawe muniments.
Nottingham Public Library.
  Elliott deeds; Framework Knitters' Papers; James deeds: Smith MSS.
    Stretton's map of Nottingham (1799–1800).
Nottingham University.
  Hadden MSS.; High Pavement Chapel records.
Nottinghamshire County Records Office.
  Ichabod Wright's Diaries; Land Tax Returns; Newark Poll Book,
    1790; Parish records (Arnold); Stenton & Metcalfe MSS; Sherbrooke
    MSS.
Public Record Office, London.
  Bankruptcy files.

Sheffield Public Library.
    Bagshawe MSS., Barker MSS.
Staffordshire County Records Office.
    Land Tax Returns; Rocester deeds.
Warwickshire County Records Office.
    Bedworth Parish Apprentice Register & Papers, 1802–21; Newdegate
    MSS.
In Private Possession.
    Castle Gate Congregational Church, Nottingham, Minute-Books;
    Cuckney Primary School; Toplis & Co.'s Apprentice Register;
    W. C. Dove, Esq., Sutton; Haslam's (Joiners) Account Book; Hayton
    Parish (Retford); Overseer's Accounts, 1786–88; W. Hollins & Co.
    Ltd., Nottingham; Accounts of Oldknow, Cowpe & Co.; Ind. Coope
    & Co., Burton; Allsopp MSS; National Provincial Bank Ltd., E.C.2;
    Ledger, 1748–52, and Summary Accounts of Smith's Bank, 1780,
    1786–88, 1790–95, 1808; Mrs G. Palmer, Lambley (Notts.); Davison
    records; Spalding Gentlemen's Society; Banks-Stanhope MSS.; Sun
    Assurance Co. Fire-Policy Registers; Westminster Bank Ltd.,
    E.C.4; Day-Books of Crompton & Co., Derby.

PARLIAMENTARY PAPERS AND OFFICIAL PUBLICATIONS

Journal of the House of Commons, XXVI, XXXVI, IL, LVI.
Specifications of Patents, 1769–1800.
Minutes of Evidence on Petitions against Orders in Council, *PR*, 1812, III.
Report of the Select Committee on Children employed in Manufactories,
    PP, 1816, III.
House of Lords Committee on Cotton Factories Bill. Minutes of Evidence,
    PP, 1818, XCVI.
An Account of the Cotton and Woollen Mills and Factories, 1803–1818.
    Lords' Sessional Papers. *PP*, 1819, CVIII.
First and Second Reports of Commissioners appointed to collect information
    as to the Employment of Children in Factories. (Factory Inquiry), *PP*,
    1833, XX, XXI.
Report of the Commissioner appointed to inquire into the Condition of the
    Framework Knitters, *PP*, 1845, XV.

NEWSPAPERS AND PERIODICALS

Derby Mercury	*Northampton Mercury*
Nottingham Journal	*Warwickshire Advertiser*
Nottingham Review	*Wolverhampton Chronicle*
Birmingham Gazette	*Gentlemen's Magazine*
Leicester Mercury	*London Gazette*
Manchester Mercury	*Lloyd's Evening Post*

UNPUBLISHED THESES

C. M. Elliott, 'The Social and Economic History of the Principal Protestant Denominations in Leeds, 1760–1844'. D.Phil., Oxford, 1962.

J. Forrest (Mrs J. Lindsay), 'The Darley Abbey Paper and Cotton-Spinning Mills, 1783–1810'. M.Sc.Econ., London, 1957.

P. J. Rooke, 'A Study of Rewards and Punishments in the Elementary Schools of England and Wales, 1800–1893'. M.A.(Educ.), London, 1962.

D. G. Stuart, 'The Parliamentary History of the Borough of Tamworth'. M.A., London, 1958.

CONTEMPORARY WORKS (*i.e.* published before 1850)

S. Bagshaw, *Derbyshire Directory* (1846).

W. Bailey, *Western and Midland Directory* (1784).

J. Blackner, *History of Nottingham* (1816).

W. Bray, *Sketch of a Tour into Derbyshire and Yorkshire* (1778).

J. Brown, *Memoir of Robert Blincoe* (1832 Edn.).

R. Davison, *Ten Letters, Principally upon the Subject of the late Contested Election at Nottingham* (1803).

A Letter to Mr. Bowles (1803).

W. Dearden, *Nottingham Directory* (1834).

C. Deering, *Nottinghamia Vetus et Nova* (1751).

W. Dickenson, *Antiquities of Newark* (1805).

F. M. Eden, *State of the Poor* (1797).

J. Farey, *Agriculture of Derbyshire*, 3 vols. (1811–17).

A Treatise on the Steam Engine (1827).

W. Gardiner, *Music and Friends*, 3 vols. (1838).

S. Glover, *History and Gazeteer of Derbyshire* (1833).

Derbyshire Directory (1829).

G. Henson, *History of the Framework Knitters* (1831).

Holden's *Triennial Directory* (1850–57).

Hosiers' and Framework Knitters' Examinations before a Committee of the House of Commons, 1778. (Derby, 1779.)

Humble Petition of the Poor Spinners of the Town and County of Leicester (Leicester, 1787).

W. Hutton, *History of Derby* (1791).

J. Jaffray, *Hints for a History of Birmingham* (Birmingham, 1857).

R. Lowe, *Agriculture of Nottinghamshire* (1794).

J. Nichols, *History of Leicestershire* (1795–1815).

Nottingham Poll Book, 1774, 1780, 1796, 1803, 1806.

J. Pilkington, *Derbyshire* (1789).

W. Pitt, *Agriculture of Staffordshire* (1796).

History of Staffordshire (1817).

W. Radcliffe, *History of Power-Loom Weaving* (1828).

Rees' *Cyclopaedia* (1819).
Sketchley's *Birmingham Directory* (1767).
W. Stumbles, 'Glimpses of Arnold the Last Hundred Years' (1859), in *Sketches of Mental Recreation after Daily Toil* (1875).
J. Throsby edn. of R. Thoroton's *History of Nottinghamshire* (1790).
The Trial of a Cause instituted by . . . His Majesty's Attorney-General . . . to Repeal a Patent granted 16 December 1775 to Mr. Richard Arkwright (1785).
Universal British Directory, 5 vols. (1790–98).
G. Walker, *Essays, prefaced by a Short Life by his Son* (1809).
Willoughby's *Nottingham Directory* (1799).
S. Woodhouse, 'Memoir of Robert Hall', *New Methodist Magazine*, 1828.
A. Young, *Agricultural Survey of Lincolnshire* (1797).

MODERN WORKS (*i.e.* published since 1860)
Anon., 'The Putrid Fever at Robert Peel's Radcliffe Mill', *Notes and Queries*, CCIII (1958).
C. Aspin and S. D. Chapman, *James Hargreaves and the Spinning-Jenny* (1964).
C. H. Beale, *Reminiscences of a Gentlewoman of the Eighteenth Century* (1891). *Catherine Hutton and Her Friends* (1895).
C. J. Billson, *Leicester Memoirs* (1924).
T. M. Blagg and F. A. Wadsworth, *Nottinghamshire Marriage Licences* (1935).
F. Buckley, 'Old Nottingham Glasshouses', *Trans. of the Society of Glass Technology*, X (1926).
L. I. Butler, *Linby and Papplewick Notebook* (1950).
J. Byng (ed. Andrews), *The Torrington Diaries, 1781–94* (1954).
W. H. Chaloner, 'Mrs. Trollope and the Early Factory System', *Victorian Studies*, IV (1960–61).
People and Industries (1963).
J. D. Chambers, *Nottinghamshire in the Eighteenth Century* (1932).
'Population Change in a Provincial Town: Nottingham 1700–1800', in L. S. Pressnell ed., *Studies in the Industrial Revolution* (1960).
Vale of Trent, 1680–1800 (1959).
'Worshipful Company of Framework Knitters', *Economica*, IX (1929).
S. D. Chapman, 'Pioneers of Worsted Spinning by Power', *Business History*, VII (1965).
'Sutton Old Mill' [Samuel Unwin & Co.], *Journal of Industrial Archaeology*, II (1965).
'The Transition to the Factory System in the Midlands Cotton-Spinning Industry', *Economic History Review*, XVIII (1965).
'Working-Class Housing in Nottingham in the Industrial Revolution', *Transactions of the Thoroton Society*, LXVII (1963).

R. A. Church, *Victorian Nottingham* (1966).
C. R. Clinker and C. Hadfield, 'Ashby Canal and its Railways', *Trans. Leicestershire Archaeological Society*, XXXIV (1958).
T. L. Coxon, 'Tutbury Cotton-Mills' (Typescript, 1962).
W. P. Crick and J. E. Wadsworth, *A Hundred Years of Joint-Stock Banking* (1936).
G. W. Daniels, *The Early English Cotton Industry* (1920).
C. S. Davies, *A History of Macclesfield* (1961).
C. Erikson, *British Industrialists: Steel and Hosiery, 1850–1950* (1959).
W. Felkin, *History of the Machine-Wrought Hosiery and Lace Trades* (1867).
J. B. Firth, *Highways and Byeways in Derbyshire* (1908).
R. S. Fitton and A. P. Wadsworth, *The Strutts and the Arkwrights* (1958).
N. Gash, *Mr. Secretary Peel* (1961).
J. T. Godfrey, ed., *The Stretton MSS.* (1910).
C. L. Hacker, 'William Strutt of Derby', *Derbyshire Archaeological Society Journal*, LXXX (1960).
C. Hall, *Memoirs of Marshall Hall* (1861).
H. Hartopp, *Register of the Freemen of Leicester*, I (1927), II (1933).
High Pavement Chapel, Nottingham. A Biographical Catalogue of Portraits (1932).
J. Hodgson, *Textile Manufacture in Keighley* (1879).
C. Holme, *History of the Midlands* (1891).
G. G. Hopkinson, 'Inland Navigations of the Notts. and Derbys. Coalfield', *Derbyshire Archaeological Society Journal* ,LXXIX (1959).
J. Hunter, *Familiae Minorum Gentium*, I (1894).
H. R. Johnson and A. W. Skempton, 'William Strutt's Fire-Proof and Iron-Framed Buildings, 1792–1812', *Trans. Newcomen Society*, XXX (1955–56).
R. W. King and J. Russell, *History of Arnold* (1913).
A. H. Lawrence, *Bedworth, A Short History* (Bedworth, 1952).
L. Lindley, *History of Sutton-in-Ashfield* (Sutton, 1908).
J. Lindsay, 'An Early Industrial Community', *Business History Review*, XXXIV (1960).
J. A. S. L. Leighton-Boyce, *Smiths the Bankers, 1658–1958* (1958).
M. H. Mackenzie, 'Bakewell Cotton Mill and the Arkwrights', and 'Calver Mill and its Owners', *Derbyshire Archaeological Society Journal*, LXXIX (1959; LXXXIII (1963); LXXXIV (1964).
J. D. Marshall, 'The Cotton Mills of the Upper Leen', *Trans. of the Thoroton Society*, LX (1957).
P. Mathias, *The Brewing Industry in England, 1700–1830* (1959).
Methodist New Connexion Jubilee Book, 1876.
R. Mellors, *Old Nottingham Suburbs* (1914).
G. M. Mitchell, 'The English and Scottish Cotton Industries', *Scottish Historical Review*, XXII (1925).

A. E. Musson and E. Robinson, 'The Early Growth of Steam Power',
Economic History Review, XI (1958–59).
F. Nixon, 'The Early Steam-Engine in Derbyshire', *Trans. Newcomen
Society*, XXXI (1957–59).
Nottingham Borough Records, VI, VII, VIII.
R. H. Oakley, 'The Mills of Holymoorside', *Derbyshire Miscellany*, II (1961).
A. Parker, 'The Nottingham Potters', *Transactions of the Thoroton Society*,
XXXVI (1932).
A. T. Patterson, *Radical Leicester, 1780–1850* (1954).
W. P. W. Phillimore, *County Pedigrees: Nottinghamshire*, I (1910).
S. C. Pigott, *Hollins, A Study of Industry* (1949).
S. Pollard, 'Fixed Capital in the Industrial Revolution', *Journal of Economic
History*, XXIV (1964).
F. Redferd, *History of Uttoxeter* (1865).
T. H. Ryland, *Reminiscences* (Birmingham, 1904).
J. Smeaton, *Designs, 1741–92* (Newcomen Society, 1950).
D. M. Smith, 'The British Hosiery Industry at the Middle of the Nineteenth
Century', *Trans. Institute of British Geographers*, XXXII (1963).
Industrial Archaeology of the East Midlands (1965).
J. H. Thornton, 'The Northamptonshire Cotton Industry', *Journal of the
Northants. Natural History Society*, XXXIII (1959)'
G. Unwin, *Samuel Oldknow and the Arkwrights* (1924).
Victoria County History, Leicestershire, IV; *Warwickshire*, VI.
A. P. Wadsworth and J. de L. Mann, *The Cotton Trade and Industrial
Lancashire, 1600–1780* (1931).
W. Watson, 'Observations on Bakewell, beginning 31st May, 1774', *Derby-
shire Archaeological Society Journal*, XI (1889).
F. A. Wells, *British Hosiery Trade* (1935).

Glossary of Trade and Technical Terms

ATMOSPHERIC ENGINE (or NEWCOMEN ENGINE). A steam-engine invented by Thomas Newcomen for pumping water out of mines. The first was erected in 1712 and many others were erected during the remainder of the century. The working stroke of the engine was effected by the pressure of the atmosphere acting on top of the piston.

ENTREPRENEUR. The person or persons responsible for the vital decisions on production and the supply of markets in any commercial or manufacturing firm. The entrepreneur may be the single owner, partners, or manager.

FACTORY. A building in which mechanical power is used for manufacturing. In this book, the factory is contrasted with the workshop, which contains only manually-operated machines.

FRAMEWORK KNITTER. A man, woman or child who operates a stocking-frame (Plate 2).

HOSIER. In the eighteenth century, a wholesale dealer in goods made on the stocking-frame.

JENNY. A spinning-machine invented by Hargreaves c. 1764 (see Plate 2). It duplicated the motions of the traditional domestic spinning-wheel.

MILL. A word used in the eighteenth century to describe any machine that performed its work by rotary motion; hence twist mill, fulling mill, horse mill, water mill. In this book the word 'mill' is used in its present-day sense, implying a water-powered factory.

MULE. A spinning-machine invented by Samuel Crompton of Bolton between 1774 and 1779. It incorporated the principles of both the jenny and the water-frame and in time displaced both.

POINT NET. An hexagonal net made on a machine developed from the stocking-frame. It was in fashionable demand from 1786 to c. 1816, when it was superseded by twist net.

ROLLER-SPINNING. The process of spinning by employing a series of fluted rollers which attentuate and apply twist to the cotton rovings, or hanks of carded cotton.

SPANISH EYELET-HOLE MITTS. One of the early fashion varieties knitted on the stocking-frame in Nottingham. The mitts were a cheap imitation of ladies' black silk lace gloves.

STOCKING-FRAME (or HOSIERY-FRAME). A domestic knitting-machine invented by Rev William Lee of Calverton, Notts, in the reign of Elizabeth I (Plate 1). It produced underwear and shirts as well as stockings.

THREAD MILL or TWIST MILL. A small factory in which a horse capstan or

247

water-wheel gave power to machines which twisted cotton or linen warps (i.e. the longitudinal threads in the looms) to give them extra strength. An early form of this machine was patented by John Kay of Bury in 1730. Similar machines were widely used in the hosiery districts of the east Midlands by the middle of the eighteenth century, though here the precise use of the product is obscure.

THROSTLE. A machine similar in principle to the mule, but adapted to spinning worsted.

TWIST NET (or BOBBIN NET). Net twisted on a machine patented by John Heathcoat of Nottingham in 1809. The machine successfully imitated the motions of the cushion-lace maker.

WARP. The threads which are stretched lengthwise in the weaving loom.

WEFT. The cross threads which are woven into the warp to make the fabric.

WATER-FRAME. An alternative name for the roller-spinning machine. Roller-spinning required mechanical power, at first usually provided by water-wheels.

WORKSHOP. A building distinct from the worker's cottage in which one or a number of tools or manually-operated machines were used.

WORSTED. A thread spun from wool that has been combed. Combing consists of removing the short fibre from the raw wool, leaving a loose 'sliver' of long fibres for spinning. Worsted fabrics were finer and lighter than the more traditional woollen ones.

Index